ROAD TO NJAWARA, THE GAMBIA

BY

DR. ALHASAN SISAWO CEESAY, MD

© 2016 by Dr. Alhasan Sisawo Ceesay, MD

All rights reserved. No part from this book may be reproduced in any form without written permission from the publisher, except by a reviewer who may quote passages in a review to be printed in a newspaper or magazine.

FIRST PRINTING

PUBLISH KUNSA.COM

ISBN 978-1-910117-82-8

INSCRIBED TO

My Parents, Wife and Children, Teachers, Friends, Colchester Friends of Manding Charitable Trust UK and Friends of Manding Alpena, Michigan, USA; and the downtrodden.

Home, sweet home! Njawara village is pearl of the Badibous every villager dream belonging.

Dr. Alhasan S. Ceesay, MD

PREFACE AND ACKNOWLEDGMENTS

Njawara village, located along border of Gambia and Senegal in the Northern Gambia, is a three hundred years old former colonial trading centre in hinterland Gambia. She was a tourist magnet that among a few villages can boost of having welcomed Queen Elizabeth 11 of England to its Bantaba in the 1960s. Njawara was home of many businesses and is still habited by Wolofs, Mandinkas, Fulas, Jolas, Sereres, Komyaginkas and Bambara tribes' men from Mali. All these tribes continued to leave in homogeneous harmony to today. Njawara is a place of a unique multicultural society rich in history and tradition and has a lot to offer to visitors and scholars alike. Njawara is home base of the author. Njawara *portrays a pulsating village government and traditions of the local. It depicts movers and sages of the times and how rural knowledge and tribal cohesiveness is maintained and passed onto the next generation. Today's Bantaba is a microcosm of former African Democratic systems. The Bantaba is doctrine of village life and village constitution. This village ritual has been going on for many millennia in hope of maintaining with high fidelity ancestral values and virtues. In this setting, which is standard in most villages, everyone participates in debate about a topic(s) or rendered decisions. Here the village settles intricate disputes fairly without resort to Western legal routes.*

The Bantaba doubles in addition to its other functions as a ceremonial as well as a wrestling ground amidst other festivities held in the area. We salute heroines and heroes like Hadi Panneh, Sefo Fafanding Kinteh, late Baba Salla Ceesay and Sisawo Ceesay, the Lower Badibou District Authority, Kerewan Area Council and all speakers and contributors to the functional life of Njawara village in various sections of the work. Without giants like these life at Njawara would have been more dismal than it already is. These sages are our Njawara alchemists. Which youngster of the 1950s would forget the great storyteller and tradesman Bakary Kanteh at the Shop at the T-Junction? Special thanks go to Dudou Ceesay, Mrs. Famatanding Tarawaleh, Njawara residents, and all whose names have not been mention but gave valuable points and coaxed me to writing Njawara Bantaba as an epic story of my birthplace. Many thanks to my wife and children, who are essential part of me, for persevering through thick and thin of my sojourn for Manding Medical Centre. In the mean time allow me express profound gratitude to my wife and children for bearing and persevering patiently through with me in thick and thin during my drive to bring medical aid and service to villagers. Also I am immensely thankful to illustrious lawyer Ousainu Darbo, Lorna Robinson, Eliza Jones, Dr. Laurel Spooner, Dr. Peter R. Wilson, Dr. Barbara Murray, Dr. Phil Spooner, Dr. Richard Murray, Dr. Malkaight Singh,

Dr. Avery Aten, Dr. Blais Tambo, Cloyd Ramsey, Howard Riggs, Rita Riggs, Dr. Charles Egli, Dr. Cooper Milner, Dr. Nelson Herron, Deidre O'Leary, Margaret Cruise, Bill Cruise, Alison Cruise, Dr. Eunice Kahan, Dr. Betzabi Alison-Prager, Henry Valli, Fr. John Milner, Homer Sheppard, Geraldine Sheppard, Dr. Lamin J. Sise B, Dr. Sulayman S. Nyang, Dr. Haidar Shali, Bishops Masson & Coleman McGhee of the Episcopal Diocese of Michigan, Detroit, the Ceesay Committee Diocese of Michigan, Lois R. Leonard, Rev. Walter White, Rev Huge White, Patricia Koblynski, Ishfaue Ahmed, Ahmed Nizami, Abdinnisir Hassan, Faisal Alim, Noora Sugulle, Mahmud Adam, Ganem Al Hadied, Abdullah Shahim, Asiya Qadri, Yusuf Ali, Ebrahima Bojang, and numerous others whose names are not mention but not forgotten.

I write to raise money for the building of a village hospital at Njawara, the Gambia. It is my hope that you would be inspired to join our dream of providing medical aid and service to Gambian villagers and children in the North Bank region. Purchasing this book or donating in cash or kind would help bring our dream to fruition of Manding Medical Centre for a much needed healthcare delivery and hope to villagers, especially children who frequently die prematurely from childhood diseases because of lack of medical service. Together we can catch a dream for the villager and children. Log on:- www.friendsofmandinggambimed.btck.co.uk; to learn more about our self-help village health project Manding Medical Centre at Njawara. Portions of proceed from sale of this work go to support goals of Manding Medical Centre. In addition it will in due course offer scholarships to rural candidates wishing to read for a medical or an agricultural degree and return to serve in rural Gambia.

One can buy my books by logging onto: www.publidhkunsa.com to support our goal providing medical aid to villagers.

Dr. Alhasan S. Ceesay, MD

Chapter 1

A Paradise village

The proverbial story is that Njawara is Paradise in her rich cultural activities and fodder for tribe and peaceful cohabitation of this millennium upon millenniums past. Hence it was no myth that Her Majesty Queen Elizabeth had to be taken to see a true African village Parliament, the Bantaba, in action and plumage.

The Bantaba is located mostly either at the center of the village or its entrance to enable residents attends meetings and dose so freely. The Bantaba serves as seat of village government and place for residents to air their views on topics to be debated or decisions to be made. A decision made here governs all present or absent residents of the concern village or hamlet. It serves as the ritual forum of village jurist purists.

The Bantaba also doubles as an open village classroom to which everyone wishing to participate does so in this village pulsation. It also serves as hall of entertainment during wrestling seasons and in major drumming festivities marking marriage ceremonies. At Njawara the Bantaba serves as an international forum where Senegalese neighbors meet Gambian counterparts. The big sprawling cotton tree at the Bantaba has witnessed thousands if not millions of village meetings and also out lived most current Njawara residents.

It proudly celebrates its 350 year in existence. In every village and hamlet an area in the village is normally chosen and designated as the meeting place to discuss affairs of the village or hamlet to which everyone yearns attend since its existence. Here is what a village Bantaba effectively stands for. In Western jargon it simply means the village town hall. The Bantaba is usually located under the shades of a spreading huge mango tree or cotton tree.

It is the place where resident of a village chose to meet, discuss affairs of the community and seek shelter from sweltering heat from the sun. It is a place to assemble, have conferences, or just to have a friendly talk with fellow villagers. Here villagers make decisions and resolutions and recount history during gatherings at the Bantaba beneath the great tree.

History narrated here keeps knowledge of the tribe alive and united. The Bantaba in some villages double as a village classroom which everyone wishing to attend dose so freely. The Banataba serves as seat of village government and here the heart of the village pulsates. Villagers eagerly and willingly participate in the communal life debates. These may be about land ownership or conflict and dispute are jointly resolved unanimously according to traditional tribal rules.

Hence, it was at such a place that Grandpa Bajoja Ceesay and other depicted speakers in this work lecture their audiences Residents are cordially invited to attend, participate as well as air their views on a topic or decision. Villagers eagerly and willingly participate in the communal life debates affecting their region. These may be about land ownership, or conflict and disputes are jointly resolved unanimously according to traditional tribal rules at no monetary cost to those involved.

Alasan Mballow & mum famatanding Ceesay

Chapter 2

Njawara village, Badibou

Njawara is a 350 years old former colonial market village, situated on the banks of the Miniminyang Bolong, a creek of the River Gambia in the lower Badibou district, North Bank region of the Gambia. It has a population of two thousand and is 95 kilometres from Bathurst now Banjul, Gambia's capital city. Njawara was the centre of trading in peanuts, rice, fish, coos, hides and vegetables and lies close to the Senegalese border. It was established or founded by the Panneh family of the Wolof tribe and initially called Mpanneh village.

The elderly still call it Mpanneh Baa. Among residents of Njawara are Mandinkas, Fullas, Wolofs, Jolas, Seres, Konyaginkas, and Bambaras from Mali, some Syrian and Lebanese business families. Wolos and Mandinkas constituted the largest group in the village. Kerewan was the nearest government post to Njawara. Njawara had been and is still without electricity, telephones, sewer system or paved roads, and water is pumped from nearby boreholes. Feeder roads are normally deep in dust and full of craters in some places. They resemble pools during the rainy season. These dusty dirt roads serve both traveller and Lories that transport goods to and from Njawara.

It was such a busy trading centre for the Gambia and Senegal that lead government ships to ply to the village biweekly. Cutters and tugboats transport peanuts and hides to Banjul. Shelled nut are shipped to Europe, and proceeds provide the country's foreign exchange. In Gambian villages people lived with nature. They fetch drinking water from wells, until the advent of boreholes, and transport the water in Calabashes or clay jugs to family jars.

The water served for cooking, washing/bathing, and laundry when needed. No one flushed gallons down the drain just to wash their face or hands. Firewood and coal is used for cooking in almost all homes. The only illumination besides the moon that served the people came from candles and kerosene lamps of various forms. After sunset the moon is all there is. No wonder there is so many romantic stories about blue skies lighted by the smiling full moon and cheering bright stars.

The Gambia, especially by Njawara, is savannah or grassland strewn with few trees. Lots of wild animals and birds of spectacular plumage could see roaming about in the grassland or bushes. The river, especially creeks like the Miniminyang bolong, is full of fish and crocodiles, and many land animals come to drink before hiding or taking repose for the night.

Also present along the banks are numerous monkeys, Baboons and other species of wild animals. Inhabitants of Njawara like their neighbouring villagers are mostly small farmers and petty traders. Father, like most residents, was a farmer during the rainy season and shopkeeper for the Lebanese traders during the dry season. Farm produce i.e. rice, peanuts and coos was sold to companies and businesses residing in Njawara and trading with its hamlets. Njawara started spiralling downward on advent of political jargonising. Most the firms have left either for fear reprisal by wining political parties or being unduly taxed.

Trade season starts in December and ends in later part of May each year or as decreed by government. Folks work at the stores and firms either as shopkeepers like my father was or as drivers, yard cleaners, security and labourers. The market was located in the centre of Njawara and buzzes with people who bring in all sorts of produce from the neighbouring villages and across from Senegal. Njawara still stands as gateway for trade between the Republic of Senegal and the Gambia. At the market one can find fresh meat, fish, rice, beans millet, coos, peanuts, peanut butter and oil, vegetables, beads, trinkets of different styles and colours. On the stalls are Candles, kerosene lamps and most spectacular tie-dye batiks of differing styles.

Also found are carvings, lots of tropical fruits, such as mangoes, guavas and kola nuts, snake skins, which tourist love to buy, and a whole host of local produce are seen at this village market stall. The market is the liveliest place where bartering and other forms of exchange go on constantly. Artwork, simple house furniture, domestic and cooking utensils made of clay or tin can be seen at most stalls. Village sales persons are experts in bargaining and are polite, if not too courteous, in their dealings with potential customers. They hardly let a customer pass by empty handed without getting them to purchase something from their stalls, even if it means for them to be selling at a loss, an item or two.

In due course, the vendor will persuade the buyer to purchase more from his long line of wares. Also at the market one can pick up on current affairs and the most recent news from Banjul. This is freely passed on to willing listeners. Lastly but not the least for sightseers are the soothsayers willing to tell any lie for a few dalasis or if lucky pound sterling.

All kinds of mesmerising magicians can at times be encountered making the market akin to Disney world for kids during my young days. We learnt a lot of wheeling and dealing from veteran traders of yesteryears. For some children it doubled as a school and a part time apprentice.

A village head or mayor called an Alkalo and six elderly homeowners permanently resident at Njawara administers the village. These men and women serve as cabinet as well as advisors to the Alkalo. The Alkalo is authorised by the district chief and divisional commissioner to hear local cases and adjudicate on local disputes of a non-complicated nature and to rule judiciously on these disputes according to traditional laws.

Disgruntle or dissatisfied persons can appeal the village head's ruling to the district chief for retrial at the risk of a long drawn procedure and heavy penalties or hefty fine and imprisonment. Njawara never had a school until 1961, when the residents, lead my uncle Baba Sallah Ceesay, decided to build one on self-help project. Money was collected from residents and hands were put to work in building the first classroom block.

A compound was provided to serve as the staff resident quarters. Two more classrooms were added a year later. The district chief, Nfamara Singated and resident appealed to the Gambia government for more improved facilities and to provide more teachers to the school. I still recall, with joy in my heart, the glow in the faces of the first pupils and their parents as the designated head teacher, Mr. Baboun Fatty, introduced his staff from Banjul and the first registered pupils of the school.

The enthusiasm was so electrical so much so that a night class, nicknamed "night school" by the elders, was simultaneously started for adults; nearly every able-bodied adult signed up for the evening classes. It was heartening to see so many farmers and very poor works trying to compete with each other about which one returns to class the next day able to count or spell all the assigned homework.

Both parent and child taught each other, and the teachers visited all homes they could during the weekends. Ladies as well as young or adolescent girls were not left behind and they in fact did lot better than most old men and lasted longer in the program than most adults. The pupils progressed rapidly because their dads and mums struggled with them over the same homework and played the same learning games, such that as rewarding each other when one scores the most or spelled every given word correctly.

In the following years the government built more facilities and expanded the school to cater for more pupils as those from nearby hamlets queued into Njawara school. More teachers were added to ease the load from the skeletal crew manning the school at the time. The school produced lots of candidates for both secondary and High School education.

Three of my cousins, Ebou Ceesay, Omar Ceesay and Ismaila Ceesay were pupils at Njawara Primary School. Ebou Ceesay is now Director of operations at Gamtel and Omary and Ismaila Ceesay are both head teachers of their schools in the provinces. Evening or night classes stopped during the rainy season because most of the adults spend the day at the fields and come home late and too tired to learn after filling their belies. Desertification and global warming has now reduced amount of rainfall in compares to the 1950s rainfall records. Njawara School still operates despite current geopolitical and economic difficulties.

The adult classes have dwindled with population shifts and migration to greener pasture at the Kombo coastal area of the Gambia. Also at Njawara were a Dispensary and a Health Centre. A trained dispenser from the Royal Victoria Hospital in Banjul and locally trained nurses and midwives manned the Dispensary and a health inspector took care of local preventive health while running the health centre.

The midwives help with obstetrics and gynaecology cases that do not need referral to the main hospital in Banjul, where specialised help may be available to patients at government's expense. A health inspector now resides in Njawara but there was none when we were born or when my twin brother died of measles at the village.

Now children are vaccinated regularly against a host killer childhood diseases that took many of my generation prematurely. The food stalls are inspected daily and regularly and all meat, fish along with other perishables have to be fresh to be displayed at the stalls. The health inspector quarantines all persons with contagious diseases and notifies the health authorities in Banjul and at the divisional commissioner's office. Quality of drinking water is checked daily for presence of larvae or harmful microbes.

Clinic days are busy as patient pour in from surrounding villages and as far as Senegal. It caters for well over five hundred patients on a full day. None of these poor villagers ever had a chance to be seen by trained qualified physician or consultant at any time because most of the doctors are stationed at the Royal Victoria hospital in Banjul, Gambia. The fortunate one had to walk fifty to hundred miles to see a physician. Senegalese travel to Njawara for treatment because it was cheaper and easier to see a dispenser than at home.

Social activities in the form of wrestling, wedding ceremonies, and dancing take place mostly in the dry season after harvesting the farms. This was show-off time instead saving money for a rainy day. Groups from Senegal come for wrestling matches with their Gambian counter parts resident at Njawara village.

The sight of wrestlers with their colourful attire is spellbinding spectacle in itself. It was the time young ladies show their prettiness and agility in dancing more than pleasing to the beholder. Boys certainly look forward to these Senegalo-Gambian friendly encounters and entertainments at Njawara. After such hard work at the farm during the rains one never wants these joyful occasions to cease.

Oh dear, how I longed for those good old days to come back again. I will chance to relish each and every moment as if though it never pass away. Those were innocent golden and youthful days of life at Njawara.

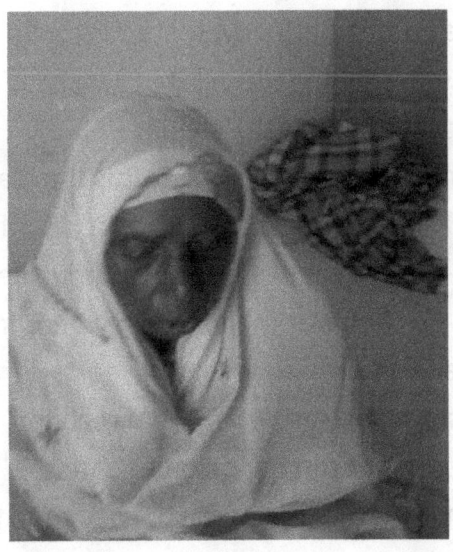

Binta Ceesay, elder sister, 2015

Chapter 3

Grandpa Bajoja Ceesay on Mandinka traditions

Children and adults both eagerly looked forward to the old sage's lecture. The expectant audience gathered beneath the shades of the spreading Mango tree to listen to the wise of the wisest at Njawara village talk to them about Marriage, christening, circumcision, leadership and other Mandinka, Fula, Wolof, Sere, and Jola culture as practiced in the Gambia. A deafening silence from eager audience of children, youths and village elders braced for the preamble marking the start of Grandpa Bajoja Ceesay's weekly lectures.

I beg indulgence to allow me digress to tell little bit about what a village bantaba effectively stands for. In Western jargon it simply means the village town hall. The Bantaba is usually located under the shades of a spreading huge mango tree or cotton tree. It is the place where resident of a village choose to meet, discuss affairs of the community and seek shelter from sweltering heat from the sun. It is a place to assemble, have conferences, or just to have a friendly talk with fellow villagers. Here villagers make decisions and resolutions and recount history during gatherings at the Bantaba beneath the great tree. History narrated here keeps knowledge of the tribe alive and united.

The Bantaba in some villages double as a village classroom which everyone wishing to attend dose so freely. The Banataba serves as seat of village government and here the heart of the village pulsates. Villagers eagerly and willingly participate in the communal life debates. These may be about land ownership or conflict and dispute are jointly resolved unanimously according to traditional tribal rules.

Hence, it was at such a place that grandpa Bajoja Ceesay gives his stories, lectures that are at times joyous and at times frightening. As usual, he starts these debates by offering prayers to all. He said it becomes his duty for him to speak to us about tradition. The shifting sands of time made his thoughts to appear a sphinx arising from the ashes of old ways. It was a pleasure and he promised to do his best at it.

He said today he was going to talk about the handing down of beliefs and customs unique to Mandinkas and other tribes in Gambia from one generation to another. He said what he embarked upon was a long established custom or method of procedures of the tribe. He started by simply letting us know that every living thing one-way or the other procreates. He said only man, through developing moral and judgmental powers enacted elaborate form of marriage. Marriage follows certain norms as per society.

In general, marriage that is the union or wedding of adult male and female into sanctified couples practiced by all civilized human beings. There are monogamous, polygamous and even group marriages in societies. He emphasized that this relation between man and women is blessed from God who choose continuation of His wonderful creation in this fashion.

The old sage stressed that marriage is meaningless without blessings that involved parents of both couples and the priest. He said being unmarried at certain age was taboo and culprits are normally severely dealt with by their community. He told us there are marriages where the couples are spoken for before being born. "How" shouted a young lady the audience?

He replied, that such an act is an outcome from desire not only to perpetuate long-standing friendships between proponents but to also reduce possibilities the young going for unwanted clowns. Usually parents of both sides had experience such an offer to them or want to maintain loyal connection through to the next generation. Above all, he emphasized the proposals are not binding to the children to be coupled. A well-meaning explanation is given to them when in their early teens as well in their twentieth year.

If they fail to expressed any doubt or have objections this would be the last chance before the intention of the involved parents is announced to the village and surrounding hamlets. Barring any objection the date is set and the marriage is consummated at the mosque on a chosen Friday or Sunday at a Church if the couples are Christians. He said there is no objection in marriages between tribes, intertribal and even Caucasian and Negro for they are all God's children.

What is bad in marriage in being unfaithful, augmentative, intolerant, and laziness. Time and seasons do not wait for any lazy couples. Some marriage do come to an unforeseen end called devoice. This happens when an irreconcilable state persist between couples for long even after intervention by parents, priest, and community. Devoice is granted to couples with understanding that the children will not suffer its ramifications in the after mirth.

In reality in African settings devoice is rare because its repercussions brakes centuries of relationship between the parents of both parties. Grandpa Bajoja Ceesay counseled that couples should do all they could never to allow devoice to happen. The couple must first make certain that their own side of the affair was immaculate. He said the pot couldn't call the kettle black while pointing fingers to their partners.

One cannot be divisive and intolerant and expect others to be very kind and accommodating to them. He out lined the following as what makes most marriage fail. Disharmony in personal relations and too many relationships, pain, medical or gynecological conditions, multiplicity of irreconcilable roles, and blaming all dose eclipse marriage.

The world is never always going to be our liking. No child should be subjected to the impact and anguish of separation between parents and psychological effect it brings along. Children who unfortunately had to endure such experiences can only better articulate this. A house divided falls miserably and is hell for children of devoiced parents. He went on to say in the event of death of a husband, the wife, if she chooses, is normally adopted by the brothers of the deceased to stay along her children in the compound or village.

Most young ladies opt to move on and remarry to another man within the village or else were, preferably not too far from the children who will now be taken care of by the family of the previous deceased husband. Having said this much about marriage the sage moved onto the outcome of marriage that is procreation and christening. In a happy marriage between healthy couples a child soon emanates.

This is another occasion for paying homage to God, gratification, festivities and a responsibility demanding more of us than we will ever imagine. It teaches us a different lesson in life and caring for the upbringing of another human being is the most rewarding as well as challenging adventure. The changing phases of newborn, toddler, teenager and eventually fully-grown adults are a marvel only parents can experience.

He rhetorically asked, "What was the meaning of or usefulness of christening our children? "A few brave ones attempted to give answers. Some said we do it to give names…. "I am Jato (lion), the strongest and king of the jungle". The old man laughed and pointed to the next eager to talk, said, "I am Mansa. My father said it was a warrior king's name." At this stage Grandpa added that a rose by any other name still smells sweet.

He thanked them for their correct contributions although much more reasons exist as to why humans have this tradition of christening. He began by saying that since man came with the spoken word he developed ability to differentiate, as we all cannot be called Jato. It would be meaningless and confusing when one wants to call or talk to a particular person. He hence gave few more tangible reasons for christening a child.

He said these areas outlined thus, "It is a way of paying homage and expressing gratitude to God for letting us continue in the new comer. It is expressing joy that our loved one survived not only the changes pregnancy brings to her state but for surviving that last risky hour of labor and parturition.

At this juncture grandpa said there was no greater sin in life than not appreciating, respecting, loving and protecting one's mother. She was more than any human on earth was the first to risk her life for us to join this earthly Garden of Eden. So we must always be kind to both our parents but more so to our mothers, and wives. Among other reasons why man christens is to provide name for that individual (s) to which society will identify them.

A name can be colorful, historical and even of superstitious nature. But what is in a name?" Someone in the shouted, "They all sound sweet as a rose. It gives both the couples and community to celebrate along with family, friends, and communities far and wide. It brings people together and creates cohesion and bondage between villagers. No one is an island. We all need the other and it is always good to share our lives and happy moments, for whatever worth it may be.

It will be appreciated when we open up our hearts to others. This is the time when we men believe our wives appreciate any gift we gave to them. Babies cement our loyalties to wives. An outburst of laughter filled the place from the elders who normally seat quietly and listen to grandpa talk. The last topic grandpa dwelt on relates with circumcision and why men do it.

He said in ancient days. Some disease occurred in the gentile of men. He also said, "Some when erective find it painful because the foreskin tightens up. A butcher found out that when he cut off a piece of men's foreskin, in effect circumcised, they no longer present with erectility problem." All of which was dramatically irradiated when this wise butcher thought removing a portion of the foreskin would just alleviate these poor men's' nightmares.

It worked miracles and men had been circumcised since. He made it clear that such surgery was not needed for women. It was just because of copy carting that lead women to the circumcision grounds. He did point out that some women do go through difficult labor causing attendants to remove or widen the birth canal to allow delivery of the child. This he said did not warrant women being subject to what tantamount to mutilation. Episiotomies are a necessary life saving medical procedure for both mother and baby.

He said that the talk must now focus on men while respecting women who already went through female circumcision. We have history telling us origin of men circumcision as above but a lot more Mandinka added aspects now exist. Mandinkas circumcised their boys for the above reasons plus it is used to indoctrinate, educate the soon would be adults into manhood and their responsibility to community.

It is a challenging ninety days that become memorable events in every mandinka male's life. He is taught to meet all sorts of challenges, find solutions unselfishly taking care of all people and circumstances of life. Here African pharmacopoeia becomes a miracle. He said the green concoction when applied to cut areas stops the bleeding immediately and allows rapid healing. Only rarely one out of a thousand circumcised boys ever suffers from tetanus.

Yet today's so called civilized African allowed all that knowledge to disappear in reliance on colorful pills, capsules, and endless creams from lands beyond. Grandpa lamented about the error and Africans depending too much on the easy way out but not the safest of having to use their brains to manufacture or modernize known local medicaments.

He warned and indeed advised that we talk to old herbalist to record things before the last traces of African Pharmacopoeia fades away. The end of the ninety days encampment molds the boys into full grown mentally matured males according our world. The boys return home ready to take reigns from their parents, elders and become husbands as soon as possible.

Yes the village has become reborn again and certain of its continuity with its traditions up hell by the incoming generation of elders. Fathers gleefully servo the occasion knowing that they too had done what was expected of them and will now continue to give guidance when sort but not enforce it. Grandpa, to every one's surprise, said let me digress and talk a bit about leadership as understood by the Mandinka.

Starting with the head of the house, priests, village heads, Chiefs governors and heads of states all have one thing in common. First, they are servants of the people they governor guide. Their role is akin to that of the umbrella. When open it shades all and everything beneath its shade. The umbrella does not engage in differentiating, an art mastered by colonialists, tribalism, trigger-happy rebels and AK47 nuts. So should all the above leaders be to their subjects.

A leader should be honest servant and not a disguised master and Mafioso to their people. Leaders should be kind and considerate of their people for they need love and support before surrendering to the icy hands of death. Man has limited time on earth and he should strive to leave worthy footprints that the next generation can follow and replicate for generations to come.

Leaders must be humane, compassionate, and competent and above all spearhead exemplary manners, hard work, love and harmony towards their people. He concluded by reminding us that tradition roles he outlined is handing down of beliefs or customs from one generation to another. It is long established customs or methods of procedures of the tribe.

What he today passed onto us is based on style of the knowledge and Mandinka tradition passed upon from centuries of creation. Grandpa admonished us to be custodian of it and pass it onto our children to disseminate to theirs'. By this the handing over of beliefs and customs from one generation to another along established customs or methods of procedure of the tribe is complete and the young now holds the baton. He said what little he told us was based on the style of the mandinka traditions passed upon from centuries of creation. God bless and give all good health, long live, security and prosperity.

Chapter 4

Why Tourist Magnet

Today's shrunken world beggeths closer interaction at heart. Ever since man became aware of his environment and ability to explore he developed culinary taste, which has never been satisfied. Njawara, a typical village located at the fringes of the Miniminyang creek on the River Gambia near Senegal, offers friendly atmosphere and display of the most colorful and cheerful people of the smiling coast of the Gambia. Njawara specializes in all African cuisines, exotic diets and above all has world-class hotel one can rest undisturbed by the roar of modern day megalopolises cities.

None have been here without wanting to return the moment chance arises. Come dine at Njawara's open beach or hotel. Both offer memorable tales to tell folks back home. Imagine the feel of fresh cool air, sweet smell of flowers, and sight of colorful birds among antelopes grazing in the Savannah undisturbed by your presence. The dancing, acrobats and folklore would make you want to extend your stay. And for honeymooners, our bridal suit is not only superb but also heavenly and offers you heaven on earth with a big, big memory to take home. Njawara is not all entertainment and no work.

Hotel Duniya Dima is tourist entity compring of sixteen hut-like accommodations. Each housing a guest or two with exception of the bridal suit, which is specially, built in luxury and pleasurable atmosphere for honeymooners The huts are buildings made of breaks with inner part having Western furnishings of tables, beds, TV, Telephone, bathroom and built-in Air Conditioners.

Guest shares a joint large swimming pool with section to serve children that may wish to take deep in water African waters. The facility was built by the Norwegian Artist who comes to Njawara annual at the school of African Music they erected at Njawara. Here they practice African music and make tapings to convert into videos and discs for sale in Norway. Our guests are lodged at hotel Duniya while the village of Njawara goes into frenzy mode in entertainment and letting the visitor mix with villagers from the region.

Everyone in the village and nearby hamlets along with the Commissioner and the Lower Badibou District Authority put their best front for the visitors. The guests visit schools and villages of Kinte Kunda, Kerewan, Suware Kunda, Sabba and Toro Bahen and many more menorable places to see, as well as learn from and develop friendship with indigenous farmers of the region.

The show starts a day after arrival to allow fatigue and jetlag to wain away. Village after village pour into Njawara to welcome their honoured guests from beyond the mighty Atlantic Ocean.

Most never met such large group of Americans or Europeans in one group hence there was the ember of curiosity in air. All gathered at the village centre known as the Bantaba would be dancing, singing, acrobatics and magic became the spell of the day. It always entertains and leaves visitors at awe and with clicking cameras not to miss a second of any performance. This is not akin to the Tarzan drama the students were familiar with about Africa.

It illuminates genuineness of culture and artistic ambiance the visitors never new existed in black Africa. The real fun dawns when it becomes the turn of visitors to enter the ring and dance along with villagers. YES, the African rhythm has it rules and one can look clumsy if a novice at the dance style. Our friends do wonders and enjoyed themselves to the fullest. On the second day visitors wolud try their skills or hands at African roof thatching.

It looked simple but it's an art carried on since time immemorial and it served to prevent our mud huts from dissolving under the pouring torrential rains during the rainy season. Those who decided to teach at the schools found an unheard of discipline and smartness in the students before them. The pupils are under normal circumstances were very respectful and not only eager to learn but also to know as much as possible about America. Both wanted to know so much about the other that they would never want the schools day over.

They learnt a lot about people and wondered what went wrong in their own to loose such stimulating atmosphere between pupils and teachers in the so-called developed world. They were ready to reveal this finding to juniors back in America or Europe. Some went fishing with the great fishermen of Njawara and did they bring a canoe full of priced fish to cook for all in attendance. The American fishermen were given the traditional reception accorded to big seafarers of ancient day Africa. Again throngs of dancers and acrobats met them for being relaying joy of their safe return home with a good catch.

Reproduced is Miss Jessica Slominski's observations and lifelong lessons learnt from visit she and her leadership class had on visitng Njawara village.

"In May 2005, I was fortunate to join other ACC classmates and our instructor, Tom Ray, on a leadership class cultural trip to Njawara village, The Gambia, West Africa. We had been invited to visit and help at the Manding Medical Centre by its founder and ACC's 2005 Distinguished Graduate, Dr. Alhasan Sisawo Ceesay. This trip proved to be one of the most difficult yet rewarding experiences of my life. Everyone asks me, "How was the trip? How was Africa?"

My first instinct is to tell them, "Hot! Very, very hot! I cannot really explain my African experience with words- it's just too awe-inspiring. I think of the people, the culture, the environment, and the poverty, and I lack the words to give it justice. I can, however, tell you what I learned more about myself and African society from this experience.

Having grown up in Alpena, I realize that I have been sheltered from many things. I have never had to worry about having enough to eat nor lived without the basic necessities our society takes for granted every day. After just a couple of days in Africa, I was already missing indoor plumbing, air conditioning, and ice cubes! After my trip, I cannot say that I came home and abandoned modern convenience, but I did take an inventory of my life and truly saw what I had instead of what I did not have.

I think one of the greatest things that I learned in Africa was from the people. The villagers of Njawara were genuinely happy to have us there. They went out of their way to make us comfortable and make sure we had every-thing we needed. They gave us so much when they had so little. The people not only gave food and comfort, but they also gave of themselves.

When I was sick and dehydrated, alone in the village while the group went to The Gambia's capital, the people would not let me be by myself. They pulled me into their daily activities and made sure I had my own special day. Looking back now, I realize that I have never been given such a precious gift in my entire life.

The African children touched the lives and hearts of all that went on the trip. Everywhere we went, the kids would come out from their compounds and wave at us, calling "Toubob", which meant "white person." They would follow us and our vehicles, making me personally feel like Miss America.

From what I witnessed in Africa, I can say that Africans take time out of their lives to enjoy each other. Africans help each other and trust each other, working together to attain a common goal. They make do with what they have and are thankful for whatever they are given. My experience in Africa was eye opening. It gave me a look into a culture and society far different than my own, and for that I will forever be grateful. I will carry the lessons I have learned, the people I have met, and the memories that I have made from this African journey with me always."

With this there was no wonder the students became herbinger to wonderful relation for villagers and visiting dtudents. Hence after a few months of their return to America a proclamation establishing sister city program was endorsed by Alpena City Council in December 2005. Alpena, Michigan, USA has as of the 5th of December 2005 ratified resolution of sister city program with Njawara and Kinte Kunda villages in the Gambia, West Africa. The full text of the proclamation document is reproduced bellow.
"Whereas, the city of Alpena, recognizes and supports the concept of global cooperation and community relationship; and
Whereas, the villages of Njawara and Kinte Kunda, through their local leaders and Dr. Alhasan Ceesay, have reached out their hand in friendship and goodwill to Alpena; and
Whereas, relationships were established by the students and faculty of Alpena Community College when they were warmly welcomed to the villages in The Gambia for a service project earlier this year; and

Whereas, mutual understanding of our diversities as well as our similarities will lead to cultural exchanges that will be beneficial to the citizens of both areas; and

Whereas, we believe that true global community is often established one person at a time; and one city and one village at a time, and leads to beneficial relations and programs for all;

Now, whereas, I John F. Gilmet, by the authority vested in me as Mayor, do hereby proclaim a sister city program with the villages of Njawara and Kinte Kunda in the Lower Badibou District, The Gambia, West Africa.

And do urge all area citizens to extend the hand of fellowship and embrace genuine fraternity to their friends in Njawara and Kinte Kunda and pledge support and loyalty as these communities of two great nations join together as "Sister Cities."

Signed: At Alpena, Michigan, United States of America on this 5th day of December, 2005"

With this development the villagers got needed boost regarding desire to build a village hospital for the region. Hence a charity status was also proclaimed or set afoot in Alpena, Michigan.

Manding Medical Centre will soon be a recognised charitable Trust in the USA. Proponents plan to register as Alpena Friends of Manding Charitable Trust, Michigan.

Dr. Avery Aten, Chairman of the Department for Women and New born of Alpena Regional Medical Centre along with the medical community of Alpena are in the verge of processing application seeking the formation of charitable trust to help provide needed medical aid to children in the

Gambia. In an email to Mrs. Lorna Robinson, Secretary of Friends of Manding Charitable Trust in Colchester, UK, Dr. Aten stated; "We have recently made some first steps in helping Dr. Ceesay with his project, and we thought to forward this message to you and ask for your opinion regarding the process of setting up a charitable Trust in Alpena.

Our college students from Alpena were very energised by their visit to the Gambia, and we would like to maintain the relationship between our communities as well as get the health care centre going that Dr. Ceesay envisions.

I have reviewed the plan for a trust with a friend who is an attorney and he is getting the forms for the application for trust, which would have 501c-3 Status. It would therefore be the appropriate entity for seeking funds from foundations such as the Gates Foundation.

We also need approval from the state of Michigan and those forms are being sought as well. Carol Shafto suggested that the trust be established to accept gifts for education and medical purposes." Bellow is full text of letter from Dr. Richard Bates of the Obstetrics/Gyneacology community of Alpena, Michigan informing Dr. Alhasan Ceesay of their interest in joining the objective of Manding Medical Centre for the villagers in the Gambia. The note read:

"Dr. Ceesay,My name is Richard Bates, and I am an Obstetrcian/gynecologist in Alpena. Dr. Aten has mentioned the opportunity in Gambia, and a number of medical professionals involved in woman's care would be interested in becoming involved. We would love to utilize our gifts of knowledge, training and experience to serve and assist those in need in Gambia. I look forward to learning more. Blessings from Richard.

Greetings from the smiling coast of Africa.

American guest enjoying a bowl of Benechin

Guest welcomed by Arfang Bah Mayor of Toro Bahen

Students pose with Commissioner and District Authority

Having the fun of his life trying African rhythm

Learning to dance the African rhythm

The real dancers at it during the welcoming ceremonies.

Guest bonding with young villager at Njawara

A typical village and environment

Aja Hadi Paneh, Mayor of Njawara village

Guest at Manding Medical Centr's furue location

Badara Jobe, Njawara's agriculturalist

Alagie Ceesay with guest at Manding Medical Centre

Dr. Alhasan Ceesay holding Africa.

Mr. Sisawo Ceesay, Father

Dudou Ceesay, brother in green with family

CHATER 5

A PRISONER OF MY AMBITION
FOR THE VILLAGER

The burning embers of a wish and hope for my people became a prison wall that kept caving onto me any time I relaxed my effort. Ambition to bring the golden Flees, in the form of medical aid, to the villager constantly hunts me and reminds me of my covenant for the Gambia.

There were no doubts in my mind that I was rightfully engaged in bringing much needed medical service to the region served by Manding Medical Centre in the Gambia. I literally became the fugue of the family as I pushed to bring my desire to provide proper medical aid into fruition for the villager in the North Bank of the Gambia.

This quest for a better medical service to neglected villagers led to my disappearing from the family horizon to America as early as 1967. There I started the challenge of my life in a drive to become a doctor of medicine serving the Gambia. The path of this adventure is well documented in my first book, "The legend against all odds" published by PublishAmerica, Baltimore, Maryland, USA in August 2002. The strength of my conviction along with a mindset to do something concrete for my people made me give up today's pleasures for a better tomorrow for the Gambia. An Armchair psychologist, Dr. Kube Lonna (nick named Dr. Hamham), once told me. "Dreamers are a pain in the neck."

I asked why? And he replied, "They wake up with one of the most ridiculous ideas and try not only to live in that nonsense but implement them for the rest of their lives. US pragmatics and wise became sceptical and weary of the dreamer and brand him either a total loony or living in a planet by himself or herself". I replied quoting Lawrence of Arabia. Who said "All men dream: but not equally. Those who dream by the night in the dusty recesses of their minds wake in the day to find that it was vanity; but the dreamers of the day are dangerous men, for they act their dream with open eyes to make it possible." I further made it clear that none the less many dreamers have converts.

I asked what converts the sage to the dreamer' path? To this he gave the most amazing reply in favour of the dreamers and people with strong convictions like mine. My armchair psychologist told me, "We only become flabbergasted as the dream unfolds to bits of reality opening up wide realms unknown to us before that day."

He continued by illustrating what he meant. "Take for example the case of the Rights brothers and their attempt to fly. Boy oh boy! Some critics who strongly believed that only birds, goblins, and angels had the privilege of flight ridiculed the Rights brothers as witches. Today you and I know better for we now use the Rights brother's dream to fly round the world at ease and by it we have catapulted to the moon and beyond".

I hope this has cleared the air for the reader as to why some of us are considered as whacks and a challenge to my friend the sage armchair psychologist Dr. Kube Lonna. Very early in my high school days friends labelled me as a reclusive person not knowing that my whole psyche was based on going aboard and becoming one of the future doctors of the Gambia.

I am fully aware of all work and no play not only turns us into monsters but also indeed a very dull one at that. I just moderated my life and made certain that I never lost track of my direction in life and my ambition for the Gambian villager. After ten years in America my family considered me being lost in zealous desire to gain book knowledge or Western education. I learnt that my father, while on his deathbed urged that prayers be offered so that I, the family fugue would return home.

Like Maco Polo or Simbad's adventures mine had seen me fly on several times to America, Liberia, the West Indies and the United Kingdom seeking more skills with which to serve my people. It is said that life is lonely at the top but I found it even lonelier when struggling from ground zero with no hope of financial assistance at sight. Every hour of my life had to be organised in a way to minimise loss of income and to maintain progress in my academic pursuits. Hence I worked on three jobs during the summer breaks and at school libraries to raise funds for my education or repayment of loans which enable me continue schooling.

To me every ounce of energy and cent spent on my aspiration to become a doctor in the Gambia was as exhilarating as becoming an overnight multimillionaire. It is a joy I wish I could share with you. Graduating from medical school and my first patient in the Gambia are indelible blessed moments I hold dear to my heart. The rewards will forever be for my people and humanity.

Binta Ceesay, Daughter, 2015

CHAPTER 6
DISTIGUISHED 2005 GRADUATE AWARD
TO DR. ALHASAN S. CEESAY

I attended Alpena Community College (ACC) in Michigan, USA, from September 1967 to December 1979. My contact with friends at Alpena never waned. Hence the wheels of profound recognition by the institute started rolling when Mathew Dunckel called me to let me know he read my book, "The Legend against All Odds." He was very impressed and intrigued by my experience and fortitude since my leaving Alpena Community College in 1979. I met Mathew when he was twelve years old. His father Dr. Elbridge Dunckle was my academic advisor while I was at Alpena community College. I will without any reservation still recommend Dr. Dunckel for academic advisor to any foreign student attending the college.

It was during one of our telephone conversation (02/01/05) that Mathew told me of the possibility of ACC recommending me for the Distinguished 2005 Graduate award offered annually by Alpena Community College to its outstanding Alumni. Alpena Community College foundation recognises its graduates annually for their academic and their career accomplishment for their communities. It simply recognises the aspirations of Alumni for their people. The Pandora's Box was opened by innocuous telephone conversation in recognising my aspiration and goal for providing medical aid to Gambian villagers.

Mathew asked me to fax him any and all possible documentation about me and work I do in the Gambia. He would then speak to the relevant authorities regarding my being nominated for the Distinguished 2005 graduate of Alpena Community College coming May 5th 2005 spring/summer commencement. Mathew did just as promised. In a nutshell, here is the letter from Mrs. Penny Boldrey, Executive Director Alpena Community College Foundation. It read:-

Alpena Community College

666 Johnson Street

Alpena, MI 49707

January 6, 2005

Alhasan S. Ceesay, MD

245 Great Western Street

Moss Side

Manchester M14 4LQ

England

Dear Dr. Ceesay,

Mathew Dunckel shared the information that you recently provided to him regarding your professional achievements since your early years at Alpena Community College. I'm extremely pleased to share with you that your many outstanding accomplishments have earned you the distinction of Distinguished Graduate of Alpena Community College (ACC) for 2005. We commend you for your humanitarian efforts in founding and developing the Manding Medical Centre in Gambia, West Africa. I'm anxious to read your book. "The legend against all odds" once Matt has finished with it. Without a doubt, you serve as an example of how a solid educational foundation from Alpena Community College can launch a lifetime of achievements. You will be honoured at our spring commencement exercises on Thursday, May 5, which begins at 7 pm, in the Park Arena at ACC. We invite you to join us on that evening.

However, we certainly understand that making a trip to the United States, on so short a notice, may not be feasible. During the commencement program, I will share a synopsis of your extraordinary career that has earned you the honour of Distinguished Graduate. If you are able to join us, you will be invited to join me at the podium to receive your award and to address the audience if you wish.

Would you be willing to provide us with the following: 1) a copy of your professional resume; 2) a paragraph on your memories of ACC and how your experience helped you achieve your goals; 3) a professional photo for use in our alumni newsletter as well as in an ad that will appear in Alpenanews.

Please feel free to call me or e-mail me with any additional questions you may have. Again, congratulations! We look forward to hearing from you in the future.

Sincerely

Penny Boldrey

Executive Director

My response to this honour and invitation to my second home America was swift and obvious as penned bellow. I e-mailed Penny forth with as my heart was overwhelmed by joy for being recognised by my Alma Mata ACC. It simply stated:-

13/01/05,

Manchester, UK.

Dear Penny Boldrey,

I am overwhelmed and do not know where to begin this note of thanks to Alpena Community College. In my mind it's the American people who deserve such honour and distinction for I am only recipient of the goodness of the Americans. I am humbled and further rejuvenated by the thought and recognition of my goals and work for the Gambia.

I remember in the 60s when people used to tell me, "You will end up just like all foreign students who came to America. They end up getting trapped by the greener pasture syndrome of America."

To such challenges my response had always been; I for one will disappoint a lot of you for I will never rest until I bring to my people the American know how and willingness to share with others. This stance has never changed and will not ever change because the only way I can, in a small measure compared to what you did for us poor ones, pay back is to be able to show what the USA is all about and her stand for the little guy anywhere on this planet.

I will look into my schedule to see if I can afford to be in Alpena May 2005. I will let you know by the end of February 2005. Mean while I'm faxing a resume and will try to send my photos by e-mail. Where it is not possible for me to attend in May, would it be okay for my first Alpena family friend, Mrs Rita Riggs to represent me at the ACC' spring Commencement Ceremony.

She was the first people in Alpena that opened their homes to me. She and her family will certainly appreciate recognition of their help to this simple Gambian. None the less rest assured that I have not yet slammed the door to my seeing Alpena once more. Timing and visa problems might make it unattainable. Again, please accept profound gratitude to all of you and to Alpena Community College. God blesses you and rain peace on earth in 2005. Cheers and regards.

Sincerely

Dr. Alhasan S. Ceesay, MD

Mrs. Boldrey replied thus:

ACC, Michigan 49707

13/01/05

Hi Dr. Ceesay,

Yes, I did receive your curriculum vitae and thank you for forwarding that to me! We are extremely proud of you and your accomplishments! Once I get my hand on your book, I will pay special notice to the ACC chapter. The best part of my job is the opportunity to meet former alumni and learn of the impact ACC had in their lives.

Please believe me that we understand if you are unable to join us at commencement on May 5. Indeed we would be pleased to have Rita Riggs accept this honour on your behalf. Rita is remarkable and kind woman. My husband speaks fondly of her and has stayed in close contact with her. I look forward to getting to know you better through our correspondence! And meet you in person someday. Regards

Its

Mrs. Penny Boldrey

Executive Director

At the end it was not possible for me to attend the ceremony in person. So Rita Riggs and her family stepped in for me.

Her elder son Robert Riggs was designated to receive the award in my behalf as representative of Rita who was in her 80s at the time. I emailed the follow short remarks to be read by Robert Riggs at the time the award is given. It is titled:-

A FUTURE FOR ALL

Mr. President, staff, Graduates, Ladies and Gentlemen; I am deeply moved and humbled being chosen Alpena Community College's Distinguished Alumni for 2005. This recognition belongs to America.

Without the good will and foresight of the staff, students and the community of Alpena in 1967, I might never have had the chance to earn education with which to help my people move forward in life. Hence, allow me reiterate profound gratitude to Alpena Community College, my fellow students, people of Alpena and America at large. My life after Alpena has been full of trials and tribulations detailed in my first book, "The legend against all odds". One relief in it is the robust blessing and peace of mind I have knowing that I am right in what I am doing for my people. There are those who claim Heaven in being rich but for me it is reaching out to help others that matters in life. Upon graduating from medical school, I returned to the Gambia and setup a self-help village Health organisation (Manding Medical Centre) at Njawara village in an effort to provide a much needed medical service to the rural sector.

I am happy to report that membership has grown beyond twenty thousand villagers. Please join me to catch a dream for my villagers. Manding medical centre will help portray the America we all dream of and yearn to be part. We are on the verge of building the children's unit and do need monetary, equipment and medicines assistance in our drive to provide this unique service to villagers. To the graduates, I would like to remind you that, the great tide of history flows and as it flows it carries to the shores of reality what binds us as one human race.

Be aware of the extent, depth and gravity of the challenges ahead as you set out to transform, reconstruct and integrate America into a global icon. Sincere congratulations for your march towards success and fulfilment. Alpena Community College has given you the first footprints. Walk your way with head held high and determination to succeed in the world. Confucius said, "Our greatest glory is never failing, but in rising every time we fail." Stockpiles of atomic bombs or weapons of mass destruction and dictators do not measure greatness.

I believe strongly and sincerely that with deep-rooted wisdom and dignity, innate respect for human right and lives, the intense humanity will make us more cherished and better leaders. This will make us able to contribute towards the future and progress of mankind.

I am happy for you and hope that you will fly the American flag for it is the great American constitution. Finally, I would like to pay tribute to pass and present staff, students of ACC and Alpena community for having given me the opportunity to forge for my people. Allow me make special mention and express thanks to the remarkable and noble friends I met in Alpena.

Sincere thanks from my family, villagers and I to Howard & Rita Rigg, Judge Philip & Viola S. Glennie, Mr. Henry V. Valli, Dr. Elbridge Dunckel, Dr. Strom, Bill & Magritte Cruise, Dr. Charles T. Egli and the Alpena medical association, Mr. Cloyd Ramsey & the Medical Arts Clinic and all who helped make my sojourn to Alpena a remarkable success. If I have a million friends, I would like many more to be like you. I hope you will believe in, as well as join me, in my dream of providing modern medical aid to the Gambian villagers.

Thanks a million and God bless America!

BY: Dr. Alhasan Sisawo Ceesay, MD

Mrs. Penny Boldrey called to let me know she confirmed the details with Robert Rigg, who was selected by the family to deliver the speech. She assured me that Bob was all set with my remarks and had been practicing many times. Rita and Donna will also be attending with other friends. To make it official she sent this note to Robert Rigg (Bob).

April 21, 2005

Robert Rigg

312 Liberty Street

Alpena, MI 49707

Dear Bob,

Dr. Alhasan Ceesay has informed that you will be representing him at our commencement ceremony and accepting the Distinguished Graduate Award on his behalf. Our spring commencement exercises will be held on Thursday, May 5, at 7 pm. There will be VIP seating near the front left section of the Park Arena for and your family. During the commencement program, I will share a brief synopsis of Dr. Ceesay's career. I will invite you to join me at the podium to receive Dr. Ceesay's Distinguished Graduate Award.

Following the presentation, you will have the opportunity to share Dr. Ceesay's remarks. I shared with Dr. Ceesay that his comments must be kept brief (2-3 minutes) because our program consist of many individuals who will also be addressing the graduating class. After the ceremony we would like to take some photographs, so if you could remain near your seats, I will come to you.

A reception at the Jeese Besser Museum follows commencement and you are also invited to join. Enclosed you will find a copy of Dr. Ceesay's remarks. I look forward to hearing from you. Please call me to confirm your participation.

Sincerely

Penny Boldrey

Executive Director

Two weeks prior to the ceremony I received an e-mail letting me know that Karen Eller, administrative assistant in the president's (ACC) office of Public information will be writing about me in the Lumberjack Link spring/summer alumni newsletter publication. Penny also told me that Kerrie Miller (also alumni) and news writer for The Alpena News would like to feature me in the local paper. I immediate e-mailed the following to Kerrie Miller at the Alpena News.

Hi Kerrie, I just received Penny's email with the good news that you want to feature me in the Alpena News. For me this would be a dream come true. Yes! By all means go ahead and feel free to contact me should you want more information about me or the work I'm doing in the Gambia. I am a simple person that loves to help others get on with life the best way they can during their short sojourn on mother earth.

I strongly believe that hose of us who had the privilege to learn from America have responsibility to share American goodwill with our people. That is the only way they, our people, can experience the real America that stands for the down trodden and the innovative. I still feel very happy when come across an American. If your paper is able to help me get Manding Medical Centre at Njawara out of its current limbo, then you would have participated in the most noble and worthy course that will out live us and will be a spring board of hope and medical service for generations we can ever dream of.

We are still on fund raising stage to build the first phase, the children's unit, which according to estimates will cost around £250,000 or about $500,000 dollars. I committed all proceeds of my book, "The legend against all odds", to the centre but it is not selling enough to get things in fast gear. I need help to bring relief to my villagers.

Well, this is enough introductions until I hear from you. God bless you and thanks a million for being kind towards us.

Sincerely

Dr. Alhasan S. Ceesay

Kerrie Miller replied and asked that I send her a synopsis of how I found out Alpena in the 60s. So I sent her the following summary. "I came to be in Alpena by simply going to the then American Consulate in Banjul, the Gambia and asked for a catalogue with information on American colleges.

As a beggar normally has no choice, I started from the top alphabets. Well, Alpena Community college was there and was the first that accepted my application among the schools that replied to my desire to pursue further education in America. This part is well expanded in chapter in my book "The legend against all odds" highlighting my experience at ACC from 1967 -1969.

I was born and bread in abject poverty and I'm only fighting for my villagers to have a chance to proper medical care etc, etc nothing more and nothing -less.

I hope you will help get your readers interested in Manding Medical Centre and its objective for the villagers. Thank you for taking upon the task of writing about me and my work in the Gambia. Manding Medical Centre is in limbo and we year for a boost or a short in the arm to get things moving faster. Please visit our website: friendsofmandinggambimed.btck.co.uk,

It's

Dr. A. Ceesay

I will later reproduce both articles written by Karen Eller for the Lumberjack Link and Kerrie Miller's in the Alpena News respectively. For now let us head to the spring commencement podium and listen to what Mrs. Penny Boldrey has in mind about this simple village doctor. Bob and his family attended in time and it was now time for Penny's remarks about my achievements from the days of Alpena Community College to now. It is simple and movingly started thus:-

"Good evening and congratulations graduates!

The Alpena Community College Foundation created the Distinguished Graduate award not only to recognize, but to honour our graduates who have gone on to contribute to society through successful careers. Our recipient tonight serves as an example of how a solid education foundation from ACC can launch a lifetime of achievements. I 'm pleased to share with you that our 2005 Distinguished Graduate is Dr. Alhasan Ceesay from the Gambia, West

Africa. Dr Ceesay received his Associates of Arts Degree in 1969, exactly two years after leaving the Gambia. He credits many individuals, and the generosity of others, as the driving force behind his success. Following his graduation from ACC, Dr. Ceesay transferred to Olivet College, on a full-tuition scholarship provided to him by the Besser Foundation. In 1971, he earned a Bachelor of Arts Degree in Biology from Olivet, and in 1973 completed his Master of Science degree from Michigan Technological University at Houghton Michigan, USA. Dr. Ceesay taught biology for several years in the Gambia before entering into medical school in 1992, he was awarded his Doctor of Medicine Degree from the American University of the Caribbean. Dr. Ceesay again returned to the Gambia, and provided free medical assistance to the villagers for an entire year before he took a position as House Officer at the Royal Victoria Hospital, Banjul, the Gambia, and was eventually promoted to the post of Medical Officer in 1999.

He is the proud founder of the Manding Medical Centre, a self-help village Health organisation located in the Gambia, which has provided much needed medical care to over 8000 villagers. In his autobiography, "The legend Against All Odds", Dr. Ceesay shares his struggle to survive in his quest for an education.

All the proceeds from his book go to supporting the Manding Medical Centre. Dr. Ceesay and his wife have three daughters, ages 14, 11 and 7. In my correspondence with Dr. Ceesay over the past few months, he shared his profound gratitude for his American education.

He said, "In my mind, it is the American who deserved such honour and distinction, for I'm the recipient of the goodness of the Americans." Due to travel difficulties, Dr. Ceesay is unable to be here tonight to accept this award. However he has asked his first American family, the Howard Rigg family to represent him. At this time I'll ask Bob Riggs to join me at the podium to accept the award for Dr. Ceesay.

Indeed, it is truly an honour to recognize Dr. Ceesay for his many accomplishments and humanitarian efforts. We congratulate him on earning the Distinction of Distinguished Graduate of Alpena Community College. – Penny Boldrey- Robert Riggs eloquently delivered my remarks aimed at the graduates and residents of Alpena city. It was welcomed as I was later told by those who were able to e-mail me. Alpena city and ACC were very happy.

This Distinguished Graduate award came thirty 36 odd years since I last visited Alpena, Michigan. Mathew Dunckel sent me the following comments about the evening of the award. "Alhasan, your address was given at commencement. It was the portion of the evening that was enjoyed by most. Partly because it was delivered well and partly because of my father was mentioned.

I think what you said was inspirational for our students and brought home the need for them to think internationally. Tom Ray is making final preparation to depart for Gambia early next week.

What a great adventure for the students. I am looking forward to hearing about it on their return. Thank you for helping make it happen.

Your friend

Matt.

I sent Penny Boldrey the following; "I received both the award and enclosures. Accept my deepest appreciation for the kind words spoken about me in your presentation speech during the spring graduation ceremony. Thank you very much for your kindness.

I suggested we pursue the possibility of twining Alpena with two villages in the Gambia. Dear reader, I hope your patience is not running out as you eagerly look forward to the publication for alumni and friends of Alpena Community College.

Karen Eller wrote to let me know that she was assigned to write a news article for the local paper announcing my receiving the Distinguished Graduate award. She read my book, "The legend against all odds," to garner more information about me to help her on the matter at hand. She continued by letting me know that she found my story very interesting and she intend to do a good job at the article. Here without further ado is Karen Eller's article about me. This idea unfolded to reality in the chapter on sister city proclamation.

THE LUMBERJACK LINK: ALPENA MICHIGAN
DR. CEESAY NAMED DISTINGUISHED GRADUATE

Dr. Alhasan Sisawo Ceesay of the Gambia, West Africa, was recognized with the Distinguished Graduate award at the ACC spring commencement ceremony in May 5th, 2005. On hand to receive the award for Dr. Ceesay was members of the Howard Riggs family, his first host family when he came to Alpena in 1967. According to Dr. Ceesay, "The Riggs were the ideal American, an average working class who readily shared the little bit God gave them with others less fortunate."

Dr. Ceesay earned his Associate of Arts degree from ACC in 1969 and went on to Olivet College to earn his Bachelor's degree in biology with the help of a full-tuition scholarship from the Besser Foundation. He earned his Master's degree in biological sciences from Michigan Technological University in 1973. In 1979, Dr. Ceesay returned to Africa and entered the University of Liberia Medical School in Monrovia.

Because of political unrest in the Gambia in 1981, Dr. Ceesay escaped to the United States in hopes of completing his life long dream; "to provide medical relief to the villager who is forced to walk miles on end to seek medical aid for his already dying child, wife or friend." During the time he was seeking political asylum in the United States, Dr. Ceesay never gave up his quest for education, and he continued to take classes at Michigan

State University and Wayne State University. He was finally accepted at the American University of the Caribbean in the West Indies, and he began the final segment of his journey to becoming a doctor. In 1992, after 25 years of educational struggles, Dr. Ceesay was awarded his Doctor of Medicine degree from the American University of the Caribbean.

He returned to the Gambia where he provided free medical assistance to the villagers for an entire year before taking a position at the Royal Victoria Hospital, Banjul, The Gambia. Dr. Ceesay founded Manding Medical Centre in 1993. This is a self-help village health organisation which provides much needed medical aid to the villagers of the Gambia, West Africa.

His autobiography, "The legend against all odds," chronicles his struggle to survive in his quest for Western education. Proceeds of his book go to support Manding Medical Centre at Njawara village and provide scholarships in medicine and agriculture for indigent rural candidates in the Gambia. To learn more about Dr. Ceesay's ambitions, you can e-mail him at alhasanceesay@hotmail.com.

Dr. Ceesay was honoured to receive this distinction from ACC and would like to "express thanks to the remarkable and noble friends" he met in Alpena. He credits the goodwill and foresight of the staff and students at ACC for giving him the chance to earn an education and help move his people forward in life. By Karen Eller.

I thank Karen Eller for this revealing commendable article. Here now is that featured by the Alpena News written by news staff Kerrie L. Miller. This is Miller's version about me and my goals.

ALPENA NEWS, MICHIGAN, USA 2005

A LONG ROAD FROM GAMBIA TO ALPENA

When he was about 14, Dr. Alhasan S. Ceesay saw a family tragedy unfold that would change his life forever. As he was walking to school, he saw a woman, pregnancy full-term, who was obviously ill.

Her husband was carrying their young son who was nearly comatose from illness. Ceesay later found out the pregnant woman's baby died in uterus and she died from the toxins built up in her body as a result. The young boy also died three quarters of a mile before his family was able to reach the health centre at Kerewan village.

"That day I said, "If God will help me, no one will ever have to go through that again. That picture is what made up my mind for me," Ceesay said. Ceesay, a native of Njawara, Gambia, is a graduate of Alpena Community College, class of 1969.

He earned his Associate's of Arts degree from ACC before attending Olivet College, Michigan Tech and Howard University, earning his doctor of medicine degree from the America University of the Caribbean in 1992. But how does a young man from a village in Gambia get to Alpena to attend its community college?

In an e-mail message, he stated that after reaching the American Consulate, and asking for a listing of American colleges, Alpena Community College was at the top of the alphabetical list. And Acc was the first to respond to his application. Once here, life was not without challenges. In a telephone conversation, he said it was the first time he had left his country, and when he got here no one spoke his language. "But I don't give up," he said.

Another goal Ceesay never gave up on was making it possible for village families, such as those like one who affected him as deeply as a young man, to have access to have access to health care services. With the creation of the Manding Medical Centre, which has helped over 8000 patients free of charge, he is doing that.

Though progress has been very slow in coming to the centre; Ceesay said officially he is employed by the central government and is only on the weekends is he able to man the centre, along with three or four other doctors who volunteer their time. Ceeesay say the centre sees no fewer than 500 patients and as many as 1,500 patients in a weekend.

He said currently the centre is in limbo and is a little more than a shed. He has been working on fund-raising to get the first phase, a children's unit, built. It is expected to cost approximately $500,000. Members of the ACC Leadership Class are currently conducting fund-raising to go to Gambia and help with the children and volunteering at the centre. The trip will last two weeks.

Ceesay is the author of a book chronicling his life's experiences called "The legend against all odds" (available at Amazon .com) and he has committed all proceeds of its sale to the centre. He said he's never regretted the decision he made to become a doctor. "Sometimes I feel like I have oil on my feet and I'm climbing a very steep hill." Ceesay said. "I have always believed I'll reach my goal… you have to be crazy like me and you have to ignore lots of things that take you away from your goals."

A typical day in Ceesay's life begins at 5 am with prayer, before boarding public transportation to the hospital where he works, 7 miles from his home. From 7 – 11 am he does morning rounds, followed by clinics, then evening rounds. Days can last up to 10 or 11 pm before he heads back home. "In between, I try to please my wife and children. It's a very simple life really," he said.

He and his wife have three daughters, the oldest of which has dreams of attending Alpena High School and ACC before going onto medical school like her father. Ceesay's long-term goals revolve around the medical centre, which he hopes will continue to grow for generations, helping thousands more patients. "I plan to stay at the centre until the day they bury me. That and have my children educated. That's it," he said.

-Kerrie Miller-

Kerrie sent me a copy of the Alpena news. And I sent the following in appreciation of the good work in the article. Kerrie, I just received a copy of the Alpena news featuring me. It was a job well done. I hope it help move my dream of providing medical aid to villagers a notch higher for Manding Medical centre and the Gambian villagers.

The Gambia and I are most grateful for enlightening your readers about us and our need for a medical facility. Extend our thanks and deep appreciation to the staff and Alpena-news. We shall definitely be in Gambia in due course. We look forward to your crew attending the ground breaking ceremonies in Gambia soon. I have started a collection of documentations about me to be placed in Dr. Alhasan S. Ceesay's achieves. Kerrie Miller replied saying that they missed me for the ceremony but she look forward to attending the grand opening of the centre.

Penny Boldrey simply said, "I will certainly make sure you receive a copy of our alumni newsletter once it's completed. Indeed, we are very proud of your accomplishments and humanitarian efforts."

CHAPTER 7

AMERICAN GUESTS VISIT MANDING MEDICAL CENTR, NJAWARA, THE GAMBIA, MAY 2005.

The telephone call on 5/01/05 from Mr. Mathew Dunckel as well as that from Mr. Thomas Ray (TOM) four days later opened the Pandora's box and became harbingers to a remarkable trip to Manding Medical Centre, Njawara village, Gambia by the Alpena Community College's Leadership class headed by none other than their instructor Mr. Thomas P. Ray.

I contacted Mr. Thomas Ray as soon as it was brought to my attention that some ACC students were contemplating visiting my centre at Njawara in May 2005. My message on the 6/01/05 to Mr. Ray ran thus:- "An old friend, Mr. Mathew, staff of ACC, had a long chat with me last night and he brought to my attention of a possibility that a class wanting to travel to the Gambia as guest of Manding Medical Centre at Njaswara.

I am more that willing and happy to pave the way for those that would venture the trip. I do need an e-mail r fax from you indicating desire to go to the Gambia on a mission for Manding Medical Centre. I will speak to both the schools and the district authority about your most welcomed trip to the Gambia. Manding Medical Centre is a self-help village health organisation I setup in upon returning to the Gambia in1992. We provide medical service to villagers and land has been donated for the location of the centre and its ancillaries.

We only have a corrugated shed as clinic. We are now on the verge of building the first phase, being the children's unit of the centre and need monetary assistance. I am delighted to know of your intentions. Please contact me as soon as you speak with the class." Thomas Ray replied on 7/01/05, "I was thrilled when Mathew discussed the possibility of a trip to Gambia for our leadership students. I will meet with the whole class next week to discuss the possibility.

As I am sure you are aware the cost of airfares from Alpena to Gambia is high, so I will need to be certain the students are committed to raising the money needed before we begin making plans. I have travelled to many locations, but never to Africa, so I am also very excited about the prospects for myself. After I meet with the students on Tuesday of next week, I will e-mail you with further information.

I wish to also commend you for your personal achievements; I plan to purchase a copy of your recent book to share with my students and for my personal reading. Thank you for your help and enthusiasm." I emailed Tom advising that to bargain for insured group tickets.

Tom further contacted me on 12/01/05 stating that he has spoken to the students and they have agreed to take on a service trip as part of the course. He told me that they would only be able to travel in a group for 10 – 14 days in May 2005.

Tom wanted to know if there was an existing program at Njawara that would be able to accommodate the students. He assured me that the students would be comfortable in a dormitory housing or make shift dormitories. In addition I let him know on the 14/01/05 that I have spoken to the commissioner, North Bank Division and the local authority in Lower Badibou district regarding their pending trip to Njawara as guest of Manding Medical Centre and the region.

I assured him that these authorities would be more than happy to have his class visit with them. I requested an e-mail from him stating that they are visiting in behalf of Manding Medical Centre at Njawara and specify what they would want to do while in the Gambia. I suggested that they can help teach in some of the schools. I assured them that even though business and some residents have moved out there is still some activity at the village. Tom in reply sent the following on the 15/01/05. "Thank you for the great news.

I am very excited about the prospect and have begun searching for group airfares with special student rates. I will inform the students on Tuesday and contact you immediately afterward via email. I have a few questions. What costs do we need to expect in Gambia and in your village? How will we travel from Banjul to the village? We need to be certain we have a clear idea what expenses we will have to help us set specific fundraising goals both for ourselves and for the foundation from which we hope to receive grants.

When I write the other e-mail, are there tasks other than tutoring that I should include? Are there other ways we can help while we are there? I am more excited about the prospect of this service trip everyday and the students are quite enthused." In another e-mail dated 15/02/05, Tom wrote, "The students in the leadership class are so committed to this project that they voted to contribute their own money toward the travel if they cannot raise enough.

This means that the number of students who actually travel will likely be fewer, but that we will be able to travel to Njawara in May. I have begun drafting the letter to the commissioner many times, but I have some questions. Am I asking the commissioner to help organise local housing for us? Do I want his permission to visit Njawara? Should I tell him what we would like to do there?

What subject might they tutor? Are there any construction projects for the centre or the village with which we could help? I would also like to know if there are any material supplies we could bring with us to donate to the centre or the village. One possible way for us to save money would be to fly into Dakar, Senegal and travel from there overland to Njawara. All the above concerns and questions were answered but a small hiccup in fundraising occurred leaving a distinct possibility that the students will not be able to raise enough to make the trip. The reason being the major source of funding for the trip fell through.

This left all of us jittery but Tom and his students were in no mood to change their plans to travel to the Gambia in May 2005. On the same day 15/02/05 I received the following from Mr. Jay Walterriet, Director of Public information for Alpena Community College. It stated that he was asked to contact me for more photos of myself and the clinic at Njawara. He wanted more information regarding the Leadership planned trip to Gambia.

I was told that the local television station would like to do a segment on the Leadership class and their trip. As part of the segment photos were needed. I sent all photos that were relevant to enable the reporter to do his TV-segment on the planned Leadership trip to Njaswara, Gambia.

Mr. Jay on the 17/02/05 emailed thanking me for providing the requested photos and assured me that ACC has received good deal of interest from the local media regarding the Leadership class trip and both he and Penny Boldrey were trying to provide all of the information they could. My e-mail was given to reporters who might want to contact me for more information. The entire twenty students could not enlist for the final take off to Africa. So Thomas Ray and 11 students took on the venture of their life time to the Gambia as guest of Manding Medical Centre at Njawara village.

On 17 February 2005 Tom sent me a copy of the final letter he sent to the commissioner and the local authority at the Lower Badibou district spelling out their intentions and wish while guests of the Manding Medical Centre for a two weeks duration. Here it is.

Thamos P. Ray

Alpena Community College

666 Johnson Street

Alpena, Michigan 49707

17 February 2005

Dear Commissioner Batala Juwara,

I am pleased to inform you of our plans to visit Njawara on behalf of the Manding Medical Centre. I am the advisor and instructor for a group of college students from Alpena Community College in Michigan in the USA. We plan to visit Njawara in May and hope you will help us find lodging with local families during our stay.

Our plan as of now is to fly out of the US on May 6th to Banjul via London and to return on May 19th 2005. During our stay in Gambia, our hope is to provide any assistance we can to the community on behalf of the Manding Medical Centre.

We would like to visit the school in Njawara and tutor the children and share stories and activities with them. I also hope that we will have the opportunity to visit the important centres of the community and learn as much as we can in our short stay about the people and life in Njawara and Gambia.

I have communicated our plans with Dr. Alhasan Ceesay, who has kindly extended the invitation to us on behalf of the Manding Medical Centre.

Sincerely

Thomas P. Ray

English Instructor

This letter was acknowledged by the commissioner and the district authority in the Gambia. Now that I was certain of the trip I set to inform my board members in like manner. The certainty of the trip was concretized by the following sent by Tom on 10 March 2005.

It simply updated me on the progress made regarding the trip; that the students have raised half the money needed to travel to Gambia. He affirms the fact that everyone concerned is working hard on the remaining sum. The arranged inoculations and are preparing to apply for visas to Gambia. He said they were all enthused and has used my address in Gambia for the visa information requirement.

Again, I was delighted for things are now heading the right direction for the historic and unique trip to Njawara. I am now certain that more doors to boost ours and the centre's goals for the Gambia will be open by this simple friendly act of ACC. Here finally is my despatch the board members of Manding Medical Centre at Njawara village.

MANDING MEDICAL CENTRE/NJAWARA

UNITED KINGDOM CONTACT

245 GREAT WESTERN STREET

MANCHESTER, M14 4LQ

ENGLAND

E-MAI:alhasanceesay@hotmail.com

Tel/Fax: 44+161-342-0854

Date: 25/03/05

DEAR BOARD MEMBER,

I am pleased to bring to your attention about American guests to Manding Medical Centre at Njawara. Mr. Thomas Ray along with 11 Alpena Community college students will be visiting the Gambia as our guest in May 2005. They will be leaving the USA for the Gambia on May 6th, 2005 and depart for United States on the 19th, of May. I would be most grateful if you give some of your time to meet them and make their visit memorable.

There are many benefits to be accrued for the centre and the Gambia. I am at present arranging in the form of scholarships or placements in various fields of study at my previous college in Alpena Michigan. I have been in constant contact with Commissioner Batala Juwara at Kerewan and I would like all of you to brain storm and make this an ongoing link between us and Alpena Community College and other Michigan cities I am now in negotiation with.

Alpena city has developed interest in our project. I am also happy to report that my former college, Alpena Community College has awarded me, "Distinguished 2005 Graduate." Find enclosed correspondence from Mr. Thomas Ray, in behalf of the Leadership class of Alpena Community College, to Commissioner Juwara and Sefo Fafanding Kinte. I look forward to your understanding and participation to help open up the Pandoa's Box of goodwill for the Gambia. This is a onetime opportunity for the Gambia that would make our two people linked for good goals and noble courses for generations of Gambians.

My regards and keep in touch.

Yours truly,

Dr. Alhasan S. Ceesay, MD

Founder/co-coordinator

cc: Mr. Ousainu Darboe

cc: Mr. Fafa E. Mby, Dr. Dawda Ceesay , Dr. Ayo Palmer
cc: Mr. Saim Kinte

cc: Mr. Sambou Kinte,

cc: Mr. Mustapha Njie

cc: Elh. Maja Sonk

cc: Mr. Dodou Ceesay

cc: Mr. Sisawo Ceesay

cc: Mrs. Mbee Sonko

On April 7th 2005, Tom updated me stating that the visa applications were going well and that most of the students have received their visas. In addition let me privilege you the reader with some of the reactions emailed to me about the pending trip and what it would mean to them. Alison Jane Smolinski said:

"Hello Dr. Ceesay. I am one of the students in the Leadership class at Alpena Community College. I am really excited about the service trip, only a couple more weeks. Right now we are trying to prepare for the trip, just getting the basic necessities and what we should be packing.

I just read about how you are building a bakery at Njawara. Even though our resources are limited, is there something we could do to help out? I thought we could help in some way. I also just wanted to say thank you for the wonderful experience you giving to us. I realize it will be truly an eye opener. I feel as if I could never be able to repay you for these two weeks that you about to give us. Thank you Dr. Ceesay!"

Another email from Brittany Posthumus simply stated; "I am one of the students from Alpena Community College that will be coming this May to help. After learning all the things that you have done I must say you are an inspiration and the world can use more people who care as much as you do. I can't wait to come to Njawara.

I am very excited to be able to help and thank you for the invitation." Lastly, Ms. Grace Schimitz sent in the following before leaving for the Gambia. "I am a member of the Alpena Community College class that will be assisting you this May at Njawara. I am greatly looking forward to my visit to the Gambia. Thank you so much for the invitation!

The Friends of Manding, a charitable Trust at Colchester had the following in its web site about the trip to Njawara, the Gambia. It read as "News flash 12 American visiting:" "A class of 11 students and their instructor Mr. Thomas Ray from Alpena Community College, Alpena Michigan, will be visiting the Gambia as guest of Manding Medical Centre from the 6th to 19th May 2005.

They will be visiting communities and tutor at local schools. Alpena has developed interest in project Manding Medical Centre at Njawara. We are negotiating to have this exchange as an ongoing affair between Alpena and Njawara." As time drew near to the flight to the Gambia Tom contacted the Commissioner on several occasions to clear last possible huddles that may surface.

None the less preparations went smoothly and Thomas Ray and his ACC Leadership class left America on May 10th 2005 via Madrid and then Dakar, Senegal before embanking at Banjul, the Gambia. As fate would have the team instead hired a bus from Dakar to Hamdali village in the North Bank which was nearer to Njawara.

I learnt they were given a VIP escort from Hamdali via Kerewan to Njawara village. As expected, I called the Mayor of Njawara, Mrs. Hadi Panneh enquiring about the American visitors. She told me they were fine and housed at the village centre, a semi motel used for foreign guest to Njawara.

Tom and I spoke at length along with Sefo Fafanding Kinte. Sefo Fafanding reassured me that every thing possible will be done to help make "our guest comfortable and like wise a memorable visit in due course. I spoke briefly to the commissioner the next day to get a feed back from him. The two week flew fast for the students most of who did want to leave at the time for kindness rendered by the villagers.

It is said that good thing never last long and this the experience of the student who went to Njawara in May 2005. Here is the reaction of Americans after the trip to the Gambia. The ACC students started sending their report and experience as guest of Manding Medical Centre, Njawara, The Gambia. Starting with Alison Jane Smolinski reported as bellow.

"Hello Dr. Ceesay:

The trip to Njawara was incredible! I did not want to leave. It was an experience of a lifetime that I will never forget. Everyone in the village was very kind and helpful. I have never met such kind people in my entire life. I found the villagers doing everything possible to make their lives better. I realized that many people work together to get a job done or finished. This is absolutely wonderful. Everyone was so helpful in the village. The people of Njawara gave us such wonderful hospitality. The food and shelter was more than we deserved.

Also your wife, Mrs Fatou Koma-Ceesay, was all too good to us. We had a remarkable time with her at Bundung, Serekunda. Her cooking was excellent. And the gifts she gave all of us, we did not deserve. Your family is wonderful and was too kind to us. I would like to thank you for the incredible experience you have given me. I could not have asked for anything more. I immensely enjoyed my self. I want to go back one day. I also want you to know that I will do my best to help in whatever way I can. I realize that action are louder than words and hope I can prove that to everyone.

Thank you Dr. Ceesay."

Another reaction came from Grace Schiminitz. "I really enjoyed my time in Njawara. The people treated us very well and it was a pleasure to spend two weeks with them. Your wife is a wonderful person and was very hospitable to us. I will always be grateful for her kind treatment.

I hope to make another visit to Njawara in the future. It is a wonderful place. It was an eye-opening experience. The people were absolutely marvellous. They treated us as their own family and welcomed us with open hands. I had no idea that they would be that hospitable. I really miss walking to the river and spending time with the children.

It was my first experience in Gambia and hopefully it will not be my last. I hope I can return their kindness. I would love to see how the kids have grown up."

The last but not the least came from Mr. Thomas P. Ray, English instructor at ACC. It read; "I want to thank you for the opportunity you provided my students on this trip. The entire experience was enjoyable and valuable as a means of teaching my students something about the responsibility that comes with the privileges they enjoy here.

Everyone was kind to us on the trip and the students came away with many great souvenirs and memories. I have many digital photos and am working on producing a CD of them to send out. I also plan to type up a version of my journal for posting on the internet and I will send parts of that to you. I plan to call the village this weekend to extend my appreciation to everyone.

Do you know anything about the proposed potential sister city relationship between Alpena and Njawara? I would like to start making some local contacts here to help that process. I am also hopeful that future trips will be possible for my students.

-Mr. Thomas P. Ray-

As you know very well man proposes but God dispose things. Tom took over the running of the department and with that came a hand full challenging responsibilities. He was not able to provide the CD until 11th of October 2005 after several reminders from me and those visiting my Website (friendsofmandinggambimed.btck.co.uk).

Finally, Tom contacted me on 4/11/05 to let me know he had the college mailing office send the CD of photos and other material registered delivery to me. Then he made donation of $1000(one thousand us dollars) in the name of Friends of Manding, a Charitable Trust at Colchester Essex organising fund raising activities for Manding Medical Centre at Njawara the Gambia, West Africa.

This cheque was duly received and forward registered mail to the Secretary of the Friends of Manding for depositing into our account at LLyod's Bank in Colchester Essex County. Tom asked about the state of the proposed sister-city program between Alpena and Njawara. Yes, this was one of my goals for inviting the Americans to my village in the Gambia. I just believe that unveiling the false masks and stigma others have about Africa will create harmony in its unique way.

People need to accept differences in the cultures. I transmitted all reactions presented by our American visitor to the Commissioner, the chief, and the village heads especially Hadi Panneh of Njawara village.

CHAPTER 8

ALPENA: THANKS FOR TWINING

SISTER-CITY PROCLAMATION

Having now been recognised as Distinguished 2005 Graduate by Alpena Community College I made a proposal for a twining relationship or sister-city status between Alpena and select villages in the Gambia. I, you guessed right, contacted Mathew Dunckel as a sound board or trial balloon for the above idea.

He replied that it was a sound idea and suggested my contacting the Alpena City Council members on the subject. He gave their web site thus: http://www.alpena.mi.us/council/members. In addition he gave the names of Councilman Dave Karschnik and Councilwoman Carol Shafto for me to initiate direct contact with the Alpena City Council.

He told me that the mayor was John Gilmet and the City manager was Mr. Alan Bakalarski. Armed with all this information and more I made my first push through Mrs. Penny Boldrey, Executive Director at Alpena Community College. I had no doubt if I get her interest in this unique wish she would do all within her power to not only contact the right people to make it eventually happen but would open up more doors for my villagers and our health project at Njawara.

Penny Boldrey upon hearing from me linked with Councilwoman Shafto on the June 14th, 2005 thus; "Hi Carol, from one Distinguished Grad to another….. I received the enclosed message from our 2005 Distinguished Graduate, Dr. Alhasan Ceesay. I' m wondering if perhaps you can help me with his inquiry regarding the possibility of twining between Alpena City and two villages in the Gambia, West Africa." Penny in turn informed me that she had contacted a good friend, Carol Shafto, who is a member of Alpena's City Council and also an Alpena Community College Distinguished 2003 Graduate, regarding my request for twining between the above communities.

She enclosed Councilwoman Shafto's response to the idea. My reaction was swift and my message to Councilwoman Carol Shafto ran thus:-"Hello Councilwoman Carol. Mrs Penny Boldrey sent me correspondence she had with you regarding a proposal I made to the city of Alpena. My initial e-mail kick starting a twining proposal between the city of Alpena; Njawara and Kinte Kunda villages in the Gambia West Africa was sent to Mayor John F. Gilmet, Dave R. Karsctunick, Mike Polluch, Sam Eller and Carol Shafto. It read, "I'm pleased to write and inform you that I am deputized by village heads of Njawara and Kinte Kunda to contact you and initiate a twining/sister city status proposal between Alpena and the above two villages. Njawara is my home village and Kinte Kunda is where I attended primary school in the early fifties. Tom Ray and the Leadership students visited both places during their two weeks stay in the Gambia.

They met the chief of the district, Sefo Fafanding Kinte, at Kinte Kunda. Kinte Kunda has been the seat of many chiefs of the region and Fafanding is the most recent of several from this village. Njawara is historically a trading centre connecting Gambia and the Northern part of Senegal.

Today she has become a tourist destination. One can easily log onto information about Njawara village on the internet. It boasts of lots of female education oriented projects. In addition it has an agricultural training centre." The contact was made in behalf of the village heads of the above and the local authority at the North Bank division of the Gambia. This twining would be a very rewarding interaction and educational for both yours and the villagers.

 The people are eager to make worth while friendship with America. The chiefs and village heads have urged me to initiate their wish for the twining between them and Alpena or any city willing to go into such relationship with the villages. You can link up with Mr. Thomas Ray and his students for feed back on their experience as guests of Manding Medical Centre at Njawara village, the Gambia. The villagers and I would be most grateful if given the chance to link up with Alpena City.

 Carol Shafto sent in this hiccup. "Dr. Ceeasy, I cannot proceed with any more discussions with the City Council of the City of Alpena until I am much clearer about what a Twining proposal entails. Could you please describe to me what you have in mind?

Although we may be supportive of your work at Njawara and Kinte Kunda in the Gambia; we cannot really act on your request until we know what we are agreeing to. Could you send me a brief outline of what you are seeking from the City of Alpena? I will be happy to act as a liaison between you and the City, but cannot do so until I have a clear idea of what I am advocating for. Thank you most sincerely."

Carol Shafto

On July 13, 2005 I sent the required clarification to Councilwoman Carol Shafto as follows. Hello Carol, I am glad to hear from you. To be simplistically clear, twining means a sisterhood relationship between two cities for the mutual rewards of those involved.

Hence it is a friendship like affair where people from Alpena can be part of and like wise the villages involved but at no cost to either party. For example Councilwoman Shafto can choose to spend two weeks in Gambia helping reorganise or create a more functional administrative system or even learn from the villagers.

In brief it is a two way international relationship. Or cultural dance -troupes from the Gambia villages can be coming to entertain Alpena, possibly more cities, during the summers. This will help raise funds for the city, the villages, like wise for our health project at Njawara. It will provide much awareness and understanding of the two people merged in friendship.

It is like adopting each other and opening up rewarding human adventures at no cost involved. In a nut-shell, it means ratified friendship between Alpena and the two villages. I hope this makes it palatable for Alpena to want to be part of such endearing relationship. I thank you in behalf of the Kerewan local authority, the villagers and Commissioner for North Bank Division, the Gambia. God blesses all of you."

Dr. Ceesay

Needless to say Councilwoman Carol Shafto was very pleased with the above clarification and appealed to Alpena City Council to consider the idea of twining in behalf of the Gambian villages. Hence, Carol on the 13/7/05 sent me this e-mail following the receipt of the above message to the councilwoman.

It simply states that, "I have forwarded this information to the mayor and city manager and offered to be the liaison if the City should consent to comply with this request. I will keep you posted with any development." I updated the Commissioner and all concern at the Lower Badibou district regarding progress of my initiative with Alpena City few weeks after hearing from Councilwoman Carol Shafto. The Commissioner and the local authority sent me the bellow covering letter in support of my push for a twining relationship with Alpena City Michigan, USA.

Njawara/Kinte Kunda

Lower Badibou District

North Bank Division

The Gambia, W. Africa

November 5th, 2005

To: Dr. Alhasan Ceesay

Manchester, England

Subject: Twining of Njawara, Kinte Kunda & Alpena Michigan

Dear Dr. Ceesay,

Your first letter dated September 23rd, 2005 has been received and the content of which is understood, both the Commissioner, the Chief and the Alkalos (village heads) of Njawara and Kinte Kunda are very much interested in having Njawara, Kinte Kunda and Alpena City twined. The Communities of both villages met and discussed the issue and they are very much happy about the lofty ideas.

Njawara and Kinte Kunda are located in the Northern part of the Gambia. They are just about 60 kilometres away from the capital City Banjul, the Gambia. Kinte Kunda is just 2 kilometres away from our administrative headquarters Kerewan where both the Commissioner and Area Council stay. Where as Njawara is located 9 kilometres away from Kerewan. Regards

Sincerely

Aja Hadi Panneh (Alkalo)

Alh. Fafanding Kinte (Chief Lower Badibou)

Cc: Mr. Batala Juwara (Commisioner NBD)

I replied to the above support with this note despatched immediately to the village Akalos, the Chief and Commissioner North Bank Division at Kerewan village.

245 Great Western Street

Manchester M14 4LQ

England

16/11/05

A BIG THANK YOU TO ALL

Dear Commissioner,

I'm profoundly grateful to you, Sefo Fafanding, the local authority (area Council and chiefs) and especially Alkalo Arfang Bah and people of Toro. Lastly but not the least a big thank you goes to the people of Badibou, Njawara and my sister Hadi Panneh Alkalo of Njawara village.

I am very happy for support and understanding given to Manding Medical Centre. I'm pleased to inform you that I have initiated a twining process between Alpena and the villages of Njawara and Kinte Kunda. I have forwarded your note of 5/11/05 to the Alpena City Council. Copies were also sent to Mr. Thom Ray and the college.

Again, thank you for making our American friends happy and welcomed to our beloved country. God bless all of you. I will continue working for our development.

Sincerely

Dr. Alhasan S. Ceesay, MD

Director/Founder

Manding Medical Centre.

I then sent Carol Shafto the letter from the district authority plus this note urging action from her end.

245 Great Western Street

Manchester M14 4LQ

England

8/11/05

Mrs. Carol Shafto

Councilwoman

Alpena City Council

208 North First Avenue

Alpena, MI 49707

Dear Mrs. Carol Shafto,

The enclosed is reply to your last e-mail dated 25/9/05 regarding the twining proposal made to the Alpena City Council earlier on by me in behalf of Njawara village and Kinte Kunda, the Gambia, respectively. The enthusiasm about having this relationship with Alpena is immeasurable. The villagers are looking forward to a warm and fruitful relationship between the two people. They all pray that you would be as eager to consummate it as they have already done in their wishes and hearts.

Finally, may friendship and human kindness be an everlasting link between all humans. God bless you and we look forward for a positive reply soon. My personal regards and thanks to the City Council and all of Alpena.

Yours Sincerely

Dr. Alhasan S. Ceesay, MD

It was not until September 21, 2005 that I sent Councilwoman Shafto the following reminder and follow up note. "Hi Carol, I hope you had an enjoyable summer. This is a follow up of that lofty idea of twining Alpena City with Njawara and Kinte Kunda villages in the Gambia. Has there been any movement forward at the Mayor's Office about the proposal made to the city?

Is there anything I or the district authority in Gambia need do to bring this to fruition? I have not heard any thing about it since your last email of 14/7/05. Again, regards and thanks. I bank on your continued interest. God Bless."

Dr. Alhasan Ceesay

The next day God smiled onto our dream to befriend America. Councilwoman Mrs. Carol Shafto sent me the following reply to the inquiry about the status of my dream for America and the Gambia. It rang in the most melodious and cherished message I ever had for a long, long time after my being admitted into medical school and upon treating my first patient in the villages.

Here is Carol's email to me.

"Good morning Dr. Ceesay: I appreciate your persistence in accomplishing this goal. Without that it surely would have failed. I do apologize for this delay. I have just returned this week from a wonderful month long tour of the UK and Ireland. My last communication, before I left, with the City Manager was that this was a good idea, will be good for public relations, and that we should go forward with the proposal.

The Mayor is also in favour. So there is absolutely nothing standing in the way of this happening. I am willing to do the work of it, but I honestly have no idea what to do. Do you know procedures or paper work or any such thing from your end? Is it as simple as a proclamation? I would like to have more information about your village, your people, and why you are interested in twining with Alpena – what connection there is.

I would then put together a presentation for the City Council and ask them to decide that we are sister-cities (the term used here, although I know the UK and Europe use "twining) with the villages of Njawara and Kinte Kunda.

We could erect a sign at the City entrance, etc. If you have any idea or directions for me, please let me know. Also any information you can provide on your village would be helpful. I will continue to work with you on this until it is accomplished.

Your friend in Alpena – Carol Shafto – This was followed by my forwarding the bellow addendum to whatever had reached the Councilwoman's desk. Being the architect of this union much was expected from me. And so I never relented supplying as much information as many times as I can afford. My phone bill sprouted to a Warping £600 etc. Most important was this addendum bellow.

SYNAPSIES OF NJAWARA/KINTE KUNDA VILLAGES

Njawara is a 350 years old market village situated on the bank of the Miniminiyang bolong, a creek of the River Gambia, in the Lower Badibou District of the North Bank Division of the Gambia. Njawara has a population of a thousand residents and is 95 kilometres from Banjul, Gambia's capital City.

The village lies close to the Senegalese border and has been the trade links between Gambia and Senegal during the colonial days. Njawara was established and founded by the Panneh family of the Wolof tribe and initially called "Panneh village." The elderly still fondly refer to her as Mpanneh. Among the residents of now Njawara are Mandingkas, Fulas, Sereres, Jolas, Konyanginkas, and Mabara tribes.

All of whom are farmers, with few serving as petty traders, growing Peanuts, Rice, Coos, and a variety of vegetables. The nearest government administrative post is 9 kilometres away at Kerewan village. Njawara lacked modern luxuries of electricity, proper telephones, sewer system, pave roads but water is now pumped from a nearby borehole.

The village has a thriving school and a dynamic citizenry working hard to improve heir lot and the future of the younger generation. KINTE KUNDA village has been the political base of Lower Badibou District for decades. It has provided us with several chiefs in the past and Sefo Fafanding Kinte is the most recent contribution. Kinte Kunda village comprises of mostly Mandinka tribes men and women.

It is the home of venerable late Sefo Njako Kinte who, in the 30s ruled the district with and iron fist. It was he who imposed one of his brothers, Almami Kinte, to take over the administration or village headship of then

Njawara(Mpanneh).

None the less he was a respected chief. Kinte Kunda was the first village that had a school in the entire Lower Badibou district and I am told that he chief insisted that the school be built in his home village leaving a row that lasted through his rein. The village is now a smaller population than Njawara and the current appointed chief of the district, Sefo Fafanding Kinte resides there. Residents of Kinte Kunda are all farmers eager to improve their lives and those of their children.

They are friendly, peaceful, charming, descent hard working people who contributed a lot to growth of the Lower Badibou District in the North Bank. These two villages along with the entire Lower Badibou District yearn for this twining/sister-city status to come to realty. Hence, I enclose relevant messages regarding the proposed twining from the district authority as per fax from the Gambia.

The villagers and I are interested in twining with Alpena Michigan n an effort to open up the Pandora's box of friendship, goodwill and more understanding of the people and cultures that would allow us relate in this shrinking globe we all share. There is a lot we can do for each other once the ugly veil of ignorance, misunderstanding and fear is removed.

And this can be done only learning and interacting with one another. I am sure the students, who went to the villages, can tell how much warmth and friendship they received from the villagers they met. Exchange visits and whole host of beneficial programs to both parties can be organised within the framework of this twining.

Once again, I personally appeal to the Mayor and City Council of Alpena to give this desire of the villagers a chance of fruition for Alpena City and the above villages in the Gambia. In short while, I received the following reply from Councilwoman Carol Shafto of Alpena City Council letting me know of the final details, date of the be proclamation for the sister-city relationship between our villages and Alpena Michigan. Without further ado I present the message as sent on the 17th of November 2005.

"Good Morning Dr. Ceesay

After many months of communication with you, I can finally announce a DATE for our Twining/Sister City Resolution! The Alpena City Council will adopt a resolution to establish a Sister City Program with Njawara/ Kinte Kinda on December 5th, 2005.

I am going to be personally preparing the resolution. Since it will be a part of permanent records for both the villages and the City of Alpena, I would like be sure all of the information is accurate. Penny Boldrey suggested that I email the text to you after I complete it.

If you are willing, you could read it for any factual errors or omissions before I send it on to the City. If you are willing, I will send that via email when it is ready, some time next week. Meanwhile I am meeting with Tom Ray from the college who led the Leadership Class expedition to the villages. He is VERY enthusiastic about this proposal and is going to give me information and even share some pictures. We will be meeting next week.

Finally, I have invited several people to come to the City Council meeting to provide testimony and support for this proposal. Both Penny Boldrey and Tom Ray will be there. Also they are inviting some of the students who went to the villages to also be present and speak to the issue.

So it would be a very nice presentation and will be more than just a formality. Also, if you would like, I can arrange to have a tape of the meeting sent to you. Our meetings are videotaped and played for the public on the public access television channel several times a week, between meetings. I can make a copy of the tape of the meeting and have it send you or to the village officials or both if you would like.

Also, the resolution will have an official seal of the City of Alpena and the signature of the Mayor. I will have as many copies as you need made and will laminate them so they will be preserved. I will send those to you and/ or whomever you designate. I will get several if necessary. I am so pleased to finally be able to bring this to completion.

I know it must have been frustrating to you to have this take so long and to have us seen to be so unresponsive. I hope this totally enthusiastic ending makes up for all of that!

Your friend in Alpena

Carol Shafto

On the day of ratification or passing of the resolution for sister city relationship between Alpena and the two above villages several speakers were heard. These included, among many, Penny Bodrey, Mr. Tom Ray, two student representatives who visited Gambia in May 2005 and Dr. Avery Aten.

This was buffered by loop of fifty photos of the villages taken by the student while in the Gambia. At the end of the presentation Mayor John F. gimlet read into the record the above proclamation and vote was tabled to pass it. This Sister City proclamation between Alpena with Njawara/Kinte Kunda, Lower Badibou District, the Gambia was moved by Councilwoman Carol Shafto, seconded by Councilman Karschnick, that the proclamation to establish a sister city program with the villages of Njwara and Kinte Kunda be approved.

The move was carried by unanimous vote. A copy of the sister City Resolution passed by Alpena City Council on December 5th 2005 is reproduced for your pleasure to read.

PROCLAMATION TO ESTABLISH A "SISTER CITY" PROGRAM WITH NJAWARA AND KINTE KUNDA, LWER BADIBOU DISTRICT, GAMBIA, WEST AFRICA

WHEREAS, the City of Alpena recognises and supports the concept of global cooperation and community; and

WHERAS, the villagers of Njawara and Kinte Kunda, through their local leaders and Dr. Alhasan S. Ceesay, have reached out their hand in friendship and goodwill, and

WHEREAS, relationships were established by students and faculty of Alpena Community College when they were

warmly welcomed to the villages for a service project earlier this year, and

WHEREAS, mutual understanding of our diversities as well as our similarities and the cultural exchanges that will result, will be beneficial to the citizens of both areas, and

WHEREAS, true global community is often established one person at a time, and one city and village at a time, leading to beneficial relations and programs for all;

NOW, THEREFORE, I, John F. Gilmet, by virtue of the authority vested in me as Mayor, DO HEREBY PROCLAIM, A "Sister City" Program with the villages of

NJAWARA/KINTE KUNDA

LOWER BADIBOU DISTRICT

GAMBIA

And urge all area citizens to extend the hand of fellowship and an embrace of genuine fraternity to their friends in NJAWARA/KINTE KINTE KUNDA and pledge support and loyalty as these communities of two great nations join together as "Sister Cities"

Signed; at Alpena Michigan, United States of America, on this 5th day of December, 2005

Councilwoman Carol Shafto read the following reply from me to Council and residents of Alpena City.

ALPENA, THANKS FOR TWINING WITH US

Honourable Mayor John F. Gilmet, Alpena City Council and residents of Alpena; please allow me convey heartfelt thanks as well as greetings from the Commissioner, NBD, Kerewan Area Council, the Chief of Lower Badibou, the Alkalos (village heads) of Njawara and Kinte Kunda.

I am today full of joy and gratitude for twining resolution ratified by the Alpena City Council. I am speechless as one of my dreams for the villager and America has now materialized in this twining resolution passed by Alpena. We are two good people now merged in good will for humanity and friendship.

This coming together will archive a lot for both of us. There is a lot for us to gain as well as learn from each other and generations to come will thank us for having taken the first footsteps of bringing people of diverse cultures and understanding together.

Enclosed is message from the Gambia in response to the most welcomed news in your last email. This is the top of the iceberg for there is lot more benefit in this act. In addition, as long as I am alive Alpena and Gambia will not only benefit from this unique venture but will smile yearly for having dreamt along with me.

Let me, in passing, mention with thanks the first harbingers of this day. They are Mr. Thomas P. Ray and his Leadership team of students from Alpena Community College who visited Njawara village in May 2005.

Thomas Ray and the students laid the marvellous foundation we today concretize. Mrs. Penny Boldrey and Mathew Dunckel deserve our appreciation for remaining interested and in constant contact with me.

The Gambia, the district authority of Lower Badibou and villagers remain eternally grateful for giving us the chance of twining with you. A Huge thanks Alpena City, the Mayor of Alpena and Alpena City Council for work well done. Councilwoman Mrs. Carol Shafto who relentlessly steered the twining proposal to completion also deserves our profound gratitude.

The villagers and I are eternally indebted to all at Alpena. In addition, we look forward to working hand in hand for the reward of all parties. Finally, I would again like to pay tribute to past and present friends at Alpena who helped me reach this pedestal. All of you helped make my sojourn to America a remarkable success. I would like many more of my friends to be like you at Alpena.

I hope you will believe, as well as join me, in my dream of providing modern medical aid to the Gambian villagers. Thanks a million and God bless America!

Signed: DR. ALHASAN SISAWO CEESAY, MD

FOUNDER/COORDINATOR

MANDING MEDICAL CENTRE

NJAWARA, THE GAMBIA

Two weeks later I received three copies of the "sister City Proclamation" along with a video tape of the Alpena City Council Meeting of December 5, 2005. Also enclosed were the Alpena news and copy of Alpena Public Notices showing minutes of the City Council meeting which carried ratification of the sister city proclamation by a unanimous vote.

I must confess exhilaration in my heart for Alpena City Council having done so much for my villages without reservation and accomplished with great speed. I sent the following communiqué to the current representative to the Gambia, Ambassador Joseph D. Stafford in preparing them for the arrival the package from the Alpena City Council for forwarding to the Commissioner of the North Bank Division, the Gambia.

MANDING MEDICAL CENTRE

245 Great Western Street

Manchester M14 4LQ

Email:alhasanceesay@hotmail.com

Date: 10/12/05

Ambassador Joseph D. Stafford

Embassy of the United States of America

Kairaba Avenue

P. M. Box 19

Banjul, the Gambia, West Africa

RE: Manding Medical Centre/Alpena USA Twining

Dear Ambassador Stafford,

I am Dr. Alhasan S. Ceesay from Njawara village and currently on studies in the UK. This is to introduce the above self-help health organisation at Njawara as well as kindly request favour of your good office's service in behalf Alpena Michigan and the villages of Njawara and Kinte Kunda, the Gambia.

I pioneered the above centre, after graduating as a doctor and upon returning to the Gambia in 1992. It became an NGO in 1994 after being fully registered by the Justice Department and recognised by the Ministry of Health in 1993. In addition, we are now a registered Charitable Trust, as Friends of Manding, in England and Wales by the Charity Commission of the UK. Our website www.friendsofmandinggambimed.btck.co.uk

It will show our home page as "Friends of Manding." Alternatively, one can used a short cut by typing in "Manding Medical Centre, Njawara" and click search. The same home page plus lot more will appear. I have also written two books and a hefty portion of proceed from the sale of both books is earmarked to help support Manding Medical Centre at Njawara and our goal of providing medical aid to the villager, especially children.

More information about my work and commitment to providing much needed medical service to the region in conjunction with the Gambia Ministry of Health can be seen in our website as above. Finally, I am more than delighted to report that Alpena City, Michigan, USA has just ratified a sister city program with my home village Njawara and Kinte Kunda village in the Lower Badibou District, North Bank Division, the Gambia.

Hence, I have asked the Alpena City Mayor's Office to send five copies of the final proclamation declaring the sister city status between Alpena and the above two named villages in Badibou to you for your office to kindly deliver the documents to the Commissioner North Bank Division at Kerewan.

Thank you for taking time to assist us in the above matter. Please feel free to contact me any time convenient to you. Best wishes for good health and achievement in the coming year. Regard to your family.

Yours Sincerely

Dr. Alhasan S. Ceesay, MD

Founder/Coordinator

Manding Medical Centre

Njawara,

The Gambia, West Africa.

This letter was followed with two telephone calls to the Embassy of the United States in the Gambia to verify receipt of the package sent from Alpena to Joseph D. Stafford. The Secretary to Mr. Stafford, in the last phone call let me know it usually take a month or more before none official mail arrives at their desk.

He assured me that the office will do as request whenever the package reaches the Embassy. I called Sefo Fafanding Kinte and Alkalo Hadi Panneh and told them to check with either Ambassador Joseph Stafford directly or one of the officers in the know at the office for their copies of the sister city proclamation of which the villagers are unsung heroes for having received the ACC students who visited Njawara in May 2005 with open hearts, hospitality, generosity and warmth.

It was not until Thursday, February 16th, 2006 that Ambassador Joseph D. Stafford and team where able to deliver, in person amid tumultuous reception and celebration, the sister-city proclamation between Alpena City, Michigan USA, with Njawara and Kinte Kunda villages in the North Bank of the Gambia.

I made it clear that the brief ceremony at Njawara on the 16/2/06 marked the end of phase one of the sister city relationship between us and Alpena Michigan. I suggested the following four areas for food for thought by all concern. They are:-

1. Education: This already started in earnest as some in Alpena have expressed desire to sponsor worthy candidates at the primary level for an experimental period of one year. Higher levels, such as college education and nursing training and or other relevant skill areas will in due course be included.

2. Health: A lot is planed for health oriented programs and Manding Medical Centre will be enhanced to a much functional status. There will be training programs for health personnel etc.

3. Tourism: I am studying ways of creating tourist attraction with facilities erected in due course to the region.

4. Cultural: Exchanges entailing having cultural dance troop(s) from the Lower Badibou District travel to Alpena Michigan, and other cities in the USA during the summers to display our fabric of entertainment, history and arts.

These are few ideas in the pipeline.

Feel free to add yours to enrich the program. This is by no means binding or final but seeking more suggestions on how to benefit both parties in this unique twining program just approved by Alpena City. Let me make it crystal clear that there is no financial commitment from Alpena. However, the cultural show can raise lot of money upon performing in America.

I thanked the Commissioner North Bank;, Sefo of Lower Badibou, District Authority and Kerewan Area Council for having worked so hard with me to provide this excellent opportunity to our people. I promised that more is on the way.

Three weeks earlier I received this e-mail from Councilwoman Mrs. Carol Shafto announcing the good news of her efforts.

"Dr. Ceesay, we have sent five copies of the proclamation to the America Embassy- which you provided the address for. I also have three copies of the proclamation for you as well as a copy of the tape of the meeting; a copy of the newspaper where the action appeared; and a copy of the newspaper with the official minutes. I will get these out to you today.

It was a most wonderful evening as you will see on the tape. Five people, your friends old and new, spoke in favour of the proclamation. This included Dr. Avery Aten who I have now spoken with and who is very enthusiastic about working on the medical aspect of things with you.

He will be in touch with you by phone he said. But you will be able to see him and hear what he had to say during City Council meeting of December 5, 2005. Also speaking where two students who have visited the Gambia; Tom Ray and Penny Boldrey. (And me, of course).

I read your wonderful letter for the record. We also had a loop of over fifty slides showing on the screen during the presentation. It was the nicest sister-city ceremony we have ever had-by far! Usually we just read the proclamation and that is it. I think this ends my part in all of this-except for one thing.

My sons and I were going to "adopt" a family through Save the Children. This involves sending a letter each month and with an amount of money. We would be happy to adopt some children from your village instead if there is an easy way to do this.

We would need a name and address and what form we could make our donation in (money order?). We are not really wealthy- but could send $20 -$25 a month for at least a year to a deserving child. Of course; we would hope that they might send a note now and then… but this all up to you. I hope you are pleased with all that has happened.

I remained your friend.

Carol Shafto.

In reply I sent my friend Carol Shafto the following.

Hello Carol;

Now I am able to response to your email. First, please accept our eternal ineptness' for having worked so hard to bring the twining into reality. Only God can reward your efforts. Please kindly extend our heartfelt gratitude to the Mayor and your fellow Councillors at Alpena. Send me the Mayor's telephone.

I need to convey our appreciation to him. I had a long chat with the village and they were in cloud nine about the approval of the sister city program. I will be forwarding the names of deserving school children you might want to sponsor/adopt. I will cal you, before forwarding the names, about it when I get the list that the parents and headmaster promised to send me.

Thanks a million and God blesses you and yours. Best wishes for good health and successful 2006. I look forward to our travelling to the Gambia soon. Regard.

Sincerely

Dr. Alhasan S. Ceesay, MD

In the mean time Mrs. Penny Boldrey was also busy doing a story for the ACC Alumni News. In addition Carol was able to have a feature about the just approved sister city program done by the local news paper. She was very happy about it as the email bellow from Carol shows. "Good Morning Alhasan, "our story" is headline, above the fold, in the Alpena News today!

It is wonderful publication for your project. I will send you copies but you can read it on-line today only at www.thealpenanews.com. It reads "Alpena's sister-city-ACC graduate initiates partnership with Gambia villages." And there is a wonderful colour picture of one of the ACC students with village children. I hope you enjoyed the story and are pleased with my efforts for publicity.

The news reporter, Sue Lutuszek, will do a follow-up story about people "adopting Children for education purposes", like I am doing with my son(s).

It is a good day for celebration. Check the website.

Your friend

Carol Shafto

Here is one of several features about the twining between Alpena City with Njwara and Kinte Kunda villages in the North Bank Division, the Gambia.

ALPENA NEWS MICHIGAN, USA

SISTER CITY PROGRAM HAS TIES TO

ACC STUDENT OF 1960s

A link dating back to the 1960s has helped Alpena establish a sister city program with Njawara and Kinte Kunda, Lower Badibu District, the Gambia.

The program was initiated by Alhasan Ceesay, MD, an Alpena Community College of the 1960s and the 2005 Distinguished Graduate who lives in the Wes African country. He was assisted by ACC staff and Councilwoman Carol Shafto.

"He feels this is his American home and villages in Gambia are his African home and wanted to link the tow together." Carol Shafto said.

When Penny Boldrey of the ACC Foundation first put Ceesay in touch with Shafto for assistance in the venture, Shafto was leery of his intentions.

"I did not get it," she said. "I wanted to know what we are going to gain?" the whole idea is simply to put out information on the situation in those villages in the public eye, Shafto said Ceesay's dream is to build a medical centre to serve the villages, since care is many miles away and roads in and out of villages aren't passable by ambulance.

Currently patients are transported out of villages without ambulances for distances to health centres from their homes. Avery Aten, MD, of Alpena also has become involved with the project. "The medical aspects of this relationship can be long-term," he told city council members.

He said so medical statistics regarding the area, such as the average life expectancy is 53 years old and 85 out of 1000 children die during birth. According to Shafto, some of Aten's hopes include sending medical equipment which is no longer used here to the villages and even possibly having nursing students experiencing practicing there. "I just see all kinds of goodwill things happening," Shafto said. "For us to have the opportunity to lead about a totally different culture is good for us."

"One aspect Shafto highlighted is the opportunity for elementary classroom in Alpena to communicate with the village school.

Although she assisted in having the proclamation made, Shafto gives credit for making it happen to individuals at ACC. "My part is minor compared to what ACC has done," she said. "They are the ones who really got this started." During the trip the students met with various village leaders who showed them what projects they were working on and where the greatest need was.

In addition, the students taught some short classes on the United States. One day the group helped with the construction of a mosque. They also visited the agricultural centre and health centre. Ray said the trip "contributed greatly" in making the sister city proclamation a reality "because it gave people in Alpena a connection to the village." "The Gambia District Authority of Lower Badibou and villagers remain eternally grateful for giving us chance of twining with you.

Huge thanks to the City of Alpena, Mayor of Alpena and Alpena City Council," Alhasan wrote. "The villagers and I are enternaly indebted to all at Alpena. In addition, we look forward to working hand in hand for reward of all parties."

 -Sue Latuszek: The Alpena News 2005-

The first hatchling of this merging of diverse hearts is as follows:-

Njawara Basic School

Lower Badibu District

North Bank Division

The Gambia, W. Africa

19/01/06

Dear Sir/Madam

RE: To whom it may concern.

These students are promising students whose parents are not able to fully support their educational needs. As a result, we would be very grateful if a concern person(s) can assist the students and their parents in taking care of some of the financial difficulties they are encountering to earn education. These include school fees, uniforms, book bills and other school needs.

Thank you and in anticipation, I remain,

Yours Faithfully

Lamin K. Juwara

Principal

These where the initial list of needy student to benefit from proposed Manding Medical Centre/USA scholarship grants.

NAME ADDRESS	AGE	CLASS	PARENT
1. Ismaila Ceesay Njjawara	14yrs	8B	Dodu Ceesay

2. Edrisa Barry Njawara	14yrs	8B		Adoulie Barry
3. Alieu Dem Njawara	12yrs	7B		Modou Dem
4. Mamud Panneh Njawara	12yrs	7A		Ousainu Panneh
5. Adama Jallow Ker Ardo	12yrs	7B		Assan Jallow
6. Kally Bah Ker Ardo	13yrs	8B		Saikou Bah
7. Njammeh Bah Toro Bah	12yrs	7B		Musa Bah
8. Hammed Dem Toro Bah	12yrs	7B		Musa I. Bah
9. Ebrima Kanteh Toro Bah	15yrs	7B		Baboucar Kaneh
10. Mustapha Jawo Toro Bah	15yrs	8A		Omar Jawo
11. Modou Touray Panneh Bah	11yrs	6A		Sohna Jaw
12. Nuha Krubally Samba Musu	10yrs	5A		Modo Krubally
13. Matarr Panneh Njawara	10yrs	4B		Bora Panneh

14. Modou Loum   14yrs   7B   Bintou Jammeh
Ker Jebal

The above list and letter were faxed to Councilwoman Carol Shafto on the 23/02/06. The fax simply read:-

Hi Carol,

I hope you are okay and back at work. I hereby forward a list of school children from Njawara school needing sponsorship. Feel free to contact those you think would like to participate in this educational project.

The first three candidates in the list are earmarked for you and your son(s). See names 1 – 3 in the list.

Send all monies via Western Union in the name of Aja Hadi Panneh, (Alkalo of Njawara village) to any Gambian Bank that Western Union deals with in Gambia.

Then email me stating amounts, date sent and for who. I will follow up by contacting the Principal of Njawara School, the parents and the chief of the district to ascertain prompt and proper distribution.

In addition, I will have Aja Hadi Panneh (Alkalo), the parents, Headmaster and were possible the recipient students to write acknowledging the amounts received. Please feel free to contact me if you have any questions or ideas to promote the above noble educational commitment. Once again, thanks and we remain grateful for your stand.

Your Friend

Dr. Alhasan S. Ceesay, MD

CHAPTER 9

AMERICAN GUESTS VISIT MANDING MEDICAL CENTR, NJAWARA, THE GAMBIA, IN MAY 2005.

The telephone call on 5/01/05 from Mr. Mathew Dunckel as well as that from Mr. Thomas Ray (TOM) four days later opened the Pandora's box and became harbingers to a remarkable trip to Manding Medical Centre, Njawara village, Gambia by the Alpena Community College's Leadership class headed by none other than their instructor Mr. Thomas P. Ray.

I contacted Mr. Thomas Ray as soon as it was brought to my attention that some ACC students were contemplating visiting my centre at Njawara in May 2005. My message on the 6/01/05 to Mr. Ray ran thus:- "An old friend, Mr. Mathew, staff of ACC, had a long chat with me last night and he brought to my attention of a possibility that a class wanting to travel to the Gambia as guest of Manding Medical Centre at Njaswara.

I am more that willing and happy to pave the way for those that would venture the trip. I do need an e-mail r fax from you indicating desire to go to the Gambia on a mission for Manding Medical Centre. I will speak to both the schools and the district authority about your most welcomed trip to the Gambia.

Manding Medical Centre is a self-help village health organisation I setup in upon returning to the Gambia in 1992. We provide medical service to villagers and land has been donated for the location of the centre and its ancillaries. We only have a corrugated shed as clinic. We are now on the verge of building the first phase, being the children's unit of the centre and need monetary assistance. I am delighted to know of your intentions.

Please contact me as soon as you speak with the class." Thomas Ray replied on 7/01/05, "I was thrilled when Mathew discussed the possibility of a trip to Gambia for our leadership students.

I will meet with the whole class next week to discuss the possibility. As I am sure you are aware the cost of airfares from Alpena to Gambia is high, so I will need to be certain the students are committed to raising the money needed before we begin making plans. I have travelled to many locations, but never to Africa, so I am also very excited about the prospects for myself. After I meet with the students on Tuesday of next week, I will e-mail you with further information.

I wish to also commend you for your personal achievements; I plan to purchase a copy of your recent book to share with my students and for my personal reading. Thank you for your help and enthusiasm."

I emailed Tom advising that to bargain for insured group tickets.

Tom further contacted me on 12/01/05 stating that he has spoken to the students and they have agreed to take on a service trip as part of the course. He told me that they would only be able to travel in a group for 10 – 14 days in May 2005. Tom wanted to know if there was an existing program at Njawara that would be able to accommodate the students.

He assured me that the students would be comfortable in a dormitory housing or make shift dormitories. In addition I let him know on the 14/01/05 that I have spoken to the commissioner, North Bank Division and the local authority in Lower Badibou district regarding their pending trip to Njawara as guest of Manding Medical Centre and the region. I assured him that these authorities would be more than happy to have his class visit with them.

I requested an e-mail from him stating that they are visiting in behalf of Manding Medical Centre at Njawara and specify what they would want to do while in the Gambia. I suggested that they can help teach in some of the schools. I assured them that even though business and some residents have moved out there is still some activity at the village. Tom in reply sent the following on the 15/01/05. "Thank you for the great news. I am very excited about the prospect and have begun searching for group airfares with special student rates. I will inform the students on Tuesday and contact you immediately afterward via email.

I have a few questions. What costs do we need to expect in Gambia and in your village? How will we travel from Banjul to the village? We need to be certain we have a clear idea what expenses we will have to help us set specific fundraising goals both for ourselves and for the foundation from which we hope to receive grants.

When I write the other e-mail, are there tasks other than tutoring that I should include? Are there other ways we can help while we are there? I am more excited about the prospect of this service trip everyday and the students are quite enthused."

In another e-mail dated 15/02/05, Tom wrote, "The students in the leadership class are so committed to this project that they voted to contribute their own money toward the travel if they cannot raise enough. This means that the number of students who actually travel will likely be fewer, but that we will be able to travel to Njawara in May. I have begun drafting the letter to the commissioner many times, but I have some questions.

Am I asking the commissioner to help organise local housing for us? Do I want his permission to visit Njawara? Should I tell him what we would like to do there? What subject might they tutor? Are there any construction projects for the centre or the village with which we could help? I would also like to know if there are any material supplies we could bring with us to donate to the centre or the village.

One possible way for us to save money would be to fly into Dakar, Senegal and travel from there overland to Njawara. All the above concerns and questions were answered but a small hiccup in fundraising occurred leaving a distinct possibility that the students will not be able to raise enough to make the trip. The reason being the major source of funding for the trip fell through.

This left all of us jittery but Tom and his students were in no mood to change their plans to travel to the Gambia in May 2005. On the same day 15/02/05 I received the following from Mr. Jay Walterriet, Director of Public information for Alpena Community College. It stated that he was asked to contact me for more photos of myself and the clinic at Njawara.

He wanted more information regarding the Leadership planned trip to Gambia. I was told that the local television station would like to do a segment on the Leadership class and their trip. As part of the segment photos were needed. I sent all photos that were relevant to enable the reporter to do his TV-segment on the planned Leadership trip to Njaswara, Gambia.

Mr. Jay on the 17/02/05 emailed thanking me for providing the requested photos and assured me that ACC has received good deal of interest from the local media regarding the Leadership class trip and both he and Penny Boldrey were trying to provide all of the information they could. My e-mail was given to reporters who might want to contact me for more information.

The entire twenty students could not enlist for the final take off to Africa. So Thomas Ray and 11 students took on the venture of their life time to the Gambia as guest of Manding Medical Centre at Njawara village. On 17 February 2005 Tom sent me a copy of the final letter he sent to the commissioner and the local authority at the Lower Badibou district spelling out their intentions and wish while guests of the Manding Medical Centre for a two weeks duration.

Here it is.

Thamos P. Ray

Alpena Community College

666 Johnson Street

Alpena, Michigan 49707

17 February 2005

Dear Commissioner Batala Juwara,

I am pleased to inform you of our plans to visit Njawara on behalf of the Manding Medical Centre. I am the advisor and instructor for a group of college students from Alpena Community College in Michigan in the USA. We plan to visit Njawara in May and hope you will help us find lodging with local families during our stay.

Our plan as of now is to fly out of the US on May 6th to Banjul via London and to return on May 19th 2005.

During our stay in Gambia, our hope is to provide any assistance we can to the community on behalf of the Manding Medical Centre. We would like to visit the school in Njawara and tutor the children and share stories and activities with them. I also hope that we will have the opportunity to visit the important centres of the community and learn as much as we can in our short stay about the people and life in Njawara and Gambia.

I have communicated our plans with Dr. Alhasan Ceesay, who has kindly extended the invitation to us on behalf of the Manding Medical Centre.

Sincerely

Thomas P. Ray

English Instructor

This letter was acknowledged by the commissioner and the district authority in the Gambia. Now that I was certain of the trip I set to inform my board members in like manner. The certainty of the trip was concretized by the following sent by Tom on 10 March 2005.

It simply updated me on the progress made regarding the trip; that the students have raised half the money needed to travel to Gambia. He affirms the fact that everyone concerned is working hard on the remaining sum. The arranged inoculations and are preparing to apply for visas to Gambia.

He said they were all enthused and has used my address in Gambia for the visa information requirement. Again, I was delighted for things are now heading the right direction for the historic and unique trip to Njawara. I am now certain that more doors to boost ours and the centre's goals for the Gambia will be open by this simple friendly act of ACC. Here finally is my despatch the board members of Manding Medical Centre at Njawara village.

MANDING MEDICAL CENTRE/NJAWARA

UNITED KINGDOM CONTACT

245 GREAT WESTERN STREET

MANCHESTER, M14 4LQ

ENGLAND

E-MAI: alhasanceesay@hotmail.com

Tel/Fax: 44+161-342-0854

Date: 25/03/05

DEAR BOARD MEMBER,

I am pleased to bring to your attention about American guests to Manding Medical Centre at Njawara. Mr. Thomas Ray along with 11 Alpena Community college students will be visiting the Gambia as our guest in May 2005. They will be leaving the USA for the Gambia on May 6th, 2005 and depart for United States on the 19th, of May.

I would be most grateful if you give some of your time to meet them and make their visit memorable. There are many benefits to be accrued for the centre and the Gambia. I am at present arranging in the form of scholarships or placements in various fields of study at my previous college in Alpena Michigan.

I have been in constant contact with Commissioner Batala Juwara at Kerewan and I would like all of you to brain storm and make this an ongoing link between us and Alpena Community College and other Michigan cities I am now in negotiation with. Alpena city has developed interest in our project.

I am also happy to report that my former college, Alpena Community College has awarded me, "Distinguished 2005 Graduate." Find enclosed correspondence from Mr. Thomas Ray, in behalf of the Leadership class of Alpena Community College, to Commissioner Juwara and Sefo Fafanding Kinte.

I look forward to your understanding and participation to help open up the Pandoa's Box of goodwill for the Gambia. This is a onetime opportunity for the Gambia that would make our two people linked for good goals and noble courses for generations of Gambians.

My regards and keep in touch.

Yours truly,

Dr. Alhasan S. Ceesay, MD

Founder/co-coordinator

cc: Mr. Ousainu Darboe

cc: Mr. Fafa E. Mbye, Dr. Dawda Ceesay, Dr. Ayo Palmer
cc: Mr. Saim Kinte

cc: Mr. Sambou Kinte, Mr. Mustapha Njie

cc: Elh. Maja Sonk

cc: Mr. Dodou Ceesay

cc: Mr. Sisawo Ceesay

cc: Mrs. Mbee Sonko

On April 7th 2005, Tom updated me stating that the visa applications were going well and that most of the students have received their visas. In addition let me privilege you the reader with some of the reactions emailed to me about the pending trip and what it would mean to them. Alison Jane Smolinski said:

"Hello Dr. Ceesay,

I am one of the students in the Leadership class at Alpena Community College. I am really excited about the service trip, only a couple more weeks. Right now we are trying to prepare for the trip, just getting the basic necessities and what we should be packing.

I just read about how you are building a bakery at Njawara. Even though our resources are limited, is there something we could do to help out?

I thought we could help in some way. I also just wanted to say thank you for the wonderful experience you giving to us. I realize it will be truly an eye opener. I feel as if I could never be able to repay you for these two weeks that you about to give us. Thank you Dr. Ceesay!"

Another email from Brittany Posthumus simply stated; "I am one of the students from Alpena Community College that will be coming this May to help. After learning all the things that you have done I must say you are an inspiration and the world can use more people who care as much as you do. I can't wait to come to Njawara.

I am very excited to be able to help and thank you for the invitation." Lastly, Ms. Grace Schimitz sent in the following before leaving for the Gambia. "I am a member of the Alpena Community College class that will be assisting you this May at Njawara. I am greatly looking forward to my visit to the Gambia. Thank you so much for the invitation! The Friends of Manding, a charitable Trust at Colchester had the following in its web site about the trip to Njawara, the Gambia.

It read as "News flash 12 American visiting:" "A class of 11 students and their instructor Mr. Thomas Ray from Alpena Community College, Alpena Michigan, will be visiting the Gambia as guest of Manding Medical Centre from the 6th to 19th May 2005.

They will be visiting communities and tutor at local schools. Alpena has developed interest in project Manding Medical Centre at Njawara. We are negotiating to have this exchange as an ongoing affair between Alpena and Njawara." As time drew near to the flight to the Gambia Tom contacted the Commissioner on several occasions to clear last possible huddles that may surface.

None the less preparations went smoothly and Thomas Ray and his ACC Leadership class left America on May 10th 2005 via Madrid and then Dakar, Senegal before embanking at Banjul, the Gambia. As fate would have the team instead hired a bus from Dakar to Hamdali village in the North Bank which was nearer to Njawara.

I learnt they were given a VIP escort from Hamdali via Kerewan to Njawara village. As expected, I called the Mayor of Njawara, Mrs. Hadi Panneh enquiring about the American visitors. She told me they were fine and housed at the village centre, a semi motel used for foreign guest to Njawara.

Tom and I spoke at length along with Sefo Fafanding Kinte. Sefo Fafanding reassured me that every thing possible will be done to help make "our guest comfortable and like wise a memorable visit in due course. I spoke briefly to the commissioner the next day to get a feed back from him. The two week flew fast for the students most of who did want to leave at the time for kindness rendered by the villagers.

It is said that good thing never last long and this the experience of the student who went to Njawara in May 2005. Here is the reaction of Americans after the trip to the Gambia. The ACC students started sending their report and experience as guest of Manding Medical Centre, Njawara, The Gambia.

Starting with Alison Jane Smolinski reported as bellow. "Hello Dr. Ceesay: The trip to Njawara was incredible! I did not want to leave. It was an experience of a lifetime that I will never forget. Everyone in the village was very kind and helpful. I have never met such kind people in my entire life. I found the villagers doing everything possible to make their lives better. I realized that many people work together to get a job done or finished. This is absolutely wonderful. Everyone was so helpful in the village. The people of Njawara gave us such wonderful hospitality. The food and shelter was more than we deserved.

Also your wife, Mrs Fatou Koma-Ceesay, was all too good to us. We had a remarkable time with her at Bundung/Serekunda. Her cooking was excellent. And the gifts she gave all of us, we did not deserve. Your family is wonderful and was too kind to us. I would like to thank you for the incredible experience you have given me. I could not have asked for anything more.

I immensely enjoyed my self. I want to go back one day. I also want you to know that I will do my best to help in whatever way I can. I realize that action are louder than words and hope I can prove that to everyone.

Thank you Dr. Ceesay."

Another reaction came from Grace Schiminitz. "I really enjoyed my time in Njawara. The people treated us very well and it was a pleasure to spend two weeks with them. Your wife is a wonderful person and was very hospitable to us. I will always be grateful for her kind treatment. I hope to make another visit to Njawara in the future. It is a wonderful place. It was an eye-opening experience. The people were absolutely marvellous.

They treated us as their own family and welcomed us with open hands. I had no idea that they would be that hospitable. I really miss walking to the river and spending time with the children. It was my first experience in Gambia and hopefully it will not be my last.

I hope I can return their kindness. I would love to see how the kids have grown up." The last but not the least came from Mr. Thomas P. Ray, English instructor at ACC. It read; "I want to thank you for the opportunity you provided my students on this trip. The entire experience was enjoyable and valuable as a means of teaching my students something about the responsibility that comes with the privileges they enjoy here.

Everyone was kind to us on the trip and the students came away with many great souvenirs and memories. I have many digital photos and am working on producing a CD of them to send out.

I also plan to type up a version of my journal for posting on the internet and I will send parts of that to you. I plan to call the village this weekend to extend my appreciation to everyone. Do you know anything about the proposed potential sister city relationship between Alpena and Njawara? I would like to start making some local contacts here to help that process. I am also hopeful that future trips will be possible for my students.

Mr. Thomas P. Ray

As you know very well man proposes but God dispose things. Tom took over the running of the department and with that came a hand full challenging responsibilities. He was not able to provide the CD until 11th of October 2005 after several reminders from me and those visiting my Website (friendsofmandinggambimed.btck.co.uk). Finally, Tom contacted me on 4/11/05 to let me know he had the college mailing office send the CD of photos and other material registered delivery to me.

Then he made donation of $1000(one thousand us dollars) in the name of Friends of Manding, a Charitable Trust at Colchester Essex organising fund raising activities for Manding Medical Centre at Njawara the Gambia, West Africa.

This cheque was duly received and forward registered mail to the Secretary of the Friends of Manding for depositing into our account at LLyod's Bank in Colchester Essex County.

Tom asked about the state of the proposed sister-city program between Alpena and Njawara. Yes, this was one of my goals for inviting the Americans to my village in the Gambia. I just believe that unveiling the false masks and stigma others have about Africa will create harmony in its unique way.

People need to accept differences in the cultures. I transmitted all reactions presented by our American visitor to the Commissioner, the chief, and the village heads especially Hadi Panneh of Njawara village.

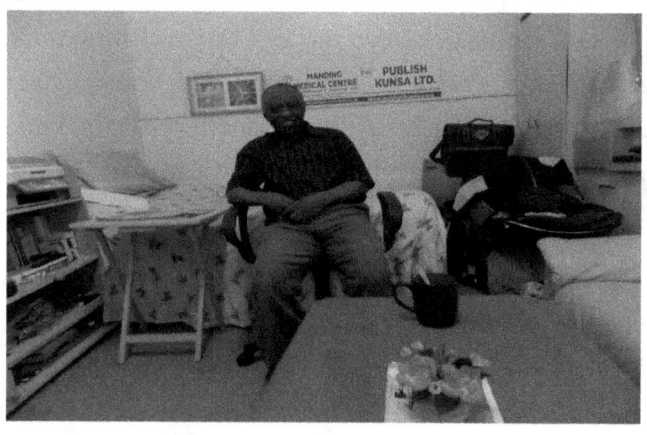

Dr. Ceesay relaxing with a cup of hot coffee: 2014

CHAPTER 10

ALPENA: THANKS FOR TWINING

SISTER-CITY PROCLAMATION

Having now been recognised as Distinguished 2005 Graduate by Alpena Community College I made a proposal for a twining relationship or sister-city status between Alpena and select villages in the Gambia. I, you guessed right, contacted Mathew Dunckel as a sound board or trial balloon for the above idea.

He replied that it was a sound idea and suggested my contacting the Alpena City Council members on the subject. He gave their web site thus: http://www.alpena.mi.us/council/members. In addition he gave the names of Councilman Dave Karschnik and Councilwoman Carol Shafto for me to initiate direct contact with the Alpena City Council.

He told me that the mayor was John Gilmet and the City manager was Mr. Alan Bakalarski. Armed with all this information and more I made my first push through Mrs. Penny Boldrey, Executive Director at Alpena Community College. I had no doubt if I get her interest in this unique wish she would do all within her power to not only contact the right people to make it eventually happen but would open up more doors for my villagers and our health project at Njawara.

Penny Boldrey upon hearing from me linked with Councilwoman Shafto on the June 14th, 2005 thus; "Hi Carol, from one Distinguished Grad to another….. I received the enclosed message from our 2005 Distinguished Graduate, Dr. Alhasan Ceesay.

I'm wondering if perhaps you can help me with his inquiry regarding the possibility of twining between Alpena City and two villages in the Gambia, West Africa." Penny in turn informed me that she had contacted a good friend, Carol Shafto, who is a member of Alpena's City Council and also an Alpena Community College Distinguished 2003 Graduate, regarding my request for twining between the above communities.

She enclosed Councilwoman Shafto's response to the idea. My reaction was swift and my message to Councilwoman Carol Shafto ran thus:-"Hello Councilwoman Carol. Mrs Penny Boldrey sent me correspondence she had with you regarding a proposal I made to the city of Alpena.

My initial e-mail kick starting a twining proposal between the city of Alpena; Njawara and Kinte Kunda villages in the Gambia West Africa was sent to Mayor John F. Gilmet, Dave R. Karsctunick, Mike Polluch, Sam Eller and Carol Shafto. It read, "I'm pleased to write and inform you that I am deputized by village heads of Njawara and Kinte Kunda to contact you and initiate a twining/sister city status proposal between Alpena and the above two villages.

Njawara is my home village and Kinte Kunda is where I attended primary school in the early fifties.

Tom Ray and the Leadership students visited both places during their two weeks stay in the Gambia. They met the chief of the district, Sefo Fafanding Kinte, at Kinte Kunda. Kinte Kunda has been the seat of many chiefs of the region and Fafanding is the most recent of several from this village. Njawara is historically a trading centre connecting Gambia and the Northern part of Senegal.

Today she has become a tourist destination. One can easily log onto information about Njawara village on the internet. It boasts of lots of female education oriented projects. In addition it has an agricultural training centre."

The contact was made in behalf of the village heads of the above and the local authority at the North Bank division of the Gambia. This twining would be a very rewarding interaction and educational for both yours and the villagers. The people are eager to make worth while friendship with America.

The chiefs and village heads have urged me to initiate their wish for the twining between them and Alpena or any city willing to go into such relationship with the villages. You can link up with Mr. Thomas Ray and his students for feed back on their experience as guests of Manding Medical Centre at Njawara village, the Gambia.

The villagers and I would be most grateful if given the chance to link up with Alpena City. Carol Shafto sent in this hiccup. "Dr. Ceeasy, I cannot proceed with any more discussions with the City Council of the City of Alpena until I am much clearer about what a Twining proposal entails.

Could you please describe to me what you have in mind? Although we may be supportive of your work at Njawara and Kinte Kunda in the Gambia; we cannot really act on your request until we know what we are agreeing to.

Could you send me a brief outline of what you are seeking from the City of Alpena? I will be happy to act as a liaison between you and the City, but cannot do so until I have a clear idea of what I am advocating for. Thank you most sincerely."

Carol Shafto

On July 13, 2005 I sent the required clarification to Councilwoman Carol Shafto as follows. Hello Carol, I am glad to hear from you. To be simplistically clear, twining means a sisterhood relationship between two cities for the mutual rewards of those involved.

Hence it is a friendship like affair where people from Alpena can be part of and like wise the villages involved but at no cost to either party. For example Councilwoman Shafto can choose to spend two weeks in Gambia helping reorganise or create a more functional administrative system or even learn from the villagers.

In brief it is a two way international relationship. Or cultural dance -troupes from the Gambia villages can be coming to entertain Alpena, possibly more cities, during the summers. This will help raise funds for the city, the villages, like wise for our health project at Njawara.

It will provide much awareness and understanding of the two people merged in friendship. It is like adopting each other and opening up rewarding human adventures at no cost involved. In a nut-shell, it means ratified friendship between Alpena and the two villages. I hope this makes it palatable for Alpena to want to be part of such endearing relationship.

I thank you in behalf of the Kerewan local authority, the villagers and Commissioner for North Bank Division, the Gambia. God blesses all of you."

Dr. Alhasan Ceesay

Needless to say Councilwoman Carol Shafto was very pleased with the above clarification and appealed to Alpena City Council to consider the idea of twining in behalf of the Gambian villages. Hence, Carol on the 13/7/05 sent me this e-mail following the receipt of the above message to the councilwoman.

It simply states that, "I have forwarded this information to the mayor and city manager and offered to be the liaison if the City should consent to comply with this request. I will keep you posted with any development." I updated the Commissioner and all concern at the Lower Badibou district regarding progress of my initiative with Alpena City few weeks after hearing from Councilwoman Carol Shafto. The Commissioner and the local authority sent me the bellow covering letter in support of my push for a twining relationship with Alpena City Michigan, USA.

Njawara/Kinte Kunda

Lower Badibou District

North Bank Division

The Gambia, W. Africa

November 5th, 2005

To: Dr. Alhasan Ceesay

Manchester, England

Subject: Twining of Njawara, Kinte Kunda & Alpena Michigan

Dear Dr. Ceesay,

Your first letter dated September 23rd, 2005 has been received and the content of which is understood, both the Commissioner, the Chief and the Alkalos (village heads) of Njawara and Kinte Kunda are very much interested in having Njawara, Kinte Kunda and Alpena City twined. The Communities of both villages met and discussed the issue and they are very much happy about the lofty ideas.

Njawara and Kinte Kunda are located in the Northern part of the Gambia. They are just about 60 kilometres away from the capital City Banjul, the Gambia.

Kinte Kunda is just 2 kilometres away from our administrative headquarters Kerewan where both the Commissioner and Area Council stay. Where as Njawara is located 9 kilometres away from Kerewan. Regards

Sincerely

Aja Hadi Panneh (Alkalo)

Alh. Fafanding Kinte (Chief Lower Badibou)

Cc: Mr. Batala Juwara (Commisioner NBD)

I replied to the above support with this note despatched immediately to the village Akalos, the Chief and Commissioner North Bank Division at Kerewan village.

245 Great Western Street

Manchester M14 4LQ

England

16/11/05

A BIG THANK YOU TO ALL

Dear Commissioner,

I'm profoundly grateful to you, Sefo Fafanding, the local authority (area Council and chiefs) and especially Alkalo Arfang Bah and people of Toro. Lastly but not the least a big thank you goes to the people of Badibou, Njawara and my sister Hadi Panneh Alkalo of Njawara village.

I am very happy for support and understanding given to Manding Medical Centre. I'm pleased to inform you that I have initiated a twining process between Alpena and the villages of Njawara and Kinte Kunda.

I have forwarded your note of 5/11/05 to the Alpena City Council. Copies were also sent to Mr. Thom Ray and the college. Again, thank you for making our American friends happy and welcomed to our beloved country. God bless all of you. I will continue working for our development.

Sincerely

Dr. Alhasan S. Ceesay, MD

Director/Founder

Manding Medical Centre.

I then sent Carol Shafto the letter from the district authority plus this note urging action from her end.

245 Great Western Street

Manchester M14 4LQ

England

8/11/05

Mrs. Carol Shafto

Councilwoman

Alpena City Council

208 North First Avenue

Alpena, MI 49707

Dear Mrs. Carol Shafto,

The enclosed is reply to your last e-mail dated 25/9/05 regarding the twining proposal made to the Alpena City Council earlier on by me in behalf of Njawara village and Kinte Kunda, the Gambia, respectively. The enthusiasm about having this relationship with Alpena is immeasurable. The villagers are looking forward to a warm and fruitful relationship between the two people.

They all pray that you would be as eager to consummate it as they have already done in their wishes and hearts. Finally, may friendship and human kindness be an everlasting link between all humans. God bless you and we look forward for a positive reply soon. My personal regards and thanks to the City Council and all of Alpena.

Yours Sincerely

Dr. Alhasan S. Ceesay, MD

It was not until September 21, 2005 that I sent Councilwoman Shafto the following reminder and follow up note.

"Hi Carol, I hope you had an enjoyable summer. This is a follow up of that lofty idea of twining Alpena City with Njawara and Kinte Kunda villages in the Gambia. Has there been any movement forward at the Mayor's Office about the proposal made to the city?

Is there anything I or the district authority in Gambia need do to bring this to fruition? I have not heard any thing about it since your last email of 14/7/05.

Again, regards and thanks. I bank on your continued interest. God Bless."

Dr. Ceesay

The next day God smiled onto our dream to befriend America. Councilwoman Mrs. Carol Shafto sent me the following reply to the inquiry about the status of my dream for America and the Gambia. It rang in the most melodious and cherished message I ever had for a long, long time after my being admitted into medical school and upon treating my first patient in the villages. Here is Carol's email to me "Good morning Dr. Ceesay: I appreciate your persistence in accomplishing this goal. Without that it surely would have failed. I do apologize for this delay.

I have just returned this week from a wonderful month long tour of the UK and Ireland. My last communication, before I left, with the City Manager was that this was a good idea, will be good for public relations, and that we should go forward with the proposal.

The Mayor is also in favour. So there is absolutely nothing standing in the way of this happening. I am willing to do the work of it, but I honestly have no idea what to do. Do you know procedures or paper work or any such thing from your end? Is it as simple as a proclamation? I would like to have more information about your village, your people, and why you are interested in twining with Alpena – what connection there is.

I would then put together a presentation for the City Council and ask them to decide that we are sister-cities (the term used here, although I know the UK and Europe use "twining) with the villages of Njawara and Kinte Kunda. We could erect a sign at the City entrance, etc.

If you have any idea or directions for me, please let me know. Also any information you can provide on your village would be helpful. I will continue to work with you on this until it is accomplished.

Your friend in Alpena

Carol Shafto

This was followed by my forwarding the bellow addendum to whatever had reached the Councilwoman's desk. Being the architect of this union much was expected from me. And so I never relented supplying as much information as many times as I can afford. My phone bill sprouted to a Warping £600 etc. Most important was this addendum bellow.

SYNAPSIES OF NJAWARA/KINTE KUNDA VILLAGES

Njawara is a 350 years old market village situated on the bank of the Miniminiyang bolong, a creek of the River Gambia, in the Lower Badibou District of the North Bank Division of the Gambia. Njawara has a population of a thousand residents and is 95 kilometres from Banjul, Gambia's capital City.

The village lies close to the Senegalese border and has been the trade links between Gambia and Senegal during the colonial days. Njawara was established and founded by the Panneh family of the Wolof tribe and initially called "Panneh village".

The elderly still fondly refer to her as Mpanneh. Among the residents of now Njawara are Mandingkas, Fulas, Sereres, Jolas, Konyanginkas, and Mabara tribes. All of whom are farmers, with few serving as petty traders, growing Peanuts, Rice, Coos, and a variety of vegetables. The nearest government administrative post is 9 kilometres away at Kerewan village.

Njawara lacked modern luxuries of electricity, proper telephones, sewer system, pave roads but water is now pumped from a nearby borehole. The village has a thriving school and a dynamic citizenry working hard to improve heir lot and the future of the younger generation. KINTE KUNDA village has been the political base of Lower Badibou District for decades.

It has provided us with several chiefs in the past and Sefo Fafanding Kinte is the most recent contribution. Kinte Kunda village comprises of mostly Mandinka tribes men and women. It is the home of venerable late Sefo Njako Kinte who, in the 30s ruled the district with and iron fist. It was he who imposed one of his brothers, Almami Kinte, to take over the administration or village headship of then

Njawara(Mpanneh).

None the less he was a respected chief. Kinte Kunda was the first village that had a school in the entire Lower Badibou district and I am told that he chief insisted that the school be built in his home village leaving a row that lasted through his rein.

The village is now a smaller population than Njawara and the current appointed chief of the district, Sefo Fafanding Kinte resides there. Residents of Kinte Kunda are all farmers eager to improve their lives and those of their children. They are friendly, peaceful, charming, descent hard working people who contributed a lot to growth of the Lower Badibou District in the North Bank.

These two villages along with the entire Lower Badibou District yearn for this twining/sister-city status to come to realty. Hence, I enclose relevant messages regarding the proposed twining from the district authority as per fax from the Gambia. The villagers and I are interested in twining with Alpena Michigan n an effort to open up the Pandora's box of friendship, goodwill and more understanding of the people and cultures that would allow us relate in this shrinking globe we all share. There is a lot we can do for each other once the ugly veil of ignorance, misunderstanding and fear is removed. And this can be done only learning and interacting with one another. I am sure the students, who went to the villages, can tell how much warmth and friendship they received from the villagers they met. Exchange visits and whole host of beneficial programs to both parties can be organised within the framework of this twining.

Once again, I personally appeal to the Mayor and City Council of Alpena to give this desire of the villagers a chance of fruition for Alpena City and the above villages in the Gambia. In short while, I received the following reply from Councilwoman Carol Shafto of Alpena City Council letting me know of the final details, date of the be proclamation for the sister-city relationship between our villages and Alpena Michigan. Without further ado I present the message as sent on the 17th of November 2005.

"Good Morning Dr. Ceesay

After many months of communication with you, I can finally announce a DATE for our Twining/Sister City Resolution! The Alpena City Council will adopt a resolution to establish a Sister City Program with Njawara/ Kinte Kinda on December 5th, 2005. I am going to be personally preparing the resolution. Since it will be a part of permanent records for both the villages and the City of Alpena, I would like be sure all of the information is accurate.

Penny Boldrey suggested that I email the text to you after I complete it. If you are willing, you could read it for any factual errors or omissions before I send it on to the City. If you are willing, I will send that via email when it is ready, some time next week. Meanwhile I am meeting with Tom Ray from the college who led the Leadership Class expedition to the villages.

He is VERY enthusiastic about this proposal and is going to give me information and even share some pictures. We will be meeting next week. Finally, I have invited several people to come to the City Council meeting to provide testimony and support for this proposal. Both Penny Boldrey and Tom Ray will be there.

Also they are inviting some of the students who went to the villages to also be present and speak to the issue. So it would be a very nice presentation and will be more than just a formality. Also, if you would like, I can arrange to have a tape of the meeting sent to you.

Our meetings are videotaped and played for the public on the public access television channel several times a week, between meetings. I can make a copy of the tape of the meeting and have it send you or to the village officials or both if you would like.

Also, the resolution will have an official seal of the City of Alpena and the signature of the Mayor. I will have as many copies as you need made and will laminate them so they will be preserved.

I will send those to you and/ or whomever you designate. I will get several if necessary. I am so pleased to finally be able to bring this to completion. I know it must have been frustrating to you to have this take so long and to have us seen to be so unresponsive. I hope this totally enthusiastic ending makes up for all of that!

Your friend in Alpena

Carol Shafto

On the day of ratification or passing of the resolution for sister city relationship between Alpena and the two above villages several speakers were heard. These included, among many, Penny Bodrey, Mr. Tom Ray, two student representatives who visited Gambia in May 2005 and Dr. Avery Aten.

This was buffered by loop of fifty photos of the villages taken by the student while in the Gambia. At the end of the presentation Mayor John F. gimlet read into the record the above proclamation and vote was tabled to pass it. This Sister City proclamation between Alpena with Njawara/Kinte Kunda, Lower Badibou District, the Gambia was moved by Councilwoman Carol Shafto, seconded by Councilman Karschnick, that the proclamation to establish a sister city program with the villages of Njwara and Kinte Kunda be approved.

The move was carried by unanimous vote. A copy of the sister City Resolution passed by Alpena City Council on December 5th 2005 is reproduced for your pleasure to read.

PROCLAMATION TO ESTABLISH A "SISTER CITY" PROGRAM WITH NJAWARA AND KINTE KUNDA, LWER BADIBOU DISTRICT, GAMBIA, WEST AFRICA

WHEREAS, the City of Alpena recognises and supports the concept of global cooperation and community; and

WHERAS, the villagers of Njawara and Kinte Kunda, through their local leaders and Dr. Alhasan S. Ceesay, have reached out their hand in friendship and goodwill, and

WHEREAS, relationships were established by students and faculty of Alpena Community College when they were warmly welcomed to the villages for a service project earlier this year, and

WHEREAS, mutual understanding of our diversities as well as our similarities and the cultural exchanges that will result, will be beneficial to the citizens of both areas, and

WHEREAS, true global community is often established one person at a time, and one city and village at a time, leading to beneficial relations and programs for all;

NOW, THEREFORE, I, John F. Gilmet, by virtue of the authority vested in me as Mayor, DO HEREBY PROCLAIM, A "Sister City" Program with the villages of

NJAWARA/KINTE KUNDA

LOWER BADIBOU DISTRICT

GAMBIA

And urge all area citizens to extend the hand of fellowship and an embrace of genuine fraternity to their friends in NJAWARA/KINTE KINTE KUNDA and pledge support and loyalty as these communities of two great nations join together as "Sister Cities"

Signed; at Alpena Michigan, United States of America, on this 5th day of December, 2005

Councilwoman Carol Shafto read the following reply from me to Council and residents of Alpena City.

ALPENA, THANKS FOR TWINING WITH US

Honourable Mayor John F. Gilmet, Alpena City Council and residents of Alpena; please allow me convey heartfelt thanks as well as greetings from the Commissioner, NBD, Kerewan Area Council, the Chief of Lower Badibou, the Alkalos (village heads) of Njawara and Kinte Kunda.

I am today full of joy and gratitude for twining resolution ratified by the Alpena City Council. I am speechless as one of my dreams for the villager and America has now materialized in this twining resolution passed by Alpena. We are two good people now merged in good will for humanity and friendship. This coming together will archive a lot for both of us.

There is a lot for us to gain as well as learn from each other and generations to come will thank us for having taken the first footsteps of bringing people of diverse cultures and understanding together. Enclosed is message from the Gambia in response to the most welcomed news in your last email. This is the top of the iceberg for there is lot more benefit in this act.

In addition, as long as I am alive Alpena and Gambia will not only benefit from this unique venture but will smile yearly for having dreamt along with me. Let me, in passing, mention with thanks the first harbingers of this day. They are Mr. Thomas P. Ray and his Leadership team of students from Alpena Community College who visited Njawara village in May 2005.

Thomas Ray and the students laid the marvellous foundation we today concretize. Mrs. Penny Boldrey and Mathew Dunckel deserve our appreciation for remaining interested and in constant contact with me. The Gambia, the district authority of Lower Badibou and villagers remain eternally grateful for giving us the chance of twining with you.

A Huge thanks Alpena City, the Mayor of Alpena and Alpena City Council for work well done. Councilwoman Mrs. Carol Shafto who relentlessly steered the twining proposal to completion also deserves our profound gratitude. The villagers and I are eternally indebted to all at Alpena. In addition, we look forward to working hand in hand for the reward of all parties.

Finally, I would again like to pay tribute to past and present friends at Alpena who helped me reach this pedestal. All of you helped make my sojourn to America a remarkable success. I would like many more of my friends to be like you at Alpena.

I hope you will believe, as well as join me, in my dream of providing modern medical aid to the Gambian villagers. Thanks a million and God bless America!

Signed: DR. ALHASAN SISAWO CEESAY, MD

FOUNDER/COORDINATOR

MANDING MEDICAL CENTRE

NJAWARA, THE GAMBIA

Two weeks later I received three copies of the "sister City Proclamation" along with a video tape of the Alpena City Council Meeting of December 5, 2005. Also enclosed were the Alpena news and copy of Alpena Public Notices showing minutes of the City Council meeting which carried ratification of the sister city proclamation by a unanimous vote.

I must confess exhilaration in my heart for Alpena City Council having done so much for my villages without reservation and accomplished with great speed. I sent the following communiqué to the current representative to the Gambia, Ambassador Joseph D. Stafford in preparing them for the arrival the package from the Alpena City Council for forwarding to the Commissioner of the North Bank Division, the Gambia.

MANDING MEDICAL CENTRE

245 Great Western Street

Manchester M14 4LQ

Email:alhasanceesay@hotmail.com

Date: 10/12/05

Ambassador Joseph D. Stafford

Embassy of the United States of America

Kairaba Avenue

P. M. Box 19

Banjul, the Gambia, West Africa

RE: Manding Medical Centre/Alpena USA Twining

Dear Ambassador Stafford,

I am Dr. Alhasan S. Ceesay from Njawara village and currently on studies in the UK. This is to introduce the above self-help health organisation at Njawara as well as kindly request favour of your good office's service in behalf Alpena Michigan and the villages of Njawara and Kinte Kunda, the Gambia.

I pioneered the above centre, after graduating as a doctor and upon returning to the Gambia in 1992. It became an NGO in 1994 after being fully registered by the Justice Department and recognised by the Ministry of Health in 1993. In addition, we are now a registered Charitable Trust, as Friends of Manding, in England and Wales by the Charity Commission of the UK. Our website: www.friendsofmandinggambimed.btck.co.uk

It will show our home page as "Friends of Manding." Alternatively, one can used a short cut by typing in "Manding Medical Centre, Njawara" and click search. The same home page plus lot more will appear.

I have also written two books and a hefty portion of proceed from the sale of both books is earmarked to help support Manding Medical Centre at Njawara and our goal of providing medical aid to the villager, especially children. More information about my work and commitment to providing much needed medical service to the region in conjunction with the Gambia Ministry of Health can be seen in our website as above.

Finally, I am more than delighted to report that Alpena City, Michigan, USA has just ratified a sister city program with my home village Njawara and Kinte Kunda village in the Lower Badibou District, North Bank Division, the Gambia.

Hence, I have asked the Alpena City Mayor's Office to send five copies of the final proclamation declaring the sister city status between Alpena and the above two named villages in Badibou to you for your office to kindly deliver the documents to the Commissioner North Bank Division at Kerewan.

Thank you for taking time to assist us in the above matter. Please feel free to contact me any time convenient to you. Best wishes for good health and achievement in the coming year. Regard to your family.

Yours Sincerely

Dr. Alhasan S. Ceesay, MD

Founder/Coordinator

Manding Medical Centre

Njawara, The Gambia, West Africa.

This letter was followed with two telephone calls to the Embassy of the United States in the Gambia to verify receipt of the package sent from Alpena to Joseph D. Stafford. The Secretary to Mr. Stafford, in the last phone call let me know it usually take a month or more before none official mail arrives at their desk.

He assured me that the office will do as request whenever the package reaches the Embassy. I called Sefo Fafanding Kinte and Alkalo Hadi Panneh and told them to check with either Ambassador Joseph Stafford directly or one of the officers in the know at the office for their copies of the sister city proclamation of which the villagers are unsung heroes for having received the ACC students who visited Njawara in May 2005 with open hearts, hospitality, generosity and warmth.

It was not until Thursday, February 16th, 2006 that Ambassador Joseph D. Stafford and team where able to deliver, in person amid tumultuous reception and celebration, the sister-city proclamation between Alpena City, Michigan USA, with Njawara and Kinte Kunda villages in the North Bank of the Gambia.

I made it clear that the brief ceremony at Njawara on the 16/2/06 marked the end of phase one of the sister city relationship between us and Alpena Michigan. I suggested the following four areas for food for thought by all concern. They are:-

1. Education: This already started in earnest as some in Alpena have expressed desire to sponsor worthy candidates at the primary level for an experimental period of one year. Higher levels, such as college education and nursing training and or other relevant skill areas will in due course be included.

2. Health: A lot is planed for health oriented programs and Manding Medical Centre will be enhanced to a much

functional status. There will be training programs for health personnel etc.

3. Tourism: I am studying ways of creating tourist attraction with facilities erected in due course to the region.

4. Cultural: Exchanges entailing having cultural dance troop(s) from the Lower Badibou District travel to Alpena Michigan, and other cities in the USA during the summers to display our fabric of entertainment, history and arts.

These are few ideas in the pipeline.

Feel free to add yours to enrich the program. This is by no means binding or final but seeking more suggestions on how to benefit both parties in this unique twining program just approved by Alpena City.

Let me make it crystal clear that there is no financial commitment from Alpena. However, the cultural show can raise lot of money upon performing in America.

I thanked the Commissioner North Bank, Sefo of Lower Badibou, District Authority and Kerewan Area Council for having worked so hard with me to provide this excellent opportunity to our people. I promised that more is on the way. Three weeks earlier I received this e-mail from Councilwoman Mrs. Carol Shafto announcing the good news of her efforts.

"Dr. Ceesay,

we have sent five copies of the proclamation to the America Embassy- which you provided the address for.

I also have three copies of the proclamation for you as well as a copy of the tape of the meeting; a copy of the newspaper where the action appeared; and a copy of the newspaper with the official minutes. I will get these out to you today.

It was a most wonderful evening as you will see on the tape. Five people, your friends old and new, spoke in favour of the proclamation. This included Dr. Avery Aten who I have now spoken with and who is very enthusiastic about working on the medical aspect of things with you.

He will be in touch with you by phone he said. But you will be able to see him and hear what he had to say during City Council meeting of December 5, 2005. Also speaking where two students who have visited the Gambia; Tom Ray and Penny Boldrey. (And me, of course).

I read your wonderful letter for the record. We also had a loop of over fifty slides showing on the screen during the presentation. It was the nicest sister-city ceremony we have ever had-by far! Usually we just read the proclamation and that is it. I think this ends my part in all of this-except for one thing.

My sons and I were going to "adopt" a family through Save the Children. This involves sending a letter each month and with an amount of money. We would be happy to adopt some children from your village instead if there is an easy way to do this.

We would need a name and address and what form we could make our donation in (money order?). We are not really wealthy- but could send $20 -$25 a month for at least a year to a deserving child.

Of course; we would hope that they might send a note now and then... but this all up to you. I hope you are pleased with all that has happened.

I remained your friend.

Carol Shafto.

In reply I sent my friend Carol Shafto the following.

Hello Carol;

I am now able to response to your email. First, please accept our eternal ineptness' for having worked so hard to bring the twining into reality. Only God can reward your efforts. Please kindly extend our heartfelt gratitude to the Mayor and your fellow Councillors at Alpena. Send me the Mayor's telephone. I need to convey our appreciation to him. I had a long chat with the village and they were in cloud nine about the approval of the sister city program.

I will be forwarding the names of deserving school children you might want to sponsor/adopt. I will cal you, before forwarding the names, about it when I get the list that the parents and headmaster promised to send me. Thanks a million and God blesses you and yours. Best wishes for good health and successful 2006. I look forward to our travelling to the Gambia soon. Regard.

Sincerely

Dr. Alhasan S. Ceesay, MD

In the mean time Mrs. Penny Boldrey was also busy doing a story for the ACC Alumni News. In addition Carol was able to have a feature about the just approved sister city program done by the local news paper. She was very happy about it as the email bellow from Carol shows. "Good Morning Alhasan, "our story" is headline, above the fold, in the Alpena News today!

It is wonderful publication for your project. I will send you copies but you can read it on-line today only at www.thealpenanews.com. It reads "Alpena's sister-city-ACC graduate initiates partnership with Gambia villages." And there is a wonderful colour picture of one of the ACC students with village children. I hope you enjoyed the story and are pleased with my efforts for publicity. The news reporter, Sue Lutuszek, will do a follow-up story about people "adopting Children for education purposes", like I am doing with my son(s).

It is a good day for celebration. Check the website.

Your friend

Carol Shafto

Here is one of several features about the twining between Alpena City with Njwara and Kinte Kunda villages in the North Bank Division, the Gambia.

ALPENA NEWS MICHIGAN, USA

SISTER CITY PROGRAM HAS TIES TO

ACC STUDENT OF 1960s

A link dating back to the 1960s has helped Alpena establish a sister city program with Njawara and Kinte Kunda, Lower Badibu District, the Gambia.

The program was initiated by Alhasan Ceesay, MD, an Alpena Community College of the 1960s and the 2005 Distinguished Graduate who lives in the Wes African country. He was assisted by ACC staff and Councilwoman Carol Shafto.

"He feels this is his American home and villages in Gambia are his African home and wanted to link the tow together." Carol Shafto said.

When Penny Boldrey of the ACC Foundation first put Ceesay in touch with Shafto for assistance in the venture, Shafto was leery of his intentions. "I did not get it," she said. "I wanted to know what we are going to gain?" the whole idea is simply to put out information on the situation in those villages in the public eye, Shafto said Ceesay's dream is to build a medical centre to serve the villages, since care is many miles away and roads in and out of villages aren't passable by ambulance.

Currently patients are transported out of villages without ambulances for distances to health centres from their homes. Avery Aten, MD, of Alpena also has become involved with the project.

"The medical aspects of this relationship can be long-term," he told city council members. He said so medical statistics regarding the area, such as the average life expectancy is 53 years old and 85 out of 1000 children die during birth. According to Shafto, some of Aten's hopes include sending medical equipment which is no longer used here to the villages and even possibly having nursing students experiencing practicing there.

"I just see all kinds of goodwill things happening," Shafto said. "For us to have the opportunity to lead about a totally different culture is good for us."

"One aspect Shafto highlighted is the opportunity for elementary classroom in Alpena to communicate with the village school. Although she assisted in having the proclamation made, Shafto gives credit for making it happen to individuals at ACC. "My part is minor compared to what ACC has done," she said. "They are the ones who really got this started."

During the trip the students met with various village leaders who showed them what projects they were working on and where the greatest need was. In addition, the students taught some short classes on the United States. One day the group helped with the construction of a mosque. They also visited the agricultural centre and health centre.

Ray said the trip "contributed greatly" in making the sister city proclamation a reality "because it gave people in Alpena a connection to the village."

"The Gambia District Authority of Lower Badibou and villagers remain eternally grateful for giving us chance of Twining with you. Huge thanks to the City of Alpena, Mayor of Alpena and Alpena City Council," Alhasan wrote. "The villagers and I are enternaly indebted to all at Alpena. In addition, we look forward to working hand in hand for reward of all parties."

-Sue Latuszek: The Alpena News 2005-

The first hatchling of this merging of diverse hearts is as follows:-

Njawara Basic School

Lower Badibu District

North Bank Division

The Gambia, W. Africa

19/01/06

Dear Sir/Madam

RE: To whom it may concern.

These students are promising students whose parents are not able to fully support their educational needs. As a result, we would be very grateful if a concern person(s) can assist the students and their parents in taking care of some of the financial difficulties they are encountering to earn education.

These include school fees, uniforms, book bills and other school needs. Thank you and in anticipation, I remain,

Yours Faithfully

Lamin K. Juwara

Principal

These where the initial list of needy student to benefit from what is now called Manding Medical Centre/USA scholarship grants.

The above list and letter were faxed to Councilwoman Carol Shafto on the 23/02/06. The fax simply read:-

Hi Carol,

I hope you are okay and back at work. I hereby forward a list of school children from Njawara school needing sponsorship. Feel free to contact those you think would like to participate in this educational project.

The first three candidates in the list are earmarked for you and your son(s). See names 1 – 3 in the list. Send all monies via Western Union in the name of Aja Hadi Panneh, (Alkalo of Njawara village) to any Gambian Bank that Western Union deals with in Gambia.

Then email me stating amounts, date sent and for who. I will follow up by contacting the Principal of Njawara School, the parents and the chief of the district to ascertain prompt and proper distribution.

In addition, I will have Aja Hadi Panneh (Alkalo), the parents, Headmaster and were possible the recipient students to write acknowledging the amounts received. Please feel free to contact me if you have any questions or ideas to promote the above noble educational commitment. Once again, thanks and we remain grateful for your stand.

Your Friend

Dr. Alhasan S. Ceesay, MD

Chapter 11

Njawara Farmers' Bantaba forum

Villagers had since ancient times met annually to discuss problems of the last season and how to get the most out of their yield. Today they are even confronted by a three-headed dragon in the form of desertification, climate change and constant attacks from voracious hoards of millions of caterpillars, Locusts and insects along with irresponsive governments.

The following is scenario of what transpires in most developing countries, especially where AK47 is king and master of the souls of the innocent. The highlight of this meeting was the secretary of state (SOS) for Agriculture's decision to attend in behalf of the government and the party the farmers' forum. Soon a trio of limos streaked through human corridors and came to quick stop at the Banataba, a place where village meetings are held. First to step out from the limo at the back was Mr. Londi Baaa, permanent secretary, Ministry of Agriculture, followed by Sansang Tio, the Director of Agriculture and then his secretaries, all of them looking fat and donning whitewashed faces.

Yes, they bleached their faces. It was a look or a fashion to signify being rich, which the farmers cared less about. Finally, in the lead limo came out a very fat looking six-footer weighing well more than a hundred and ten kilograms, Mr. Korda Tio, who could hardly move because of his weight and the exhausting heat. On taking his place at the Bantaba the village priest offered a hasty short prayer commencing the meeting of the farmers' forum.

The SOS for Agriculture, Korda Tio, stood up and confidently greeted the gathering and added, "Fellow farmers, ladies and gentlemen, I represent the government and I am here to discuss with you and find about your difficulties, search for solutions and plans government has in helping improve your lot and the cash crops you toil so hard to produce.

We in government are very proud of you and your contributions to the welfare of the state. We take great pain and in measured form do try to get help for you." His long rambling speech did not interest the farmers and Fondinke Sire Fatajo eventually interrupted it. He told the SOS that, "The forum was not a political platform and that farmers are no longer interested in oratories, which even the deliverer, forgets a few hours after the meeting. You sir, look like a fat bull while farmers continue to shrivel to pencil seizes.

We would like you to know that the meeting was about how to ward off insects that ravaged our farms and acquisition of more disease hardy seed and cash crops able to stand the scorches of climate change of the day."

At this point, the party chairman stepped in as a damage control move to calm down opponents. He had the nerve to tell the crowd," The honourable secretary of state (SOS) was there for all of us and would transmit our concerns to the president in due course." This made some of the young radicals asked that he be seated and stop being mouthpiece of the party that cares less about the plight of the farmers.

The crowd was happy that someone stood up for them and they in unison booed the chairman to sit and remain quite for the rest of the meeting. He did as requested reluctantly to avoid being lynched by angry farmers. The SOS was also rattled for he now knew he was not in friendly territory nor was the party a favourite in this Badibou gathering.

He pretended not being afraid and continued saying, "It was governments' intention to provide tractors and combine-harvesters for use by the farmers In the next planting season." Foroding stopped the SOS on his track by letting him know his predecessor made the same promises some ten years ago and none ever saw a fly more over tractor coming to plough the land for farmers. Instead, less seeds were issued leaving most of the farmers to fend for themselves from neighbouring countries.

"Hence, Foroding insisted, you should stop lying or not show up again at the farmers' forum." The embarrass SOS managed to beam a smile at Foroding in so doing infuriated more people in the gathering that expected much concrete things than delivered by the SOS. The discussions continued with Bokari Fula, a party militant, trying to palliate matters and found him being physically evicted and thrown out of the bantaba and asked never to return again.

Foroding told the crowd, "We are here to see about what can be done to curb desertification and how to overcome unexpected difficulty climate change caused and how to ward off marauding insects. I suggest each village planting more than 100,000 trees every rainy season and for them to start using crops that survived climate change in neighbouring countries and those far away."

Foroding concluded by admonishing farmers to heed to diversification of their cash crops and for cooperatives to help in the storage, transportation and sale of their produce, These guidelines when followed would help the farmer rather than listening to the SOS' repetitive promises. Majula Jonfolo in her modest way told the crowd "It was time they desist being treated as subhuman morons lead by party like cows with ropes around their necks obeying every tug by their Sheppard.

I know and insist that the only thing a party dose was dividing us and bribe loads of lairs while giving farmers unfulfilled promises. We should press on and forget about party interests. Lately, my rice fields along with many in my area were all devoured by insects and no government official ever came to our village to assess the damage or cared to help farmers like me."

Majula begged the people thus, "let us please put aside party elegancies and work together, as in the ancient times, when communities come to the assistance of the misshaped without expecting money or party praises. Our children and bedrock of the next generation are disillusioned by the half-baked school system they attend.

It demands premium school fees from parents and yield nothing at the end of the student's educational experience. It does not give money for value of education." She added, "Many children run to the big cities and the capital believing that job opportunity exist for them in these God forsaken places. These children only end up finding themselves as street people, drug pushers, pimps and addicts, and most of the girls are turned into prostitutes.

Yet the government SOS of education regurgitates high enrolment numbers as proof that many more children are being in school and educated. What a farce! If the education and certificate it produces was worth the diploma or worthless paper it was printed on why is it that all the rich folks, government high officials and ministers stealthily send their children to be schooled in Europe and America?

You and I, the little ones, are left to feed on crumbs, while the big shots lavish in luxury having the best food and drinks." She concluded saying, "Independence was not meant to be one-sided affair as observed in Africa. In Africa, to benefit one has to be a member of the ruling tribe, taw the party line, whether right or wrong, step on toes of any other tribe member wanting to get a piece of the national cake and above all the tribe in power is automatically privileged or entitled to post most of them never dreamt of or qualify to man.

One wonders why the rampant corruption and unrest in the continent. It is land or country for president and party not for the electorate." Majula Jongfolo thanked the gathering of devoted farmers and asked that they think of each other's welfare than false promises the government or governing party promises every meeting with none fulfilled.

The crowd love it and cheered repeatedly at the end of her deliberation for almost ten minutes, which did not go well with the SOS in attendance. It was getting late in the afternoon and simmering hot for the fat SOS. Now the last speaker for government, the Director of Agriculture stepped forward to chat with the farmers. He was instantly met with boos and heckling one could hear being miles from the Bantaba.

However, he mustered courage and confronted the booing. "Ladies and gentlemen," he began amidst greatest noise one cannot imagine happening to such high-ranking government officer. He persevered and said, "As you heard from the SOS for Agriculture the Honourable Member of Parliament this government dose have your interest at heart.

My department was doing all it could to bring relief and usher in new cash crops. A larger consignment of farming tools is on the way for this year. Your area would be the first to receive consideration." At which juncture someone in the crowd asked, "Would the Director of Agriculture please name just one?" The Director replied, "Cashew nuts, Potatoes and hardy rice specie from China." The gathering got really angry by this repetition and reminded him that these were the same items mentioned 15 years ago at a rally and no one ever saw any new crops or Potatoes.

Hence they accept that he had no new things to add nor dose his department care or represent interest of the farmers. The entire department plays with statistics government wishes for mare foolish public consumption or propaganda. Paul Baldeh stepped in and told him, "Even the few working machines colonial masters left behind were in such irreparable state and none functional for lack of repairs and needed maintenance. Maintenance was lacking and now the cost to the country would be unfathomable."

He asked, if that "Was not that the reason for government agents dashing to China and Malaysia to purchase fifth hand machines that are polished but break down after three months usage? He continued by reminding him thus "All the Mersey Ferguson tractors left to us by the Brits were no longer functional and parts have been said to be sold to farmers in other countries right under his watchful eyes.

Was that a right thing or in the interest of the farmers in this country?" He jokingly added, "Yet Ministers and high officials put on weight to a point most now looked like a cross between a hippopotamus and an African Rhino. One look at us farmers tells how scrawny and starving some of us are."

The crowd applauded over and over for it loved Ministers being poked, as this was the only time they can ventilate face to face with such officials without risking arrest or their lives. My dear friend in current Africa, freedom of speech is a dream thing. Right after Paul's speech a contingent of soldiers and police conducted arrests.

The securities napped all or most of the key speakers who were identified by moles of the governing party. These were later accused and charged for spreading malicious propaganda information against the president and interest of the state. Oh yes! It is always against the president and Godfather of the nation, which he assumes ownership, and not the country in question, which does not matter.

The next day government mouthpieces claiming to be newspapers rained in headlines that portray and claim that hooligans disrupted the farmers meeting. Well reader, you now saw the attitudes of governments and how they illegally use the arms of the security forces for their benefits and not those of the people. This is one aspect, which gave impetus to coup d'etats in Africa. There is no rule of law. Simply life here is worse than that faced by the red Indians of America or the wild, Wild West movies.

In Africa one has to either taw the line while helping the government rain havoc on freedom, human rights and freedom of speech or loss out under yoke of torture and murderers. Paul Balde was a lawyer by vocation and his firm along with international agencies backed his challenging of the action taken by the security forces in carrying out orders issued by advice of the government. He and his detained comrades were carted or taken to an unknown destination for interrogation.

It was later revealed that they were brutally torture in effort to extort false information and allegations against the state from them. It was so unbearable that most signed confessions under duress they had no idea or ever participated in the crimes documented in those confessions. However, they rather sign than die a very slow painful death for nothing. Signing the document only lands them in prison with scared minds for life but there was the hope of seeing ones loved ones again no matter how long the jail sentence was going to be.

The government prosecutor was so out of order in proudly and happily waving and brandishing these false confessions they squeezed out of innocent people in the air at the next government rally. Mean while all the thirty arrested were denied bail on the grounds that their act or crime was deemed treasonable and they are likely to escape to other countries before the trial begins.

How heartless can these puppet autocratic governments be? In the end out of the thirty-arrested only Paul and three other refused to sign the confession government concocted, which promised leniency by the judge at the end of the proceedings. The case was finally brought before judge Junewunna, ten months from the day of the arrests.

The judge immediately told the accused, "I would remind each of you before this court of the seriousness of the charges against you and the court needs nothing but the truth to allow it pass fair and just verdict." Paul Baldeh chuckled and was immediately removed from the courtroom and never allowed to attend the rest of the proceedings in the life of that trial.

Defence council Foroding Darboe protested the decision of the court to remove his client for something that everyone in the room including judge himself chuckled at. HIs protest fell on deaf ears for Judge Junewunna was only carrying out government plans for the case by removing the most talented lawyer and to show that it can embarrass and humiliate a Barrister in court. It serves to intimidate the other defendants into cooperating with the prosecutor during trial. Lawyer Foroding Darboe, in his opening statement made it crystal clear thus, "My lord justice, none of the thirty clients pleads guilty as the prosecutor accused them under none judiciary means.

They are innocent good citizens that do not deserve this harassment and misused of the judiciary functions of state. They were just adding option to discussion the farmers invited their participation." He then asked, "When was it wrong for anyone to ask for help or to find ways of solving problems besetting their lives? I besiege your honour and court to examine itself and squash the charges against my clients and unconditionally realise my clients who were wrongly arrested by the securities, subjected to torture and wrongfully detained by the security force. In reality this should have been a police case not solders ramming innocent people with gun butts."

He asked, "When did we, meaning the country, turn into such anarchist state?" People in attendance cheered and had themselves cleared out of the court forthwith for government allowed the television in to make a media circus of the proceedings but does not like the public see that advocate for the victims is receiving sympathy from those in court. Some of those evicted had few slaps from the security men manning the doors. Yes, this is dictatorship at its highest order. The president in tinkering with the judiciary requested that he be given the report about the pulse of the farmers who were already getting masses to march on the capital in protest to the illegal seizure and arrest of innocent descent citizens of the country.

The farmers believed it was orders issued by the president through the Inspector General of Police and the Army Commander of state. On getting the report the president ordered the postponement of the case until further notice on the guise of new evidence being present for the prosecutor to study properly before the next court date to be announced in due course. Mean while the accused are to stay under strict detention orders with no visitation rights from any other than the prosecutor and police.

The injunction included and extended to defence lawyers and families of those arrested. By dawn the next day Lawyer Foroding Darboe and family had unwanted visitors breaking into their home. Masked men using unmarked cars, which later were identified as belonging to the security forces, raided the compound. These masked men collected computers, files and any other item of interest including jewellery. Yes, the defence lawyer and his family were brutalized by these tugs. They were hospitalised for more than a week. On the next daylight the governing party organ headlined the atrocious attack and said, "Such savagery should not be allowed in this country.

The SOS for local government will do all he could to bring the perpetrators to justice." Well and good but it lacked sincerity and Innocence for some of those writing the piece were indeed present at the planning table of the very crime they are condemning. How much double standard can there can be from one sector of the country. By noon the same day the president went on radio and television to denounce the act as barbaric and uncalled for in this smiling coast of Africa.

What a farce! He ordered immediate investigation into the matter and now pretending to be in sympathy with its victims. "Be assured listeners that my government will follow these bad men to any crook they may or might be hiding in the world. I deplore such heinous acts." And he even had the nerve and shamelessness to visit the defence lawyer and his wife in hospital.

At the hospital the staff told him it was the request of the patients that no visitor is allowed in their rooms. The security right then knocked the doors down to let the president proceed to the said rooms. On finding the lawyer he shamelessly offered to shake the hands of the lawyer who refused to shake hands with him. The lawyer knew he was behind the dirty intimidation game and hence rejected shaking his hand outright or even saying a word to him.

The president left embarrassed because the whole event was televised to other countries too. The case was of regional interest and that was why the president went into this cosmetics and theatricals sympathy displays. Being humiliated by this fiasco rejection by the defence lawyer the president left horridly and angrily because he wanted to be seen shaking the hands of his adversary and the very victim whose hospitalisation he might have caused.

He was disguising himself akin to a wolf in sheep's clothing just to gain support from the farmers and quell the pending threats posed by farmers all over the country. He in his heart knows he no long enjoyed their support and must do something quick not to lose his standing amongst the farmers who are the majority voters.

This would be made worst if he had to shed blood to quell the uprising. It was certainly his hope that his sham visit to victims at the hospital would divide opinion among the farmers about their organising against his rule. The whole fiasco confused the president to lead him to summon all his party chairmen to an emergency meeting at which he asked each to try and identify key dissidents and send the list directly to his office in two days.

Special secret ambush points were earmarked and reinforcement by elite trigger happy brutes of the army, most of who came from his tribe, were put in these places awaiting the innocent farmers make the first move towards the capital. List at hand and all the security in place the president again went on radio and television asking the farmers not to demonstrate and to obey the countries law and the courts and his departments of government can redress their grievances.

He warned, "The state would not tolerate any uprising for there is always the peaceful discussion route for good citizens to follow in a dispute of any kind. "Be aware, he with stern face told listeners, "That should this warning fall on deaf ears the full force of the law will be enforced mercilessly. Hence, I urge all to be calm and go about their daily life as a peace loving people."

 This announcement made the farmers angrier and more determined to march on the capital no matter how ugly it might turn out at the end. They will demonstrate and present their petitions to the president and would in addition ask for release of the detainees to avoid repetition of such arrests any time farmers choose to deliberate about their work and farms or any group not liked by government met.

The looming dark cloud was not something the government wanted, as it has to resort to force to stop the march or back down as whims giving the opposition fodder to feed on. Some government insiders in sympathy with farmers told the farmers of traps and plan to disrupt their demonstration. Hence, instead of going in large numbers the farms choose what they styled the drip' drip train to the capital.

Weeks passed without the hoards people expected to march in the streets of the city. By the time the security knew more than twenty thousand farmers had made it into the capital ready to march as soon as the leaders gave the signal. These gather at the market place on market day helping their disguised and then all of a sudden head to the state house some five hundred meter away with most the security taken by surprise and sheer numbers of farms to either have to kill or let them into the compound.

The president was himself surprised at the efficiency and delicate way the farmers outwitted him and hence he opted to meet those delegated submitting the petitions signed by nearly a quarter of a million farmers. The sheer weight of it made him call of all plans and asked his forces to retreat and halt all operations against the demonstrators. He had agreed to meet them and hear their cases and complains.

Call it the African Magna Cater was poised for ratification and signed by king/dictator Africa. By this simple acquiesce a miracle had taken place in history of African politics for president do not backs down for "little rats like farmers and villagers." However he knew backing down was the only way he could save lives and preserved peace. He told his Ministers, "I now want to hear the genuine complain these people have against my government and to amend things to benefit all instead party exhalants."

Throngs upon throngs of farmer paraded the streets of the capital after having met the president. There was music and dancing, instead of bloodshed, for almost three days before the farmers headed to their respective villages with assurance that such attacks will never happen to them again.

The thirty detainees were released and personally given fat compensations to apace them and their families. Most of that money was donated to the cause of the entire farming community of the country. The detainees later became heroes of the farming community and are still talked about by those in the know and were at the farmers' forum. Unlike most African confrontations this one ended up peacefully and even made the government to revamp its Agricultural plans.

The government brought in many experts to help the farmers and provided needed tools for use by the farmers. Some said it was wise move on the president's side to make a u-turn before matters got out of hand and turn nasty, which would send the country into oblivion. Others deemed him a coward not fit to be president of country. These were the bloodthirsty fools who enjoyed carnage than living in peace.

My friend this is how simple gatherings in today's Africa can turn into huge balls of fire once it was not the ruling part gathering to discuss matters at times irrelevant to the state's prosperity. As for Lawyer Paul Baldeh he could not leave matters rest and after fruitless litigations with the government he ended up becoming senior law advisor to the opposition party.

It was rumoured that the opposition on coming to power would appoint him attorney general of the country. However, that dream seem quelled at present by the resent acquiescence of the president to demand made by the farmers. At least the president still enjoys support of most, if not three quarters of the country's farmers. It is said that all is well that ends well. This country's leader has for the time being saved his political carrier. This story had a good ending but in the case of the Tutsi and Hutus or in Darfur there is much to be said about African Administrations.

Chapter 12

Grandma Aminata Kassa On pregnancy

Today the topic at the Bantaba was a muted one as it involved more or less women than men. Unlike grandpa Bajoja, grandma Aminata was a shy to almost reclusive sweet person. However, when it comes to the Bantaba forum she lights up brighter than the Northern start in the firmament.

On this day she decided to talk on a very exciting and challenging phase in a woman's life. She went straight for the bull's eyes saying, "Pregnancy is the zenith of love and most rewarding of all romantic and erotic relationships. It is an endowment only the female gender experiences. We are so lucky that men do not get pregnant."

This comment drew in loud laughter and support from young and old ladies who nodded in approval. The men refused to remain silent. One man asked, "Do women get pregnant in absence of men? Are we not the key to pregnancy in women?" This remark angered some women and a few in the audience with a little knowledge of biology retorted, "Pregnancy in reality connotes the scenario of the egg and the chicken. Which one came first? The sperm and the ovum are all prerequisite to a woman becoming pregnant. Hence none is more significant than the other."

The women in support clapped the loudest. It was at this juncture that the sage lady of the day intervened and said, "Both are indeed significant but more so is it for the female who carries the evolution to full term and parturition of the new entity.

Men cannot claim responsibility for this phase; hence part plaid by women is more significant in procreation as without them there will not be any more new and vibrant forms of human life." This remark generated another sarcastic comment from an 80-year-old male in the audience. He stated, "We men set you restless and give you the joy of your lives and so you are tailored to nurture children for us."

A young lady in the crowd yelled, "Not for you in a million years!" The man looked at her directly, laughed and said, "Child watch your mouth and ask your auntie whom you were trying to embarrass. It may teach you to think twice before opening up your mouth." The girl apologized and sat quietly for the rest of the debate on pregnancy. Well, well, any time the genders gather there seem to raise questions of who is the dominant one among the two and yet, I dare say we cannot live happily without the other.

Grandma having heard from all sides and having given enough chance for debate between the genders told us, "From the day Eve made Adam to eat the forbidden fruit women embarked on a spiraling challenging path. Pregnancy is not a simple single-phase affair. It has body and mind as well as hormonal and gustatory changes that pregnancy causes most women to endure. One of the most difficult phases is, for few unfortunate ones, vomiting endlessly up to the 10th week and at times beyond.

This state of hyper emesis gravidarum has a devastating effect on both mother and child to be." She warned that, "Women should plan for the event when young and able and not allow pregnancy to occur when old. Pregnancy requires strength, patience and perseverance to cope with the changing phases of the mother and growing baby.

The nourishment demands of the new baby make us eat like hungry Elephants and leave us with an unbearable craving for more food. The weight gains makes one look like an inflated giant caterpillar tires, the kicking and turning movements of the baby as it position itself can be nerving for first time pregnant women. None of our preferred dresses fit and hormonal changes goes out of hand to making some pregnant women turn into a temporal wild beast as they become irritable, angry at their male partner for delivering them into such confusion and inability to cope with their usual life style.

The experience could be made worst from complication of drugs or disease and when the mature baby starts descending. A series of short contractions heralding labour commences earlier in the third trimester of the pregnancy. The most challenging moments of this forty-two weeks or less of ups and down encountered during pregnancy, is the last two hours when painful uterine contractions of increasing strength accompanied by breaking of water commonly known as a show, and dilatation to allow passage of the baby's head in parturition.

This is the most difficult and cause of many would be mothers loss their lives along with their pretty babies." During this explanation the crowd was as silent as midnight in the middle of the Sahara Desert. It scared a few of the young ladies and couples and reminded the menopausal their day and encounter of the first time they went into labour.

Grandma asked, "Why in the dickens do we still repeat this deadly experience over and over without hesitation or fear of what may happen to us?" The only answer she said, "lies wholly and solely on love and love of holding our own unique replica. It is not about proving our love to our husbands or lovers, for they will chicken out after the first term of pregnancy and will never allow such experience to occur in their life for any price offered.

We repeatedly get pregnant for love and because nature assigned such coveted role only to women of the species. And we do carry it out with gusto and joy of having children in our lives." She ended the debate by advising ladies not to get pregnant when they are sick or old. These make them vulnerable and may risk theirs' and life of their unborn babies in so doing.

Chapter 12

Grandpa Bajoja Ceesay Discourse on war

In one of the village weekly meetings grandpa Bajoja decided to touch on the very sensitive issue of war and warring. After the normal prayers initiating the Bantaba meeting grandpa told the gathering that he had chosen to dwell on the subject that should be of the wild beasts and thing of the past fit only in the pages of history books.

He reminded us that the greatest enemy that lies in us is fear but this could be replaced with confidence. He said, "Fear leads to hatred and fodder for conflicts which could be fought by replacing it with love. Fear makes us powerless but we can improve our sphere of influence to enable us overpower powerlessness and deprivation in this life."

He spat his tobacco out and with eyes as red as a ball of fire said, "War is the raw barbaric and wanton way men at times chooses to settle difference amongst themselves. War has never yielded winners but only misery and loss of property while setting entire regions into chaos for centuries. War is the killing of another because one is afraid of negotiating or facing raw truth of guilt in causing mayhem.

War spares neither children nor the innocent men and women and destroys at will in the name of religion, government or an idea such as democracy or communism and at times for no reason other than wanting to blindly bully another to death." He then paused and asked the crowd what they were told about the reason to fight the Nazis headed by the monster Adolph Hitler.

He asked, "Were we not told that it was wrong for one's freedom to be taken by another. It was then wrong to be dominated and governed against ones wishes. Did early conflagrations or world wars one and two teach man any sense and to learn to negotiate with one another? No, it is about bloodthirsty tugs using and whipping up your emotions about ideas or believes they lack but would nudge you into wasting your lives to kill or be killed in the conflagration.

The outcome of war includes occupying the home or land of the people by brutal means and massacring people, the awarding of so-called war heroes medals and the stealing of all that was good and the wealth of the conquered. War, my dear friends," he said, "some said it started from the twilight of life and will continue as long as armies and difference between nations or tribes exist. War is an unnecessary use of young men and women in uniform.

Warring is the coward's way of comforting themselves but not confronting evils. It is not right to kill a fellow human being. The great books of religion told us that we must turn our swords into ploughs and till the land to grow food for the people. Did these not constantly emphasize the sanctity of life, which is God's greatest gift to the living?" He said, "I have never met an old veteran solder that felt happy or comfortable having killed so many innocent souls even though his side ended up being the victor.

Today our ingenuity to murder causes mayhem and plunder has been made a billion folds more devastating in comparison to the days of lances and sword fights. We have even gone a step further to use blind bombing machines such as drones, chemically laced bombs, atomic bombs, and bombs that kill indiscriminately because of thousands of deadly shrapnel's they release on impact. What caused man to develop this numb feeling towards his fellow being? He asked. The brutality of man has gone to the lowest levels; bellow that of the wild beasts in the jungle. Lions, hyenas, and even despicable snakes kill once to feed but not destroy sawed of land along with millions upon millions of its inhabitants at one go."

He asked, "This being the case against man who is there to dare class us civilized if this way is our mode of settling differences? War is evading the truth, justice and turning bully boy. The law of the jungle has been misinterpreted by over zealous war mongering mercenary governments and rebels. Tribal wars are fanned by whipping up hate and false rumours about intent of the other tribe.

It is called banging heads to create havoc which eventually flares into huge confrontations between the concerned tribes. The motivation may just be to get the other's animals; arable land even with intention to make love with their wives or daughters while turning them subjects and slaves." He admonished that this barbaric and capricious way of the past must be brought to an end. He told listeners, "Some accused me of being in dreaming state in thinking in the lines as stated above. I normally asked my critics since they do not want their children killed were it equally right for theirs to kill another's child?" The attitude of the so-called developed world and United Nations have made it possible for rebels and rouge governments and AK47 dictators pop up all over the world challenging the UN any time they want because of barking the gun industry has and welcome purchases from the warring factors.

The gun industry and supper powers care less which child dies from bullets it made once it is not affecting its own and allows full employment of its work force as well as ill-gotten profit gains. These bad elements are certain that both the governments and UN who supposedly are able to quell things more often than not turn the other way or give a blind eye while innocent people, Hutus, Tutsi, Darfur, Chinaman Square, Tibet, Burma, child solders, purported child Witches, the suffering of the Jews and the Palestinians and even armies of drug barons and pushers in our street world wide sponsoring merciless killings.

None of these would have dared to rain the above terror and hell had the UN used its mandate correctly instead of swaying along with wishes and dictates of so called supper powers only interested in keeping their work forces and ideologist afloat, especially the gun industry. Killing is weakness but not power, as the perpetrators of war and its mongrels can testify.

Power lies in having a heart, reason, and willingness to debate than fight, to tolerate and accept or accommodate differences. The world is made up of myriads of hues, sizes, languages all of which lived on mother earth. Why then should one insist that his or hers' should be the only way to carry on with? Every thing in life varies and the very brute's body is asymmetrical.

Why do people believe war solves their problems is beyond comprehension. Moneys used to fund the combat could have been well spent if put into research for cancer, aids, building of better homes for people, food production, provision of clean and safe water, creation of environmentally friendly energy sources, for use than wasting young men's precious lives in war zones.

The above challenges would be more noble way of using public fund than the wasting in wars. There is only pain and no gain in war. Avoiding war is being reasonable and not cowardice but humane. Man must desist from war and provide avenues that make collaboration possible. Life is very short and irretrievable once lost." Grandpa paused and asked, "Are there any war veterans in the crowd?"

A few raised their hands hesitatingly knowing that they might not be the welcome heroes they were few minutes before the sage's thought on war. The crowd had swung to the side of the wise of the sage's and a backlash of gears followed which made them pull their hands fast. One of the Warriors dared to challenge the sage and asked, "Would you be standing before the gathering had others not laid their lives to make the day possible for you and others gathering at the Bantaba?"

An eerie silence followed while the sage ponders over the question. He cleared his throat and replied and retorted by asking, "Was God not kind to let the Warrior be in attendance? There was no need to rationalise barbaric acts by making others having to have to be grateful because one killed others at the behest of governments or rebels.

A spade is nothing but a spade hence both those who ordered massacre of people and the ones that carried it out are the same and they defy reason to please their weak minds." He asked the warrior, "How would you feel if the gathering raped and slaughtered your wife and daughter before your very eyes? Would you class that as saving lives of others?"

The warrior replied, "No, indeed." Grandpa then said, "God gave life. Let us please allow it to take its natural cause before returning to God. The warrior was just one of many who destroyed life and then pride themselves in being called warrior instead of the coward they were and are still masking one." This comment made the Warrior furious and he stormed out of the meeting mumbling profanities to him.

The old sage told the crowd, "What you just witnessed is the way of cowards and murderers. They cannot face facts over confrontation or truth for fear of being unveiled and they always resort to force instead of debate and giving chance to ironing out things with their so-called advisory. Warriors have nothing noble to show for their heinous acts of brutality other than scars, guilt-ridden minds, which they internalise.

Warriors are not squeamish in wantonly killing but fear the truth about the needless atrocities the like of him caused for centuries upon centuries. He will remain remorseful in silence for the rest of eternity or his natural life on earth." It was getting late in the evening but the ladies would not let the men be the only voices of righteousness.

Hence and an old lady told the silent gathering that, "Had it not been men's supper egocentric ness which run hay wild most of the time, their big empty heads misguiding them, there would have been more love and caring than wars."

She said, "Man's ego commits him into such unforgivable state of mind and willingness to kill for mythical power beyond the devils' capabilities." This indictment of men being zealous war mongering devils did not sink well as most of the men refuted her observation and allegation of men being blood thirsty criminal from birth.

The old sage intervened and told them that what exchange was going on was how wars were started. "Allegations and counter allegations lead to tribal conflicts and wars. Man never could accept guilt where it befalls him. He is only good at throwing the ball at the others' corner but not reasonable enough to accept his filthy part in the disarray or conflagration that ensues." The women cheered gleefully.

Grandpa Bajoja Ceesay concluded by urging the next generation to commit to settling differences peacefully and in co-existence. He told them, "Only through sincere and frank negotiations on equal basis can peace be achieved. Never, never loose feelings for each other and must refrain from malicious rumours or rumour mongering."

Roheyata Sey-Corr, Cousin

Chapter 13

Grandpa Bajoja Ceesay On race/tribal relations

A big story was normally afoot any time Grandpa Bajoja Ceesay collected us children under the big cotton tree, commonly known as "Bantaba", where meetings are held at Njawara. He would first half fill his mouth with either chewing tobacco or kola nuts before commencing his epic stories or lectures as most of the "Bantaba" conversations were styled by him.

From the time he commences to the end of his historic point of views a pin drop on the sand could be heard because of complete silence from his fifty or so children eager to hear every word or phrase the old sage had to say. They all seem to fall into a sleepless, tranquil state as they absorb every sentence the revered storyteller says. Our eagerness to hear him marches, if not surpasses, the silence in anticipation of the good story or advice the old sage entertains us with.

This particular meeting was neither about our ancient kings nor about victories worn by past African heroes. Everything Grandpa Bajoja dose starts with a prayer. The reason being according to him all creatures most pay homage and gratitude to their God. At this time grandpa would spill the agenda of the day to the curious awaiting tender ears.

And the children followed this with a loud chorus, "Please tell us grandpa, wisest of the wise." With a smile and a nod of his head in approval he begins thus: "Children, today's topic would be one you should not only listen attentively but must pass onto the next generation. It is about how things are and how a good human being relates with others.

First, a human must have faith, must be good not only to himself/herself but to others as well. Faith is the only path to your maker and embodies needed self-discipline. A human must earn a living and be ready to share the proceeds with family and community. You are not alone on mother earth nor do you wish to remain in solitude or be alone on this planet.

One must accept difference and like wise be tolerant to others, especially the weak and sick ones needing our help." The sage laughed and asked us to stand up and look at any direction we choose. He said, "Now look straight forward before you for a moment. Then ask yourselves what was it that you saw?"

We wondered what this exercise was all about or meant to our future lives. Why look in open wilderness, fields full of different wild animals and birds or through canopy of trees and leaves? We all in unison asked Grandpa Bajoja Ceesay if there was something unique about the exercise we just did.

To us it was nothing more than looking into an unappreciable void. Grandpa knows better. Only he at the time knew the importance of the exercise. Grandpa laughed; spat out some of the kola nut he was chewing. He looked at us straight in the eyes, his being as red as a ball of fire, and said, "All of you must remember the different things you noted while gazing in front of you. God created all the different things each of you behold but lets them all exist, if not, act and live in unison. Hence, never look down on your fellow humans no matter their stations or seeming deference from you or yours. They are as good as **you.**

Never be guilty of racism or tribalism for both are callous, ignorant, pigheaded bigotry, unjust, inhuman, and hurts the innocent. Racists and tribe-oriented people are lost idiots needing salvation. They are inconsiderate, weak minded, self delusional fools believing they are the best race and the chosen ones above all others.

They think themselves more special than the ones they look down on. They are the lowest of the low in the human race. In God's eyes everyone is precious and for one to choose to mock that is a failure of being civilized, mentally immature and not realizing or acknowledging the power of the Almighty creator. Children, do not ever be back stabbers.

I urge you to just remain loyal friends to each other and for humanity. And it is your duty to pass the above advice to generations after you. May God bless you and protect you in life. What this seemingly innocent exercise left me with was that one must at all times refrain from racist or tribal attitudes and rather we must all be our brother's or sister's keeper. "Long live Grandpa Bajoja Ceesay," the children normally say at the end of the august epic story telling/lecture meetings with Njawara's grand storyteller.

Chapter 14

Sisawo Ceesay On tolerance

If there be any broad-minded person at Njawara village it had to be Sisawo Salla Ceesay. This elderly man was among few very akin to Mahatma Gandhi of India. This peace-loving full of endurance man was today to address youngsters who could hardly tame their energies and aspirations of forcefully conquering the universe.

Like his father, grandpa Bajoja, he was an adept orator that could easily sway you to his side in a debate. With this gift though, he hardly says anything unless invited to speak.

Today we gather at the sprawling Mango tree at the Bantaba not only to cool off from the scotching heat but also to learn the art of tolerance from the master himself. The meeting started with a prayer and then he said, "Children, we are here to learn from each other." This surprised most of the elders who were more eager to hear earth-moving tactics or séance that may help them control or hold their short tempers.

Not learning from these small babies before them. Sisawo said this deliberately to trigger uneasiness in those unable to give chance to patients. The children were well behaved but one of them could not perceive teaching this sage of sages an iota about tolerance. Impatient Dinding Kanjara stood and asked, "Grandpa, everyone here knows you are the most tolerant and amongst the wisest and all of us children attest to that fact by the jokes that you accept from us unlike the other grown ups.

Hence, what is there that we can teach you about tolerance? Everyone came here to learn from you but not you from us for we are minors compared to your encyclopedic knowledge on the subject." Sisawo smiled and thanked Dinding Kanjara adding, "You have just proven my point as your impatiens forced you to speak out honestly.

Tolerance is guided by discipline and discipline without patients only yields trouble out of misjudgment and wrong assumption parked with stereotyping. Many elders in the crowd were moaning because they wanted a quick fixed to their uncontrolled attitudes towards life and those they touch. Tolerance is the simplest art to acquire once one answers the question, "Would I like to be treated so and so?

It follows the saying, "Do onto others as you would like do to you." The sage said if the answer is negative then one should find better ways of dealing with the situation than hastily concluding erroneously. He said, "Tolerant people are not cowards but reasonable folks willing to give peace a chance which eventually could be an eye opener that may yield friendship and understanding." The huge crowd nodded in approval while some applauded loudly as they never though of it in that light. Now, a sixty year old man asked, "What should I do with my nagging young bride whose demands my back no longer endures?"

The sage as well as most elders in the crowd laughed angering the ladies. The men knew what the sixty-year old man was going through as it reminds them their experience with young brides. The Sage let the laughter simmer down, cleared his throat and said, "My dear friend two wrongs never make a right.

At your current age you should be contended with one fifty-year old wife than having to add a twenty-year young heifer to your burden to show or because you have the money. Nature does tolerate but it teaches us lessons too. One of them is that our function depreciates as we age and there is no need to be impatient with the young bride.

To tolerates her you have to accept you own fault for erroneously believing you can perform as if you were in your twenties. Patients and honesty would be the most effective approach to your dilemma." He then asked to be allowed to address the youths on tolerance. He told the children, "Tolerance is accepting yourself and those around you. The "I and I only agenda" do not anoint tolerance.

Tolerance is being able to forgive when you are hurt knowing that peace would avoid repletion of the incidence. The tolerant is knows that a person is acting silly at the time and you let it pass away with out adverse reaction to it. Tolerance is part of respecting oneself and those around. Tolerance is to live and let live venue needed by all. Tolerance is faith and armor against misjudging. Tolerance is embracing differences in people and community. Tolerance is being a scout, a Good Samaritan, or passion to leave in affable life.

My dear friends heed no one forcing you into a fight which you could avoid by being a bit tolerant and nudging reason from the other." The children listened wide mouthed as the sage drove these simple but hard principles of self-preservation home. It was getting late as some attending had to walk ten miles to get home. The meeting ended with a prayer and promised to provide more aspects of tolerance next meeting of the Banta. All left happy and eagerly looking forward to Sisawo's next lecture on tolerance.

Chapter 15

Herbalist Sallah Hantie Sey

Discusses Death

Today an almost tabooed topic is on the lecture cart. Njawara's venerable herbalist will be offering a briefing on death at the Bantaba a little after midday. Some call her "Medicine lady" while others refers to her as Njawara's supper herbalist.

It is a difficult topic as it would remind her audience about their departed loved ones and at the same time bring to light how they may face the inevitable end to life they now possessed or carry.

The briefing started soon after the formalities of prayer. A dead silence ensued in a skewed crowd of almost only elderly and middle age men and women. There were very few youths for these believe indifferent to death and that youthful energies would help them swart or ward off death. Hence today's macabre topic was not for them or their interest.

Nonetheless a few did attend. Grandma Salla, Njawara's herbalist, went straight on the delivery stating, "Every living thing faces this end at certain unknown time in its existence. Some console themselves by agreeing that death is a necessary ending and will come when it will. Others agree it's the only factor of life that levels both the servant his king or master." She was immediately interrupted by a question from an elderly ninety-year man.

He asked, "When do we know its arrival and having dealt with several patients did they tell you what transpires during the last few minutes to the end?" In response grandma went into deep thought for a minute or two before offering an answer to the village elderly man. She said, "Sir, we are glad to have you with us and do pray to have you many, many more years in good health. The question you posed is difficult one but no one knows when in the uterus, on being born nor do we really know when and where death will meet us.

We know that microbial invasion, trauma, and insufficient immunity can accelerate death's arrival if we do not obtain medical assistance. Even these experts do inevitably loose to death. No patient of mine was able to tell for at that state the things of life no longer function and none of us have ever met a person who returned from the dead.

Yes, there are many survivors from near death but they were not dead. These talk of having seen angels, bright lights and rainbows or had very scary moments before loosing thought. This may be a form of hallucinatory effect than seeing things in the world beyond this one. When the angel of death departs it leaves its victim still, stiff and chilled.

The interplay between actin, myosin and troponin no longer function and the cadaver becomes rigid. As you rightly know one neither respires nor have pulsation in the vessels and nor elicit able neuronal function exist in that body. The scotching heat of our region makes it mandatory to perform all rites as soon as possible before the body start decaying for temperature accelerates that process. It is said that the evil men do lives after them and the good is often interred with their bones. Hence it's worth while to try to leave foot prints that others can immolate after our departure."

A middle-aged woman interrupted by asking, "Mama why do we have graves? Do they not serve as painful reminders of the deceased?" The sage answered by simply saying, "Graves are resting places of our departed beloved ones and they are also historical markers for generations of the linage to offer a prayer or just to know where their great grand parents finally rested on this planet of ours. The grave does continue historical ties of a family and community.

In some advance countries they even place encased pictures of the person in tombstones so that others can see the person." Another question came from a young crippled fellow who asked, "Mama would you kindly enlighten us as to why life on earth and is it not a waste as death takes it away from us?"

The matriarch medicine lady pondered for a while and said, "Man does not know the faintest idea why creation of life despite endless hypotheses of how temperature and gases collated, cooled and gelled to result in this miracle universe. This is no fact but mare speculation for it cannot account for the source of the first grain of sand, mountains, and myriads of starts in the firmament. Life is never a waste of time no matter how short or long it may last. There are always some exhilarating moments in it and also good deed that accompanied those days.

Hence, be advice to seek to do good until your time to leave mother earth arrives. Never waste it in foolishness, binge drinking or anti-social behaviors and fear of the end." Religion has it that there had to be some mysterious force of greater architectural endowment that invented life for its own amusement. This merciful and all-powerful force they called God.

By the way men should be on their guard for the way they treat their wives should or if that God turns out to be a woman, who is most likely for creation continues through procreation in which only women are empowered to conceive babies." This drew support from all women in attendance and disproval from the old men who stand to loose their earthly mythical power over women.

The temperature had become unbearable even under the spreading Mango tree where grandma was delivering. Hence she asked for closure until the next meeting in a month's time. The crowd concord thanked her and dispersed knowing that the medicine lady had spoken by telling the simple truth about the most inevitable end to life.

Chapter 16

The ramification of Party Politics

Change however slowly or fast it approaches comes with seismic and cosmic waves. The first thing it affects is the known or existing status co or norms operated upon. Chiefs and village heads gradually lost their parochial or assumed powers they normally exercised and people started questioning motives of those wishing to stand for Parliamentary posts in their regions.

Families almost tore themselves apart because of disagreement on various political party manifestos. The PPP held its ground as party of the farmers for quite a while before loosing its head and grip on the political landscape through the mistake of allowing the city tsars to encroach into the entrails of the PPP and dominate its operations and the Prime Minister turn President along with it.

This unfortunate development was the start of the fall of the Jawara regime. Hence, trading centers and villages like Njawara, showcases of the colonial rule, were hard hit when party politics surfaced in the Gambia's new political landscape in the early 1960s. To be frank the interior was neither equipped nor where the villagers given full political franchise until 1962.

The villagers organizing into a political force, namely the Protectorates People Party (PPP) later refurbished with the new name of the Peoples progressive party, caused jitters among old and fledgling Banjul city parties and tsars. The tug of war as to which one control the new state took bitter divisive ends in some quarters. It led to some founding fathers of the PPP to split and form the National Congress Party and Sheirif Sisay's short-lived Democratic Party. Njawara was no exception.

The village was divided center and left between diehard supporters of the PPP and the United Party (UP), a prominent political party led by former Barrister Pierre Sarr Njie, PS Njie for short. UP being the dominant force in Banjul it landed the Chief Minister's job to P. S. Njie despite protest from the PPP leadership led by Vetenery Surgeon Dr. Dawda Kairaba Jawara of Barajali Kunda further down Central Division in the Gambia.

Party wrangling and poor organization on the part of the city politicians gave the PPP a resound victory over the three Banjul parties (UP, Congress, and the Alliance Party of Rev. J. C. Faye). Dr. D. K. Jawara was catapulted to first, to a ministerial post as the Government affairs tsar and later the Prime Minister after independence on February 25th 1965. Dr. D. K. Jawara steered the country to a republican state in 1975 and was deposed by young Lieutenant Yahya Jammeh on July 22nd 1994.

This will go in history as one of the darkest moments in Gambian national history. The all too-familiar tune of rampant corruption and misuse of post were heard over and over for months after the surprised coup d'etat while commissions of enquiries did the so-called cleaning or mopping up assigned jobs. Nothing came out of the exercise except that the devil reared its ugly head in different fashion to evade the talons of the law and justice.

One can comfortably say corruption is still fabric of the society and remains in full force along with all its inhuman heartless tentacles. The military junta under Lieutenant Yahya Jammeh resigned from the army and took civilian camouflage and brags of wining the electorate's minds and hearts and has now been reining for fifteen years.

A few physical changes such as the Kerewan and Sankoley Kunda Bridges, a few more hospitals being built, the establishment of the Gambia Television, the Gambia University with a medical college included along with the building of senior Secondary schools in some provincial villages along the interior of the country, but more so in the Kombo region, were brought into play as showcase achievements of junta.

Lately, president Jammeh had let it be known on 9/11/10 through Senegal's West Africa Democracy Radio that he was not going to stand or run for the presidency in the forthcoming election and would handover the reins of government to the democratization process after his current term expires early next year, 2011. Most Gambians believe the announcement to be one of his publicity stunts and that he was again merely whitewashing people's faces or distracting attention from the real situation of the country, i.e. the vandalizing of justice, insecurity of the people whose freedom of speech remains in dreamland, massive poverty, Army and the National Intelligence Agency (NIA) incursions and over ruining lives.

The army and NIA are believed by most to have overused their mandated powers to the country in serving or pleasing the president and party. Everyone is praying while holding his or her breath hoping to live long to witness the coveted day this fellow would finally step down from ruining the country.

It is certainly premature to celebrate for hard work now awaits us and now faces each and every Gambian at home or in the Diaspora. We must learn from previous regimes' mistakes and jointly wrest ourselves from nepotism and tribalism of any kind.

We need and must encourage good governance through democratic means and also formulate rules that would prevent rigging of votes, life long presidency and where possible limit the powers of the military and the NIA to the barest minimum under the Law. These have turned cancerous gnawing the soul of the Gambia. We just hope keeping fingers tightly crossed that this bloke would be decent enough to act on his aired none solicited unilateral declaration of not running for office at the end of this current term next year 2011.

He need be reminded Justice Robert Jackson's speech after the Nuremberg trials that, "When a nation is stung with injury and stays away from vengeance voluntarily submitting perpetrators of heinous crimes to the judgment of the law is one of the most significant tributes that power has ever paid to reason." If Jammeh happens to vacate the office Gambians would be blessed and will christen it as the birth of the third republic adjunct to true independence and not the downward spiraling state we are currently faced.

It is my hope and prayer that the International community would for once has heart and political will to join in and help us institute proper democracy in this land of the improbable nation. It would be fair enough to commend President Jawara for having the courage decency, and a very rare common sense to allow the country to move forward and not backward, as is the current state. It will be prudence and wisdom Gambians never ascribed to him. It takes a brave and patriotic solder to take such crucial steps as announced last month. We say hats off and hooray to the Emperor of the Jola Kingdom of the Cassamance.

The future leaders at the helm should now learn the art of tolerance, negotiation, and in addition to patriotism to adhering to principles of democracy. The judiciary and the press must be free of interference and intimidation from the governing and we must debunk from current bullying of opponents no mater how much their manifestos contradict those of the governing regime. The press must respect the rights to privacy and refrain from sensational journalism and personalization to sell unfounded fictional news.

That is all counts poor journalism. The new force should direct its energies into making the country self sustenance in food, shelter, education, health and above all respect of law and order without which there would be no peaceful living together side by side irrespective of tribe, religion, and political affiliation. We should do away with all imported bad cultural behaviors inimical to our African traditions.

Let us only allow the good in the others and not the drug, alcohol and Sapphic behaviors of the so-called civilized. Our culture is magnificent and suits us best than any in the world. It ache my heart to see youngsters from the continent trying to emolliate such filthy live style calling it trendy and fashion of their generation. I just want to ask what is trendy in having metal buttons on the tongue, nose, eyelids and other ugly anatomical places mangled with un-blending ray of colors all over one's already tastelessly tattooed torsures.

A look at some of today's trend reminds one of gazing at some thing like a cross between an iguana and a Chameleon. Where did the natural look go wrong? Hence, fellow Gambians we must try to gingerly retrieve our children to believing in the real rather than frenzy feeding of the coffers of industry in the name of fashion. Jammeh's voluntary departure will do us all a great favor as it will deter blood shed and would allow us move forward in peace and as one Gambia instead of fragmented tribal and tsars' unhealthy vigilantes. God, on our knees do we fervently seek your mercy and protection from the type about to leave office. Never should we be faced with such nightmarish life nor allow hierocracy and greed to overshadow honest service to our country.

Chapter 17

Njawaras' none political

No nonsense Priest

Many a theologian headed Njawara Mosque but none is as qualified as the current one about to give a short Khutba on God. We shall call him Imam Tonya Fola, alias wah kati degga. First let us decipher his uniqueness. He studied languages, i.e. English, French, German, and Arabic in the UK before going to Persia and Egypt to solidify his koranic knowledge.

His PhD dissertation was titled, "What if God were a woman?" Hence being this radical villagers expected new approaches while quite a few skeptics thought this fellow would not last a second at helm of this austere ultraconservative congregation ran for too long by copycats. Wrong and double wrong did it turn out against the skeptics? Why?

Tonya Fola was frank priest that threw out the political garbage that cloaked religion at the cost of too many innocent lives for too long. He started the khutba by saying, "In God's name I will speak to you about the simple God of all and not the politicized, fictionalized and it pleases you individualized God of hypocrites.

No we are going to do away with views of pressure groups and try to know about the omnipotent and merciful but simple God. You must accept that God created all living things and that includes those you deliberately designated, heathens, or unbelievers and even had the daring mine to be certain that if these failed to follow your way they will not see the gates of heaven. Who are you? Did God request your permission when he was creating those fellows or did God relinquished his power to you and take leave of absence?

No one group or individual has the key to heaven. All we have is to carry out the perquisites of our chosen believe, live and let live at the same time plant good foot prints for coming generations emolliate. Today's religious killing field is nonsocial and God shall punish all those who wantonly destroy life created by him. It not matters whether one is Christian or Muslim.

In fact a Muslim is one who believes in Islam, religion of peace, and seeks to live in peace with all and not be murderer of society. Believe it or not both muslims and Christians do want to leave in peace at any given time. We hear people creating divisive wedges by recognizing some as members of the axis of evil or vies visa.

In God's eye none is evil for He created all out of love and mercy. How will my fellow men react as well as explain brutal and sadistic act they subjected their women when they come to find God to be a lovely lady? Hence fellows, be kinder to our love ones. Please do not subject them to veiling their beautiful faces. They do it only for love but there is no iota or verse in Koran supportive of it or any theological or spiritual truth in the in the act."

The women in attendance giggled making the men frown at them. Our venerable priest continued telling the dumfounded congregation that war is beastly and has always been the way savages and wild animal settle scores. A middle age lady hazards a question by asking, "Venerable, what are your thoughts on today's social mores?"

Our learned Imam thought in silence for a minute or two before offering the following, "Thank you for the challenging question which sage Bajoja Ceesay would be the best to ask. However, we all had passed through our youthful days. You know fully well that we too, like any new generation, did experiment and as well as challenged the then systems. Today's social parameter makes pale ours and leaves us amateurish in retrospect. The bugbear of all antisocial behavior emanates from lack of faith and also the media and industry's surreptitious encroachment that destroys our traditions.

The current social situation propositions that the media and backboneless politicians have hand in the brake down of the familiar ancient social norms and family fabric. With that in mind, I would opinion that the new social phenomenon being due to increasing ubiquitous Internet and television bombardments may have warped the minds of the current generation against religion or any disciplined formalities as had been in our days. In today's brave new world everything and anything goes regardless of who may be hurt.

We see it in dresses, social mores amidst lack of morals and political will to draw line on the sand on what is appropriate." Most in a sort of titivating nod agreed with what they heard but are not able to commit change of attitudes and habits for industry had a strong grip on the minds of today's youths. He said, "Today's trendy oriented 18 – 24 year old aficionados who spend most of their time on either television or the Internet loathe traditional taboos and religion.

The spirit or soul is different from this frame that encases our bones. It's the only aspect of us that moves to the next phase of life. This is why archeologists find nothing in their digs but bone and some hair or mummified bodies. This should not by any stretch of the imagination make you not believe in your creator or accept that there is no after life.

Mama God is waiting for your return to her." The audience chuckled and women loved to hear them being elevated to such high steppingstone to the really Mama God. The ladies murmured, "May you live in good health and long happy years!" The sage Imam said, "Have faith my friends but not the hypocritical type that insists upon its way.

Be charitable and tolerant to your fellow men and women and to the differences in this world. This planet earth is the only place we can exist without artificial support gears which by the way fails easily. There are those who still persist on denying the existent of God. They must concede the metaphysical possibility of him existing from the mare fact that they do have an idea of a God in their heads.

If so then God already existed because we imagine his presents, which lend support and proof of his being. Many more tangibles exist in favor of God's exist which cannot be dismissed out-rightly. Please do not allow Science, Industry or the media to hoodwink you into blotting God out of your life. C'est la vie!" Only Imam Tonya Fola could dare refer to Almighty God as "Mama God" without being lynched by the mob. He ended up the sermon saying, "I am preaching and like a drowning man placing his message in a bottle into the sea. Who will it reach?

Well believing is a unique force that no one can take away from us unless through death that ends everything in that life. Hence, we most be tolerant and peaceful towards each other. People understood what he meant and appreciated the simplicity it was delivered to enable them understand the power and gift of the almighty and merciful God.

He was happy that he got through to the audience and hope that they will pass today's sermon at Njawara' Bantaba onto their absent peers and politicians. This marked the end of the unusual khutba. The congregation thanked him and prayed that Mama God keeps him alive and well and to continue enlightening them and their progeny.

A few disgruntled clerics tried to remove cleric Tonya Fola from the post of imam but ran into such resistant that they had to run into exile in Senegal to safe their necks from Matches of lynching angry supporters of the venerable Tonya Fola. This stopped push to dethrone the "Mama God" none political priest.

Chapter 18

Njawara Bantaba's annual

Thanks giving festival Mansa Bengo

No tale about the Banta would do justice in absence of the annual grand festivities and wrestling that takes place at this open hall of the village, called the Bantaba. Here is Njawara's way of marking the grand occasion of the farmers' year.

Societies and communities since the arrival of Adam and Eve to mother Earth have designated a day or special week in which to pay homage or express gratitude to what they took for granted and referred as Supreme Being for being kind and having seen them through the previous year and its challenges.

In the Mandinka tradition, Mansa Bengo takes place annually after the harvest. In this day every villager in his or her best attire, queen, king and dancers gather in one large village for a week or two weeks long celebration and thanks giving. The festivities are marked by dancing, music, magic, acrobatics, wrestling and abundant free food and drinks for every attendant.

Normally, word is sent out early in the year, well before the festivities, for the wrestlers and other contestants to prepare them for the challenge. Great competition exists between villages until the end of the grand festivities.

Each contesting village wants their representative to be crowned that years' champion. The most lucrative rewards go to the wrestler who finally ends up champion over the rest. The contest is divided into three categories thus, welterweight, middleweight and supper sized wrestlers. Show starts on the second day with the welterweights battling it out. The winners of that level go into a semi final two days later.

The middleweight wrestlers sought themselves in manner similar to those of the welterweight group. Winners continue to the final grand wrestling day. The biggest battle is waged with supper sized heavy wrestlers. Theirs go to the wee hours of the night before final winners emerges to contest for the crown or trophy at the end of the festivities.

Almost always a surprise winner to proceed to the next phase emerges. Prices are offered for all categories on the final day. The welterweight champion likewise that of the middle weight are normally given specially embroyed trousers and trophies but not as high quality as that the heavy weight champion get nor are they entitled to the privileges accompanying being victor of the heavy weights.

These not only get trophies, money or animals, supper decorated imbroyed trouser but they are privileged by tradition to have to choose the most beautiful single dame of the gathering to be their future wife. Hence young twenty years old ladies try their best in looking presentable and beautiful so that the champion selects them.

It is pride and hounor if their dreams come true by being chosen by the champion of the day. The physique and strength of the winner is some thing that entices women. They dream to have children for such supper humans and so they pray that a champion from Senegal, Morocco, SeraLeon, Ghana, Mali, and Badibou select them.

 All the neighboring villages send in dancers, acrobats, poets, singers, soloist along with their medicine men, commonly know as voodoo men in your (Europe) neck of woods. Yes, the medicine man served two purposes for his amulet are accepted as strength providers and also it wards off the powers emanating from the opposing camp.

Believe can be delusional but stands unique until proven illogical. None other than following principals, Sefofo Fafanding Kinte and Alkalo Hadi Panneh crowns the champion of the day, which alone is a cherished honor never to be forgotten by the recipient.

The festivities normally come to close on a Friday night. It is commonly referred to as the jubilant night and drumming, dancing and singing goes on through out the night to near midday on following Saturday before everyone finally heads home to repose. Both attendants and wrestler return home contended.

Every event takes in a disciplined manner and most admirable fashion. The contestants go home happy that they were able to participate and enjoy themselves while entertaining and keeping the Mandinka Mansa Bengo tradition alive.

Chapter 19

The crowning of the champion

This ceremony is vital exercise of Mandnka tradition and scribes mark the occasion with historical chants about previous champion's generations past. Hearing this curdles the blood and draws ones' sinew to action. It is moving and full of pride and cultural history of Mandinkas.

Previous champions and old or retired wrestlers open up the show by dancing and showing off their muscles and how they brought their opponent tumbling to the ground like a heavy log.

Many chiefs and mayors/village heads are invited to the ceremony, which lasts two days during which one of the Alkalo of Njawara crowns the recent victor, and give presents to the lady selected as his bride. With dignitaries and guest assembled the chief priest is asked to open the affair with prayers.

This is followed by throngs of colorful dancers with each of several villages performing their unique version to entertain and mark the historic nature of the day. Such festivity goes on until late in the evening before the drums and dancing temporally yield place for the audience to hear the Alkalo's speech along with that from some invited dignitary. Hence, at the end of all prerequisite formalities the Alkalo of Njawara calls the new champion and the former to stand in the center of the square and be recognized as winner and strength of the Badibous.

Njawara Alkalo whose pages carry with them bags of money, gold and lady the day's champion choused to wed joins them. Scribes chant songs that proclaim Mandinka history and tradition eons of the tribe's life. The Alkalo, along with loads of presents from the state and visiting dignitaries, hands over the supper embroided trouser to the victor of the day.

He wears it and is also declared ambassador of congeniality for the state and travels to many nation exposing the values of sports and friendship it builds among nations and tribes. The ceremony turn to the phase were the chief priest and his assistants joining the Njawara Alkalo, champion and bride to bless the two in marriage?

The bride and bridegroom head to unknown quarters for their honeymoon. The festivity continues and now takes an even more festive form commemorating the union of the champion and his bride. His peers from all villages give out money, presents and carvings to put a special seal to the marriage. Hence, dear reader, you can see why men struggle hard to become champion amongst these unique traditional achievers. The Mansa Bengo Champion!

Chapter 20

Bajoja Ceesay's Political Discourse

Today the living encyclopedia of traditional politics will be speaking about politics among tribes and of international intervention politics. Hence large crowds from near and far villages and hamlets poured into Njawara to listen to wise man talk about a very divisive topic and a hot bed of fire which has already caused cracks among families, friends and relatives.

Some asked "What is his solution to this new devil that reared its ugly head since the advent of independence? By noon the village had swelled to three times its normal population. People were meandering about buying fruits, drinks and umbrellas to provide shade while they listen to the sage delivered on this difficult topic.

As soon as he got through throngs of admirers and after offering prayers grandpa Bajoja went straight at the heart of the subject. He said, "Tribe, there nothing wrong belonging to a tribe. It is intact a blessing from God to enable to be identified and to speak the tribal language. It so happen that even in the lowest group of animals a leader always emerges and man is not an exception to this rule. The way we arrive at the leadership or call it representation is politics. It is canvassing to win opinion and votes in canvasser's favor. The flaws in it are many but no human is perfect.

Hence modern elections, unlike ways the ancient chooses leaders, can be rigged, bought, or arm-twisting tactics are at times brought into play. Politics was more open in ancient times when villagers meet at the Bantaba and choose their leaders after having heard open opinions expressed about their aspiring leaders.

In those days leaders had mores and certain traditional principles were at play." He told the gathering that the worst outcome of this modern-day politic is creating division among good people as it whips up irrational emotions instead letting people see through the fallacies of their manifestos.

The moment one starts analyzing and exposing X and Y's platform he or she is deemed an opponent that should not be heeded. Grandpa said, "The truth is kept from would be voters and false promises that cannot be fulfilled in thousand years continue to deafen listeners who are normally carried away by shameless and heartless paid orators.

On top of this deception came another hideous nightmare worst than politicians. It is the AK47 era of butchery, mayhem, and blatant dictatorships over lives it was supposed to serve and protect. AK47 has lead to the self-exile of millions of Africa's intelligential for fear of safety for their lives and those of others. It has set Africa spiraling backward to worst than slave days.

Super powers play checker games on how to retain African mineral resources without having to pay much for it. In so doing they prop up puppets whose string they pull any time there is need for certain mineral, oil or raw material like timber or cotton.

Africa has become the dumping ground of poor quality goods as we are turned into blind consumers of every useless item made by them. The gun industry is at the forefront of all the evil in Africa as it openly sells weapons to rebels, gorilla or so-called freedom fighters as long as it keeps their employees and the company's coffers lined with billions of blood money from child-solders, dictators and corrupt officials. The little development the colonial occupier left is no longer there and few if any new ones are in their places.

This is why we still have millions of shantytowns than modern cities. The current juntas rather stash the money in foreign banks than have a Marshall plan to enable food production and sustenance, good housing, clean and safe drinking water, education, and health of their populace catered for. The slightest seemingly indifferent or being forthright against certain undemocratic moves of the junta in most cases lands one with treason charges and soon executed after a Kangaroo court theatrically adjudicated by high official of the junta

. All camera trial closed to media and international observers are nothing less than Kangaroo court marshals that land the victim to the firing squared. The AK47 tugs fear any one who would wake the populace to their dirty deeds and thievery." Grandpa Bajoja lamented the fact that such undemocratic governments of force and dictators head more than a quarter of the OAU.

Sad as it is AK47 came to force only because of how the tribe and corruption misused the seat of government entrusted by the voters. The national cake has never been shared fairly and this lead to uprisings which impetus caused the AK47 trigger-happy tugs to move in and stay put till dooms day come what may. So what is the solution to Africa's political woes?

First there has to be a universal local language taught in all our institutes to foster understanding and communication among the majority of Africa. As it stands unless a few revert to using a foreign language the African is completely at lost to what language the other is uttering. It is a shame we can learn Latin, English, French, Portages, Spanish, Chinese, Italian or German but not ours. Listen to our Roman Catholic priests regurgitate Latin verbatim but if challenged to speak the local languages they become quite as dead rocks for being ignorant or incapable of saying more than a few phrases at time.

Second, Africa most agree on use of one currency which most be call Africa to avoid the language nightmare. Thirdly, a rapid re-action force to counteract any coup d'etat in Africa should be established and maintained in the earliest possible time in other to stop the current AK47 mayhem from becoming cancerous.

Lastly there should be no place for life long or royal presents on African soil. Hence the constitution should make it mandatory that no head of state run or stands for election more than three terms be it consecutive or not. Once a head of state had ruled for three parliamentary live times that person should opt to serve in an advisor capacity but should not be allowed to run the affairs of state till death.

This way there will be stability at the helm and it may give chance to other tribes to handle the steering wheel of their ship and help direct it to safe harbor. In conjunction to the above Africa most insist on self-sustenance, develop skill force in computer, IT, business, higher learning and research, industrial technology and above all agriculture for a full Tommy spells a healthy none dependent nation and also gives chance for our innovative minds to go to work." At this time one could hear a pin drop on the sand because of silence and eagerness to learn from the sage.

However, a member of the United Party (UP) who most likely wanted his party's present noted by the gathering asked the sage, "Sir, all what you said were correct and laudable but how do you propose to implement such a mammoth task? Rest assured that the UP would advocate for what we heard from this unique meeting of hearts."

Grandpa told the man that this was not a UP forum nor was he in any way bedfellow of any party in cohorts with any party and he would not allow these lecture be politicked. "The answer to your question is for Africa to turn inward and accept its endowment of diversity and at the same time to be creative and communication is the key to opening up the Pandora's box of progress for the continent.

Further more all Africans should be accepted as citizens of Africa and all border controls and immigration, tax tariffs should be thing of the past for the African coming from any city or state.

It was getting dark and the meeting ended with prayers and chants of "long lives the sage. May we always have honest people like you amongst us". Some promise to make amends with their friends and family over riff they had about politics.

Chapter 21

Njawara residents discuss Climate change

The dialog bellow is direct reproduction of discussion on climate change as perceived by villagers. These were farmers affected and hence very concerned by the desertification and unusual frequency of floods they have been observing recently. As readers will note it has no scientific data backing it but the discussion carried a human aspect and why the current floods and how those responsible could solve or prevent the pending catastrophe and devastating event about to engulf our planet.

Now let us follow the villagers pouring their hearts out as to what caused the current state of change, why the unusually freaky floods and sporadic rains. Those who lived in the Caribbean Sea now expect hurricanes on a weekly instead of quarterly occurrence in a year as was known by most residents in these island-nations. Some European countries now experience shorter winters followed by long spells of very wet, at times dry, hot summer weather.

Samba Njie said, "I heard in Europe, China and America people are talking about the new phenomenon of climate warming of the earth due to some gas that is emitted into the atmosphere by cars, manufacturing and even cow dung.

They say some of the cause is due to deforestation because there are fewer trees to absorb the gas they are emitting." Saini Kassama told them; "Oh, I heard about it too. The solution in part, they said, is for us in the poor countries to stop buying cars made by none other than the developed countries and to stop producing children for this increases the world population rapidly.

They keep building polluting cars and produce children but we must tighten our belts and do none of the above for it exacerbates climate change. What a farcical!"

Musu Kinte said, "Fellows, some of my observation along with what my grand father told me seem to support the outside opinion but we are not to be blamed for the changes in climate. True we cut the forest trees for fuel and cash money and that might have an impact on the level of the gas they are talking about. Our people must eat and only coal from the wood serve as fuel for us.

There are no artificial energy sources such as electricity for us as they have in their countries. We depend on what nature provides and the wood from the forest becomes the easiest source. Our people fail to harness the rivers to produce the cheapest and clean energy source of electricity for the citizenry." Boy Jatta said, "True, true indeed.

The amounts and frequency of floods is unusual but my grandfather remembered similar cyclical happenings when he was 16 and the last was in his 60s. The current huller-hoses are all a commercial gimmickry for people to buy their new machines and inventions than the climate being avasive.

My grandpa who has been a farmer all his life said climate warming and wet spells had been the way of nature since ancient times and no fear mongering changes Mother Nature."Samba Bah added, "No, you are not all right my friends. My animals now have to travel miles on end before getting to munch on a green shoot. The situation has nothing to do with ancient or ancestral oracle's predictions or God getting angry, as in the days of Noah, to swell the rivers of earth to cleanse our sinful life styles.

It is far from that but it is something man had irresponsibly done in pursuit of his greed to amass wealth. He even now stands as polluter of the surface of the moon." Musu Seyabao said, "How can you be so naïve? Which one of you remember just a few years ago when some scientists and commercial enterprises were telling us that all electronic devices, especially computers would stop at 12 midnight on the dot December 31, 2000? Did KY2 happen?

Off course not but millions threw their worthy machines for more useless plastic gadgets of today making industry richer than ever but not worth money value spent on such devices. My son is still using his Olivet machine with no problems at all. I agree we must reduce our tree cutting and plant more trees for the next generations to have fuel for their pots. Industry is heartless and full of gimmickry.

I just wished that most of mankind would care about the Environment and Mother Nature". Saini Njie told them, "Climate change as chanted else was simply connotes material change than having to do with natural cycles of the weather.

If these people were serious and concerned enough about climate change they would by now have stopped making oil products, plastics, building gas gosling cars, do away with all those bright neon signs of advertisement and stop planning on profits instead of allowing lower market price so that we can live and let live. It is the dream of every merchant in those countries to be amongst the worlds richest and not the kindest company."

Boy Jatta said, "My God, you are right. I threw my computer away in the river on December 31, 1999 believing what was rumoured about to happen to electronic gadgets come the year 2000.

I then sincerely believed those scientists and industry that told such spotless lies to the world even though they knew the contrary was the case. A day latter I visited my friend Kebba Sonko who I found cheerfully using his old computer. Mine was even more recent than his but it now seats at the bottom of the deepest part of the river worthless even when salvaged. I lamented my instinct of having thrown a good machine on wrong commercially oriented information.

This is why lots of people in Africa and the developing world perceive this huller-hoe about climate change as another game to get their new machine bought without fail. The rest of the world must first be serious and curtail all polluting substances they produce and dump upon us poor innocent consumers.

The developed or industrial world must put its money where it mouth is and not kill us with rhetoric and dangers they do not agree would eventually happen. The G7 and G20 always give lip service to curving climate change but are more interested in having their manufacturing industrial power machines churning out pollutants while maintaining employment of their work force to the detriment of the developing people who have long ways to catch up with these giants of industrial envision.

They are producing cars by the hundreds of thousand a week and yet expect us to ride horse drawn carts of the 12th century. They disregard the environment and ecosystem than any on earth yet make more noise about climate change as if the rest of us are stupid not to notice their polluting habits and industrial greed.

We plead with them to stop polluting Mother Earth, to use what they genuinely need for existence than throwing away tones and tones of Consumable food because a franchise or supermarket label in its commercial interest says best before or not later than date so and so." Sani said, "You are right they should stop putting their heads in the sand and be true to finding solutions on how to curb their dirty contribution to the dethronement of our planet.

They should desist from keeping their industries churning and employment going while condemning similar efforts by others. Our produce is always condemned and classified by them as unfit for consumption or for purpose.

Yes, we are guilty, as charged, of deforestation in Africa but on the other hand their timber industry and need has an upper hand in this as it motivates farmers in dare need of cash to cut trees to sell to timber companies. Hence the pot should desist from calling the kettle black for they are both the same tarnished black colour.

Deforestation would have not happened as fast as it did in Africa had the rivers been harnessed to produce much needed hydroelectricity and as well irrigation source for the farmers. Sadly enough people cut trees to convert it to coal, furniture, and building materials.

The supper powers curtail our level of productivity by allowing AK47 ruling the developing world". Jungfolo Fatajo: said, "Hi fellows. I have been listening to you most of the time and some of the things you said about the reason for the frequency of floods and indeed this very dry dusty farm of yours had sense.

Some of the things covered in your discussion were right about cyclical changes as was in ancient times. Let me add and agree with you that greed has a big hand in the soup of climate change. No one in the industrial world cares as long as their toxic produce and greed was annually netting them humongous profits.

Coal can be cleaned into environment friendly fuel for the production of energy but this will not be done because industry sees it as unprofitable and cares less and only pretends about health of its consumers. Efficient electric and solar powered cars would dramatically reduce carbon emission but the hydrocarbon industry deems this too adventurous and costly and at the moment only playing lip service.

Such cars are on our streets worldwide. They still want to rely on cheap labour from developing countries and sell the product at huge profit margins because of sky rocking pricing system they agreed upon. Finally, you are right villagers should embark on replanting forest they destroy to allow the next generation to have wood and for their animals to grace in the field.

Without the forest there would be no rain and that means no grass for the animals to feed on. Hence nature is an interlinked entity breaking any link leads to unbelievable catastrophe". Hassan Bahol (a teacher) added his ideas thus "Friends your debate drew me to you and hopes you will not mind few comments from me. One area your discussion failed to cover was the part plaid by our governments.

How many here know or learnt about solutions offered by our own government beyond the rhetoric's of belt tightening and party tree planting exercise? The climate is too serious a thing to be politicised and our politicians like their effigies else were care less about you and your animals. All they seek is the votes they get from you every five years should they fail to rig the election for they do not believe in the justness of the ballot box.

The rest of the world send money to our governments only to later discover these being used for building of private luxury villas, purchasing special or tailor made prestigious cars and with the rest stashed in international banks.

Mean while the peasantry is left to go hungry and dare not to speak about it to the media in or out of the country. Those who speak risk their life under the AK47 heartless and ruthless guillotine. Agriculture the main source of food is dying because of lack of forth rightness from politicians and their henchmen.

Africans should not starve but we do. Africans should not cry for energy but we woefully lack it and Africans should be amongst the most educated because of gift we are endowed and yet we even lack an alphabet.

Africans are proud to be multilingual but lack or still refuse to select a single language the continent can use for channel of communication or can boast of having so that it inhabitants can communicate instantly other than the use of past colonial languages which are less poetical than ours. Friends we have long catching up to do. The world moves by rocket leaps while Africa drags its feet in a spiralling backward move.

Had the so-called supper powers not looked the other side to allow AK47 destroy us at the same time allow our minerals and raw materials filter to them at throw away prices life would have not been as miserable for the our farmers as its today.

Imagine villagers yearning for what they doped the golden days of colonial rule. This is a shameful indictment on our political systems, which only want to amass wealth by any unscrupulous means but cares less about the indigenous it govern.

Thank God to the African's resilience, which enable us, get over slavery and Apartheid. I am certain we will, with head and shoulders help high, cross this seeming unconquerable mountain of a challenge for our survival. God bless Africa and humanity!"

Chapter 22

Haruna Njie the Master fisherman

Some skills are life savers i.e. medicine but Haruna's was a unique one that seafarers would not like to be without. Hence most of those gathered to hear him talk about the sea and fishing or sheer leisure trip up the meandering rivers and creeks of the region. He was one simple in language but can, like a professor deliver volumes in short forum.

Remember in his days there were no tape recorders and 99.95% attendees were illiterates with spongy brains that literally absorb stacks of information delivered in such Bantaba gatherings. In that era people were happy to share whatever little they know as long as the community would benefit from such information. So the likes of Haruna Njie were welcome addition to village sustenance and safe practice while at sea.

All meetings start with a prayer before the speaker takes the microphone less public podium. All the Chubalos, these are Africa's best divers, and armature fishermen present were more than happy to hear this sage of the sea. He started with a joke and a myth about his tribe's way of initiating male children to the sea.

He said, "Can any of you fathers imagine having to throw your seven year old son into deep waters knowing that he is heavier than a tone of rocks nor could he swim for false believe that if the child floats it makes him a Sere and a good seafarer? This is murder and not true behavior of my venerable tribe.

Thank God my parents were not that crazy for I would have not been here to talk to you about the sea. Today we will continue on boat construction, times to be at sea and time permitting how to rescue those drowning or about to drown at sea. In our last meeting at the outcasts of the village we cut down a two hundred and fifty footer cotton tree with girth of 45 feet circumference.

When the canoe is completed it will measure a 100 feet long by 3 feet wide and it will be the longest locho in the region. It will be capable of carrying up to quarter of tone weight from Banjul to Njawara village. We will now walk to our local canoe builders and find out progress made in getting us a boat within few weeks."

The eager crowd followed as he led the way to the boat builders. They had done a superb job and even faster than he envisaged. He said, "Here we are the locho is taking shape. What you need to know is that not every tree qualifies for canoe building, as most plants will rot after several weeks in the water.

Second one must leave a margin of at least three feet at both ends during the construction and excavation phase to adjust the length or hollow. The sides must never be less than four inches thick to allow a solid wall against stormy weather and rough sea waves.

This work will go on another two weeks before our boat emerges. A big naming ceremony would be arranged when building and every thing is complete. The ritual comprises of the boat being blessed by a priest who chant verses as he utters the name for the first time. The name is usually kept a secret, even the builders of it would not know, until the hour of lunching the canoe to sea.

Then an elderly retired fisherman is asked to embark the canoe while it is been push into the river by very strong hands and ropes to steady it on the way. The elderly man connotes long life for the new entrant into the water and he too offers prayers when the boat touches water. He paddled his way round the creek and back amid drumming and dancing.

The new name of the cane is Bahol meaning "good heart." African life is full of rituals and none is more serious adhered to than the lunching of a new boat. One canoe builder asked why some trees like Baobab never serve as good boats?

The sea master replied, "The Baboon has a soft trunk and water porous than the cotton tree after endless tragic disasters at sea from Baobab tree boat it was decreed that any found selling or using such boats should be thrown in jail for recklessness about lives of innocent passengers."

He said, "Let me digress a bit and tell you what to look for in the weather. First try to gage the strength of the wind. This could be done by just watching the height of the waves and looking above to check the clouds. The darker they are the likelihood of lightening, thunder and stormy weather.

This made it unsafe to venture far from the coast as many a canoe capsized in such tempestuous rises. Fishermen will tell you that certain fish like the Kujali come out in abundance during such turbulent times but be sure of your chances of escape in the even the canoe looses balance and capsized.

You must always tell friends and other nearby fishermen which creek you are heading and for how long. Return home when the weather is friendly even if you had only half your normal catch that day. By and large the life you save would be yours. Your rescue is certain when it happens near the Mangroves than far away in the middle of a stormy river.

The only thing one has to be on the lookout in the Mangroves was man-eating crocodiles. You must get as quickly as possible to the highest ground or climb the nearest tall tree and look for women coming to rice fields. Yell to the top of your voice because your next problem would be Hyenas trying to get animals that came to drink at the riverside.

The safety of your Locho now lies in the way you man it. The sails most be properly fitted and maintained regularly to avoid leaking when you need wind to speed the canoe. Let greed not tempt you to over load the beast. The best load level is when the canoe and load is eight inches above water level. Use smoke signal with intermittent blowing of the horn to alert others about your being in stressful situation and whatever the circumstances do not panic.

This leads to misjudging your life saving moves. Avoid Hippos by all means for they can capsize your canoe at lightening speeds. Hippos are not known to be man-eaters but males can drown one. If you happen to catch a huge Shark do not attempt to bring it to the surface for you and your canoe may just be sank by its sheer weight and force in water. I believe you have had lot of information for today.

I will speak about the types of fishing nets and rods or hooks one need at different fishing expeditions during our next meeting after the christening ceremony of our new Locho/canoe." The Sea-master then asked if any had question on what was said. Everyone was more than pleased and not only eager to attend the next meeting but also looked forward to christening of the new canoe in a month's time.

Dr. Alhasan Sisawo Ceesay, MD

Mr. Sisawo Bajoja Ceesay, Father

Mrs. Famatanding Tarawaleh,
Mother holding baby Penda Dibba

Mrs. Binta Ceesay, Elder Sister

Dudou Ceesay, brother (in green) with family

Dr. Alhasan and wife Fatou Koma-Ceesay

Famatanding Ceesay, Daughter

Binta Ceesay, Daughter

Miss Roheyata Ceesay, Daughter

Dr. Alhasan S. Ceesay graduating from the American University of the Caribbean, Plymouth, Monserrat, West Indies

Dr. Alhasan Ceesay and friend Bishop MsGehee, Detroit, Michigan, 1982

Chapter 23

Mass Kangie at the Steering wheel

Mass was phenomenal engineering gift to Njawara. This man never attended any college of engineering nor can he even read and right his own name much more to unravel intricate designs of car motors. Mass Kangie was the only driver that can turn a dead world 1 vehicle into a functioning machine in three weeks by using local black smith and designs he foresee to work.

No wonder he had an endless list of apprentice during his heydays as Njawara' supper driver. He was the only one able to tackle the road from Badibou Kerewan to Nuimi Barra during the rains. All other vehicles fail for lack of expertness this master local motorist had.

He literally repairs any bran or make brought to his garage at Njawara. He had rivals in drivers like Samba Cham, Ndula Jallow, Tamsir Njie and Omar Kangie but none was as good at the steering wheel or the road like the Njawara doyen of drivers. Passengers to Banjul would rather wait for Mass' vehicle than board others because it would be time saving when Mass takes them. The others either are stuck in deep mud or suffer serious engine damage that leaves them with no idea of how to salvage the day.

People lost money and business in boarding other highway vehicles than Mass Kangie's. Mass Kangie's 1950 Bedford lorry's roof was normally parked with yams, millet, Guinea fowl, a few bags of rice, and bales of batik heading to Albert Market in Banjul. Inside, the lorry's long rectangular box was divided into two with humans closer to the driver's side and the rest being used for beasts heading for slaughter at the Abuko Abettor. Latecomers perch on the floor because the eats would have all been over utilized.

The lorry traveled at 45 miles per hour and stops at every village along the Kerewan- Barra highway, to either offload or take new supplies of human and animal cargos. The entire 95 kilometers distance takes Mass three and half hours to disembark his cargo at Barra Ferry Terminal for passengers heading to Banjul, the Gambia's capital city. Of his long life of 75 years Mass remained at the steering wheel from 14 years old until he was no longer able at age 70. His children never took to driving and most of them are nowadays in petty business in the Kombo area.

Chapter 24

Sefo Famara Singateh's

Wednesday meetings Njawara Bantaba

One Lower Badibou District chief that made his tenure felt in Njawara was Sefo Famara Singateh from Saba village. Njawara being the hub of trade between Gambia and Senegal was good place to exercise regional politics and to gather information from.

There were also major Lebanese, Syrian and French business operating at Njawara from which he collects tax for the government in Banjul or the divisional commissioner above him.Like his predecessor Sefo Njanko Kinte, Sefo Famara Singate never missed coming to Njawara to attend the regular Wednesday village meetings.

He rides to the meeting on a huge almost five high, definitely seven feet long red Arabian horse flanged by three of his select guards. Children line up his rout just to glimpse the beast even though it scares the dickens out of most of them. However curiosity kills the cat. The saddle was one most decorated and it left an impressive regal impact on the children and admirers. Sefo Famara Singateh wore his traditional dress and carries the golden staff of authority with a small crown at the top issued by the colonial governor.

He lays it besides him and asks that prayers be offered before the meeting commences. He was very gentile person who never used his authority unnecessarily. He normally allows villagers to speak out on any topic they feel need to be address by him or the village head. For some reason he was my father's best friend from boyhood days till the two departed to their maker.

It was Sefo Famara Singateh who calmed my father when I insisted upon acquiring the right to enroll at Kinte Kunda School to earn Western education. At the meetings and upon lifting his staff all present would listen and old sage would either acknowledge what had been debated upon or add his own suggestions.

He always sad, "If I may be allowed, I think so and so would be additional solution to the problem or would improve the situation." Everyone knew him to be too diplomatic and polite hence he had few opponents during his reign as chief of Lower Badibou District. His elder son, Kitabou Singateh succeeded him and like father like son the people loved him.

Ketabou Singateh was my classmate during our Primary school days at Kinte Kunda. I left and went to Kinte Kunda and he headed for France until his appointment as chief of the Lower Badibou in place of his father Famara Singateh.

Sefo Ketabou Singateh was instrumental in helping me set up NGO Manding Medical Centre at Njawara village. He did continue his father's weekly meetings at Njawara even though political divisions and incursions now had great dived between residents which led to most of the shops closing and moving to the new settlement of Farafene 16 miles north of Njawara.

There is no longer revenue to collect from Njawara as the village tragically dwindled from a populace of not less than 5000 residents in 1963 to fewer than 2000 in 1997, most of who are elderly and could not relocate. Ninety percent of the youth moved to the capital area in pursuit of greener pastures and better education facilities for their progeny. Sefo Ketabou like the father had a short reign and we miss them both and pray they rest in peace in Heaven.

The current young chief, Sefo Fafanding Kinte from Kinte Kunda is doing his utmost best to revive Njawara's traditional Wednesday meetings. He is a regular visitor to the village even though not in the grand Sefo Famara's pump and grandiose style. Sefo Fafanding Kinte was a former teacher brought to the chieftaincy by the current regime. He is loved and respected by the region and he contuses Sefo Ketabou's footsteps with regards of Manding Medical Centre at Njawara.

He is a young man I owe a lot for being able to rally the troupes to the cause of the region. Together we were in 2005 able to twin Alpena City in America with two Gambian villages, Njawara and Kinte Kunda villages respectively. We are still standing on one leg for a possible fun-raising trip to Alpena with the Badibou Cultural Dance Troupe we formed years back.

This will come to affect once the visa and air ticket cost is met. The recession in Michigan dampened the first initial attempt but I am doing all that is possible to rejuvenate venues into receiving us when the State's economy peaks up. Kemo Kinte, coordinator of Alpena-Njawara-Kinte-Kunda relation also works relentless and diligently with us and he never lost hope that one day there will be light at the end of the tunnel for Manding Medical Centre at Njawara.

One business head Njawara has was Baba Salla Ceesay, alias Abdoulie Salla Ceesay but commonly known as Baba Salla the business acumen. Abdoulie Salla Ceesay is Njawara's business wizard. He is younger brother of my father and one very popular at Njawara.

He worked as a shopkeeper for the Bijawdies from his adolescent days to his early sixties when the Syrians and Lebanese business closed shop at Njawara for fear of political repercussion as happened in other African independent countries.

This fear never held water in Njawara because of the gentility of the average Gambian of the smiling coast of Africa. However the abrupt departure of a majority of the businesses in the village sank the village to the low depth it is currently at.

Baba Salla forth hard to help revive the village but political tug of war and unfounded rumor monger created more divisiveness in the village to deprive it rising from the mud up to day. Baba and Fasana Sonko did their best to reunify the village to the good old golden days when Njawara was business and business buzzed 24/7 at the village.

Unfortunately none of Baba's children took up business but Fasana's Son Elh. Maja Sonko has bent the historical arch of business to his advantage. Maja Sonko is today one of Badibou's business tycoons and has in many ways constantly contributed cash and kind to wards the goals to rejuvenated Njawara to its admirable days of the 1960s.

We lament the premature departures and lost both Baba Salla Ceesay and Fasana Sonko. May they rest in peace for good job rendered the Njawara.

Chapter 25

Famatanding Tarawaleh on

What nurtures marriage

Famatanding Tarawaleh is a quite amorous person who is imbued in tradition. It is her turn today to speak to the girls and women about how to keep their marriages alive and well above the competition of step-wives and concubines. She bags sixty years of married life before her beloved husband passed away a few years back.

The Bantaba was jammed with ladies from all corners of the region who traveled to Njawara to hear the sage matriarch speak about how to maintain marriage, one of the most pleasant and at times difficult if not the most challenging human institutions. After the prayer formalities she said, "I hope to have seen more men than my peers in this gathering."

It drew loud laughter and applause from the crowd while a few men shouted, "carry on my lady." The matriarch Famatanding spent a few moments lost in thought, then started by telling the crowd, "Marriage has been enacted by civilized society because it serves to maintain love, family and the protection of children.

Marriage is nourished by love, perseverance and team work, never to expect an angel or perfect being in your man, pay less heed to outside rumor mongered, be trustworthy and work hard to being a team member in the relationship. These will be our topic tonight." She told the audience that all before had some love or later developed it for their male partners.

She said, "Love is the key to marriage. Love of the self will enable one love as well tolerate others especially our life partners. It does need constant rejuvenating or it will fade away. It demands one to give in at times for the shake of peace and the children. It is a tangible link between two foreign hearts that becomes one in two people.

Do it for loves shake the elders advice us." Hence without love there is no marriage. The most difficult part in this gig saw is that of maintaining perseverance in the relation. One must have the determination to keep the marriage alive and well under thick and thin moments. It requires diligence and doggedness if not tenacity beyond emotions. We persevere because of love and the children that come out of it. It is our duty to stand by these children until they too become able mature adults of society.

The greatest fallacy in marriage is to expect one's partner to be right most of the time. He would be first to admit that he is no angel and it would be great if he were told when he is off the tract in the relationship. Most husbands are amenable to polite correction, especially when done in the privacy of the home.

Marriage is a two-way traffic and you must be ready to accept your short comings in a relationship." She paused to allow the audience to digest the above. In the interim a young lady asked, "Mama, what should I do with my stubborn husband who thinks or believes he know it all and is always right?" Famatanding cleared her throat before responding and said, "Daughter, first you should not be addressing your husband in this sort of language in public. I would ask that you publicly apologize to him now if he is here."

Men in the audience cheered loudly in support of cautionary advice given by the sage but most of the women frowned at her. However, frisky Jambanding Kanjara stood up and said, "Never in my life would I ever apologize to an obstinate ingrate male. Mama you are just echoing your time when men where uncrowned kings. You are not speaking for our present day liberate woman.

The matriarch laughed and looked at the girl straight with eyes as red as a fireball and told her, "It is great to be at your tender and inexperienced age. I was there and was more stubborn than you are but time does tame the shrewd and make one mellow. In answer to the previous lady's question, one must not base solutions on negative premises. Perhaps your husband seemed obstinate to you but may be reacting to you in manner you just displayed right before us.

Your question brings us to the next topic of discussion. Perhaps you have your ears leaning more to the outside than paying heed to what goes on in you own back yard. Let me make it abundantly clear that there are no sexual apartheid going on or a secrete society against women even if you happen to accept that a woman's place is in the home.

This is outright false for women do what they do because of love and family. Listening to rumors can cause a serious rift in marriage. The rumormonger's aim is to place a wedge in your marriage life so that she can gain access to it. You never know what you have until when you loss it for good. Rumor breaks marriage at the wrong time as it affects the future of children of that relationship. She told the now absolutely silent crowd that love or marriage without trust is a joke and ends in a roller scatting cavalcade of woes.

One must be trustworthy at all times to breath hope and continuity in relationships such as marriage. Deceit and lies only add up to more trouble at the end of the day and will definitely end the marriage. The greatest fool is one who believes to be wiser than all others. The most painful thing in a relationship is for one to find a partner being a deceitful cheat.

Dishonesty engenders trouble and heartaches. Swindlers will never see daylight in their marriages. Love deserves honesty than deception." The matriarch told the gathering that love is neither an idea nor a dogma, neither an art nor a science but something much more intricate that holds us blindly glued together and its force is stronger than the heart can bear to do away with. She said, "Love makes us admire and venerate our men.

It is a phenomenal that blindly enthralls us to attraction. Its spellbound holds us to our partners. Hence we must work as team member with our partners to nurture to allow marriage to it blooming heights. A divided house falls just like a disunited army.

We are each other's keeper in a marriage and community. Again to everyone's surprise Jambanding Kanjara stood up and asked, "Would it be correct to expect my husband to do the laundry, and to baby sit the kids while I try for some fun in my coup up life?"

It was getting late and darkness was creeping on but the sage had to answer this burning question of the present generation. Hence, the matriarch summarized the answer thus, "My child a household divided due to irrelevant requests, and assignment or perceptions only end up falling apart.

Today's men do not refuse helping when they can but if you throw the dishes or pots in other to attend an unnecessary activity in the name of liberation. You might just be liberating yourself from a good marriage and would regret having done so. My late husband washed the dishes and calabashes and at times did the laundry without my asking.

The chores are not gender marked but due to the nature of subsistence or breadwinning men are most of the time out in the field or office trying to get food, shelter and security for a rainy day." Jambanding mused and said, "Thank you mama for enlightening us. We are forever indebted to you and may God keep you in good health and live long enough for you to see our grand children." The crowd liked it and applauded her for coming to her senses and for speaking so eloquently for them.

All is well that ends well. The sage nodded in approval and appreciation and asked that the audience meet in a forth night at which time she would continue on this very important life and linkage in marriage.

Chapter 26

A snippet of Njawara Residents

Let us take a moment to browse though snippet about other golden hearts and movers at Njawara were the following residents of the village. **Dudou Ceesay,** Njawara's Oustas The locals call him Oustas meaning Teacher. Without use of this designated ID very few could tell whom one was asking for.

His simplicity made him almost a recluse and yet this all rounded Quranic mentor is well like and loved by the village. He has indeed been member of most of the committees and as my elder brother had stood by my cause, Manding Medical Centre from day one of my having revealed my intention of providing medical aid to villagers in rural Gambia.

Dudou Ceesay is his real name and he today serve as the oldest male of the Njawara Ceesay Kunda clan. He is the one the rest of the siblings of Sisawo and Baba Ceesay recognize as leader of the family. We take his wise decision and counsel as sacrosanct and with it direct the Ceesay Kunda clan at Njawara. Oustas Dudou Ceesay spent twenty-one years at Ker Cherno Mama learning the Quran and Islam. He taught religion at Njawara Primary School until his retirement in 1995.

Unlike grandpa Bajoja he is a bit shy of being an orator. He and his wives and children are still domicile at Njawara and he act as our custodian of the Njawara Ceesay Kunda dynasty. Although and frail, he enjoys our full support and relish his guidance. His daughter Fatou Ceesay has now become the second medical doctor in the Ceesay Kunda clan at Njawara, Lower Badibou. Bakary Kanteh of the shop at the T-Junction near my home was my friend and another able businessman was gentleman Bakary Kanteh. He like my great, grandparents originated from Mali.

On migrating to the Gambia he decided that Njawara was his Garden of Eden on earth. He married Njungi Kante from Njaba Kunda village in Central Badibou and adopted Njudou Ture in addition to his son Samba Rakal Kanteh. Bakary Kanteh coined revered friendship with the Ceesay Kunda clan at Njawara and as such mum and Mrs. Kanteh became twins as they shared family concerns and attended children of both families.

In short, they were like blood sisters that had trusting relationship upon which collaborative partnership emanated. Father usually sends one of us to get Kerosene, Matches, candles or sugar and sundries from this shop at the T- Junction.

In those days streets were not named and everyone in the village called or identified Bakary's shop as the 24/7 general merchandise shop at the T- Junction. It was a stone throw from where we leaved and it stayed open from 7 am till 11 pm daily.

Name it you will chance to find it stashed up in one of Bakary's shelves. He was very friendly sales person that keep costumers coming over and over because of anecdotes and stories he tell to both young and old. He was a much liked storyteller by all counts.

He never turned a millionaire but compared to his peers and the times he was considered a wealthy man. Bakary lived up to the age of eighty-four years before returning to his maker. The shop lost its fame because both Njundou and Samba Rakal never had zeal or knack the old trader Bakary was endowed.

Njawara misses the old 24/7 shop at the T-junction not far away from Njawara's famouse Banti Yasin where young men congregate daily to watch beautiful ladies pass by. At one time the shop grew so famous that it became the talk of town even though it is tucked miles away from the center of Njawara village where trade and battering ran wildly.

Yes, the "who is who of ladies" of the village rather buy from his shop at the fringes than those of high priced Syrian and Lebanese shops lining the center of Njawara village. Like Baba Salla Ceesay, Bakary Kanteh was a gifted salesman whose pitching woos and in the end cultivates an everlasting friendship.

Children loved to congregate at his shop to hear him tell stories that keeps them spell bounded and yearning for more the next time. The children of his day missed him dearly for his premature depart was a loss Njawara would never recoup. Mangoneh Njie exemplifies a typical village carpenter. The always-smiling ever-ready carpenter of Njawara was none other than Mr. Mangoneh Njie. Name it he can tackle it or would try other means.

He was the village's roofer, furniture manufacturer, and above all very accessible to all at any time required. He was so eager to leave his mark that he lured many to the trade and volunteered training young men and women to the art of carpentering. He had large followers coming from far and wide at times as far as the lower Senegal.

Mangoneh builds boats from huge chunks of trees, nails corrugated roof with lightening speed and before you know it he is at the black smith requesting a new type of saw that he believes would work better than the made in Honkon blades.

I met him several times running dad's errands. He would say, "Son is your father up to sending without a loaf of bread for the village carpenter?" I would smile and in protest or protecting my dad would reply, "Uncle you know he has ten loafs on the way. He just wanted you to help in fixing so and so roof at home of x and y in Torro Bahen village. He promised to pay you as soon as he sends the ten loafs of bread this evening."

Mangoneh Njie, besides being the region's best carpenter a freak for bread and children teased him to his last days about hot bread fresh from the local wood oven. The all-adept Mangoneh, gifted carpenter of the region let us after an attack of malarial bout.

There were no hospitals and the dispensaries were poorly supplied with drugs and to make matters worst the dispenser catered for entire districts with very bad impassable roads. There were no ambulances and patients relied only on the able hands of local herbalist at hand. Njawara missed its golden trade's man, Mr. Mangoneh Njie.

Among those uplifting Njawara's spirit of giving was her great hunter Ismaila Sey was the only son of gGandma Jainaba Sey. He was a tall lanky fellow with broad shoulders. I met him when I was five and he inspired me. He was the first to show me how to use a bow and arrow.

One of his instructions at the time was that one never shot at pregnant deer or antelopes. He simply said, "It was unkind and unnecessary to deprive their babies the chance to be born." He definitely, despite being a hunter, would have been regarded as an animal conservator. He drew fame for bringing home nearly a dozen deer and some time two full-grown male antelopes.

Villagers, in their drones, lined at his yard daily to buy fresh deer or antelope meat. Leftovers of which were given to the poor children and orphans to take home for them to eat. It was this generosity that brought endearing notoriety to Njawara's hunter.

The village and all hamlets went into morning when this great man died from a bout of pneumonia. Village still speaks well about his uniqueness kindness to orphans of the district. He stand remember for the good he stood for to the community. A village's story exclusive of musician is solemn solitude. Hence I present Njawara Musicians What soul would thrive without music?

A person without music is definitely heartless by African standards. The village throbs to life and tradition and also history that follows the rhythmic drum beats from our able musicians. Njawara had two types of entertainers who are the Wolof drummers and occasionally the Fulani acrobatic performers.

Once long time ago before the advent of independence and at grand weddings Syrian or Lebanese, Njawara had the luxury of being entertained by an orchestra from Lebanon that came to grace wedding of their comrade. This was the only foreign musical group that came to the village until the arrival of the Scandinavians, who now run a college of music in the village. Until then Njawara was entertained by its local griotes and traditional festivals passed on eons ago by our ancestors.

So we had the Seckas on the Fulani harp and Modo Ceesay as master manager of the Wolof drummers. By the way because of the insignificant number of Mandinkas in a Wolof village, Njawara was graced with occasional Seruba drumming from visiting Mandinka musicians. The list bellow is that of the new generation musicians, the Badibou Cultural Dancers, which have joined Manding Medical Center at Njawara village in its fund raising drive to build the children and maternity unit of the medical center.

NAME	PERFORMANCE
Attikan Jorbate	Kora Player
Abdoulie Bah	Fula lead vocalist
Ousman Marr	Lead Wolof drummer
Ebou Secka	Drummer/dancer

Dembo Camara	Mandinka drummer
Alhajie Dampha	Mandinka drummer
Fabakary Manjang	Mandinka Drumer
Samba Kolley	Fula harp player
Alhajie Jallow	Fula Calabash player
Mariama Bah	Fula vocalist/dancer
Momadou Bah	Fula Tama player
Kemo Kinte	Siko drummer
Dagan Joof	Lead Wolof vocalist
Sukai Njie	Wolof vocalist/dancer
Sali Jobe	Wolof vocalist/dancer
Mariama Sanneh	Wolof vocalist/dancer
Jainaba Barrow	Mandinka vocalist/dancer
Sainabou	Mandinka vocalist/dancer
Jambanding Kallow	Mandinka vocalist/dancer

OFFICIALS

Dr. Alhasan S. Ceesay	Head/Manager of group
Sefo Fafanding kinte Badibou	Head Chief, Lower

Kemo Kinte   Coordinator/
                      Alpena-Njawara

Dr. Avery Aten, a physician in Alpena, Michigan, gave your names for me to contact on behalf of the NGO and the Badibou Cultural dance Troupe about to tour American cities in fundraising drive for building of the children and maternity wing of centre's hospital. The Badibou Cultural Dance Troupe will be performing in Alpena coming August 2007 to mark the first anniversary of a sister-city status we have with Alpena.

The dance troupe is an authentic cultural troupe that entertains whilst maintaining history and cultural values and arts of the people in Badibou, the Gambia West Africa. They entertained presidents and would be eager to intrigue you by bringing joyful and memorable evenings to your audience in August 2007 autumn activities.

The dance Troupe is helping the NGO raise much-needed funds to build the children and maternity wings of our hospital at Njawara village in the Lower Badibous, Gambia. Hence, it is one of many reasons why we are appealing for your organization's participation in any form available to you.

We are also enquiring as to whether your organization or university would kindly sponsor us and include us in your 2007 autumn activities. Rest assured that the unique performance of the dancers would leave you and the audience flabbergasted and asking for an encore. Inviting us in your 2007 activity would add enriched gains from diverse cultures. One can learn more about the work I do for the villagers by logging onto: www.friendsofmandinggambimed.btck.co.uk, then click on our home page, Friends of Manding, Browse on the left links for more information. Dr. Aten, coordinator of the program at Alpena, Michigan, will send you copies of the video documentary and dancers in practice with adverts for tour. Dr. Aten's e-mail is: marten@chartermi.net.

We hope the videos and adverts will help. Dreamers like me never stop flabbergasting minds about goals others perceive unattainable. The idea of traveling to Alpena, Michigan with a well-tuned dance group from the villages of Njawara and Kinte Kunda to mark the first anniversary of the sister-city status entered into on the December 5, 2005 commenced from the day I wrote to US Ambassador Joseph D. Stafford letting him into my intentions.

In part, the letter simply informed him thus:

245 Great Western Street

Moss Side

Manchester, M14 4LQ

England

Dear Ambassador Stafford,

In pursuant to my last contact with you, I am currently negotiating for a contingent of Gambian Cultural dancers and Artists from the village of Njawara and Kinte Kunda, in the Lower Badibou District, NBR, to travel with me to Alpena Michigan and other Cities and Universities for a fundraising drive to build the proposed Manding Medical Centre at Njawara.

The accrued cash will be used to build the children and maternity unit of the hospital. Secondly, the trip will, I hope, help us establish concrete friendship between the Gambian villages and America.

I am a dreamer who fulfils his dreams. I plan to travel with these dancers to entertain Alpena and other cities coming December 2005. We look forward to your personal assistance with regards to our securing visas when the time comes. Regards and best wish to you and your for good health.

Sincerely

Dr. Alhasan S. Ceesay

Founder/coordinator

Mandig Medical Centre, Njawara.

I continued this line of approach with numerous e-mails to the Commissioner, NBR, Chiefs and village mayors while keeping my right hand, Mr. Kemo Kinte, secretary and coordinator of the Njawara/Kinte Kunda- Alpena relations in the picture Both Sefo Alhaj Fafanding Kinte and Kemo Kinte became my focal points of contact and transmittal point to and from relevant local government authorities.

They have sine done superb job at that and everyone in the district is grateful for Kemo's youthful enthusiasm about the sister-city hood. Together we compiled several list of would be dancers and travelers to the USA with me.

We reduced the number because of money problem, the fact that most of the officers wanted or jockeyed for a place in the list to go to America and cost of air tickets. However, we were at the end able to draw upon the best talents of none partisan list of dancers, as indicate in an earlier section of this work, that was inclusive instead of being exclusive and one party affair.

To emphasize my intention of making the list as fair and party neutral as can humanly be achieved I e-mailed this note to Kemo Kinte and Sefo Fafanding Kinte. Kemo, I have reviewed your 26/07/06 list regarding those to travel with us to Alpena coming December 2006.

Please make it crystal clear to all concerned that the added councilors should not come from the same party. There most be parity and diversity. Politicians will set our momentum backward. We are rural oriented and none partisan. Pass this information to governor Seckan, Sefo Fafanding Kinte and all it may concern.

The Americans are not interested in propping up a particular party; instead they want to work with the poor people of the region as a whole needing health assistance. Hence, my aim is for this unique event to an all-inclusive and not excluding others because they do not agree with us or see things the way we do.

Exercise of raw power always ends in tragedy. We want the benefit of Manding Medical Centre to filter out to everyone in the Gambia and Badibou and to out live us. We want our efforts to be footstool for generations to come. All names in the list must be representative. I am not sending APRC, UDP, NADD, NRP, NCP, UP or PPP to America but simple villagers from the Badibous and their local authority. God be with all of you in good health.

Dr. Alhasan Ceesay

In my usual tradition of introducing Manding Medical center I welcomed then Commissioner of the North Bank Division on board and seek his full participation along with that of the Kerewan Area Council. Through the cooperation and good will of Sefo Fanfanding Kinte we were able to register the above dancers at the Attorney Generals' Chambers in 2005. Our travel visa processing went on well until when our attention was directed that we have the P1-vsas to enable or allow the dancers proceed to the US.

From hence a series of delays followed one after the other until sudden global financial meltdown, which devastated most businesses and affected Michigan where our venues were located. The trip to Michigan became casualty of the economic down turn and eventually was postponed until the economy of the state picks up. It was then that I decided to become a writer hoping that one or two of my novels may help provide needed cash to build the maternity and children's unit of the Manding Manding Medical Centre at Njawara village, the Gambia.

I have since 2005 had published books but sales on these remain dismally low and so we are still unable to achieve our goal for the medical center. One can view or purchase my books by entering: Dr. Alhasan Ceesay/books; then google search or just log onto amazon.com, books, enters my name as above to purchase a copy or two. The center, villagers and I deeply appreciate any help cash or kind one could contribute to enable us provide a much needed medical aid to children and farmers. I remained in touch with my right hand man Mr. Kemo S. Kinte, up dating him as to progress or difficulties delaying our ascent for the people.

Dreams come true only if we word hard on them and never take our eyes away from them. The wall seems to cave on me any time I falter or seem to give up the dream, Manding Medical Centre at Njawara. Hence, rest assured that I would continue to fight on to the last breath of my life to avail the above charitable service to the region.

Chapter 27

Babou or Hadi, who was the Alkalo/Mayor,

Njawara and Badibou had their share of iron ladies but none rivals Hadi Panneh. In the days when her husband, the late Babou Panneh, was Alkalo of Njawara, everyone agreed that Hadi's good personality; connections at the helm and her political shrewdness overshadowed Babou Panneh, the then affable reining Alkalo of Njawara (Mpaneh).

Hadi has not been to school but is a better politician than most past or present representatives of the region. She survived the independent era under the civilian government to a point that people hardly contact Babou and so she overnight became chairperson and women leader of the Badibous. She can neither read nor write but runs the local women's bank in the area at Njawara. Hadi Panneh made smooth transition to the junta when the civilian, her PPP mentor, fell.

 Not many politicians are so gifted or are able to make such transformation as Hadi Panneh of Njawara. I personally used to teas the late Babou Panneh by calling him "deputy Alkalo" or just outright ask for his lady boss. Babou was such a sweet simple person that he had a laugh any time I made such jokes.

He would sometimes joke and say, "I know where I am not the boss." Jokes they are but a majority of the region believed Hadi's strong arm ruled the place and most of us where not surprised she replaced her husband although with a narrow margin of votes according to the electoral and commissioner's office records. She has been fighting relentlessly to bring Njawara to its heydays of at least the colonial days and beyond it.

She has links with Njawara scholars, residents, businessmen and women within and outside of the Gambia. She initially had doubts about my stance for Njawara but calmed when she realized that there is no selfish or political motive in what I am trying to bring to the greater region of the Badibous.

She has turned into a new leaf and is now well behind Manding Medical Centre and projects likely to be accrued. Hadi Panneh made certain she and her Njawara welcomed my American guests to the village. The Alpena Community College Leadership class guests of Manding Medical Centre to the village were made to be at home and Hadi Panneh also saw to it that they had a warm and memorable two weeks at Njawara.

Warm comments about the kindness and hospitality of Njawara and Badibou from the student visitors at the end of their two-weeks at Njawara reverberated to another good accolade for Hadi Panneh and Sefo Fafanding Kinte's achievement as it made Alpena City happy indeed. Because of my confidence in Hadi Panneh and the District authority I personally selected Njawara, Kinte Kunda and Torro Bahen to be in the list of villages to twin with Alpena city in America.

The first two names were accepted for twining on December 5th, 2005. Colchester mayor, after three years of consideration, wrote to say they would like to twin with Torro Bahen but it has to be at a later date as they have already twined with three other European countries. This email was sent to Torro via Kemo S. Kinte, coordinator Alpena, Njawara and Kinte Kunda relations. Here are a few of the many positive reactions from the Americans after visiting Njawara.

Allison Jane Simolisky said, "The trip was incredible! I did not want to leave. It was an experience of a lifetime that I will never forget. Everyone in the village was very kind and helpful. I have never met such kind people in my entire life. I found the villagers doing everything possible to make their lives better. I realized that many people work together to get a job done or finished. This is absolutely wonderful.

Everyone was so helpful in the village. The people of Njawara gave us such wonderful hospitality. The food and shelter was more than we deserved. I would like to thank you and Njawara for the incredible experience given me. I could not have asked for anything more. I immensely enjoyed myself and want you to know that I will do my best to help in whatever way I can.

Thank you doctor Ceesay and many more thanks to Njawara." Grace Schiminitz reported, "I really enjoyed my time in Njawara. The people treated us very well and it was a pleasure to spend two weeks with them. I hope to make another visit to Njawara in the future. It is a wonderful place. It was an eye-opening experience. The people were absolutely marvelous. They treated us as their own family and welcomed us with open hands. I had no idea that they would be so hospitable.

I really miss walking to the river and spend time with the children. It was my first experience in Gambia and hopefully it will not be the last. I hope I can return their kindness. I would love to see how the kids grown up." Finally Thomas P. Ray (TOM) the Alpena Community College English instructor of the leadership class wrote: "Dear Dr. Ceesay, I want to thank you for the opportunity you provided my students on this trip.

The entire experience was enjoyable and valuable as a means of teaching my students something about the responsibility that comes with the privileges they enjoy here. Everyone was kind to us on the trip and the students came away with many great souvenirs and memories.

I plan to call the village this weekend to extend my appreciation to everyone, especially Hadi Panneh, Mayor of Njawara and Sefo Fafanding Kinte, District Chief as well as the local authority.

Do you know anything about the proposed sister city/twining relationship between Alpena and Njawara? I would like to start making some local contacts here to help that process. I am hopeful that future trips will be possible for my students." Tom Ray. The Americans left delighted and its now time for us to ever redouble effort to bring good to the region for the benefits of all and especially future generations.

Political wounds must be healed to allow the village to move forward, if not the least, to catch up with the times. I once told the venerable Hadi Panneh that her role as Alkalo is akin to that of an open umbrella. It shades all and everything under beneath it and does not engage in differentiating between supporters or none supporters.

Njawara village is in daring need of a unifier and this is skill not beyond her political acumen. Hadi's successor will need a magical warn to bring back the village we had in the fifties and sixties. Hadi Panneh is, to say the least; trying her best but Badibou is not an easy political wrestling ground. There are too many potholes on the way and any false move could bring a good person down forever, as happened to former Vice president S. M. Dibba.

The Badinbounka is a self-reliant being. Hadi Panneh is atypical Badibounka for swings she made are very dramatic but one must credit her for being able to bring two political warring factors APRC and PPP under her umbrella and is still making best use of them. Allow me say hurray to Badibous' iron lady and a shrewd political sage in action.

Some teasingly call her the Dugula lady while others say she is a marvelous political juggler. Say of her what you may but Njawara's iron lady plies on in hope of restoring Njawara back to pristine days of recognition for being the template of regional hub for trade and development not only in Badibou but Gambia at large.

One need call a spade for what it is and history will record controversy and stamina predicated on genuine desire from your iron lady and with gratitude we all salute her for work she did for the region in her political stewardship of Njawara and the Badibous. She will go down in the annals of Badibou as one who stood for her people in thick and thin moments of our political evolution. Well-done! Hadi Panneh, Sefo Fafanding, and Lower Badibou district authority as well as input of the Kerewan Area Council.

Bintou Ceesay and Famatanding Ceesay, 2015

Chapter 28

Almami Kinte, Njawara's voiceless Alkalo/Mayor

Born in the heydays of colonial rule and duped to the post of Alkalo by his brother Sefo Njanko Kinte render Almami Kinte politically toothless. Almami kinte being forced onto the village of Njawara created more animosity between him and the residents than his brother dreamt of.

However, it was a good political move and vantage on Sefo Njako Kinte's quarters. It affords him reliable eyes being kept on Njawara the only source of cash revenue at the time and also it kept his brother out of the compaction for the post he holds. Chieftaincy in Badious is a hot bed of molten larva ready to flow any time a political tsurmmani or volcano ruptures and it no new thing to find brother taking over the reigns of the chief at some areas. Hence Alkalo Almami Kinte had to rule using the softy-softy approach to keep the residents' happy while at the same time reporting any swings against his brother as soon as possible.

His hotheaded son, Lang Kinte Mama was one of former police officers involved in the first ever-Gambian insurrection against our newly post colonial civilian government led by a Mandinka like him.

Lang Kinte Mama served as village development officer (VDC) and ran for the Alkaloship of Njawara on several occasions and failed to replace his late father Almami Kinte. Babou Panne thrashed him at what was said to be an open and fair election contest. His father's reign came to hunt him at the end.

The Wolof, Serere and Jola resident of the village would not allow a Mandinka rule them any further than the days of Alkalo Almami Kinte. Badara Jobe: Badibou Agriculturist started maning the centre at Njawara in the later part of 1960s. Every region has its seedling and one of the sons of Badibou who dedicated his life to agriculture is Badara Jobe of Njawara.

I recall when this young man was selected by the Ministry of Agriculture to come and train village folks on bull-drawn ploughs and reforestation. Badara soon garnered name for himself in that he trained a lot during those early years and because of it he was given Malina trees to grown at what the village commonly called "the center." The center became Njawara's first orchard and also doubled as animal husbandry.

There were goats, sheep and few cows when I last visited the Centre in 1966 before leaving for the United States. Now Badara is the Toubab of Njawara as he speeds in his four by four vehicles to villages to teach more and rewarding use of the land etc.

He operates within the grass-root farmers in believe that agro-sustenance is the way forward for rural villagers. Badara is building confidence and so help in capacity and self-reliance, especially when it comes to tackling long run climate change effects in the region.

He was elected to the Ashoka fellowship in 2008 in recognition of good work he is involved with at village grass root level. Hurray to my boy Badara Jobe founder and currently Director of Njawara's Farming Centre, one of the region's most successful organizations in the North Bank Region of the Gambia. Among Njawara residents, Badara Jobe shined when guests to Manding Medical Centre were at Njawara. Bless his heart for being so gracious.

Chapter 29

Quintessentially Gambian Badibounka

In the north bank region of the Gambia leaves a special combination of tribes i.e. Mandinkas, Fulas Serere, and Wolofs, who most fledgling politicians and political parties pay great attention. Politicians of all parties take off their hats to this region for it is well known no nonsense talk and attitude towards Gambian politics and politicians of the day. Their fort rightness bewilders even seasoned politicians.

The Badinbounka does not meander in telling their feelings and the truth to one's face. In short they do not subscribe to the new idea of "politically correct stance" as happen in other countries. Nor do they take it lightly when others assume them fools or want to take them for a ride. The Badibounka is a known enigma to aspiring politicians.

He is peaceful and amiable but never yields to threats or covert carrot and stick cohesion from political parties. Why? Well dear reader, the Badinbounka is born pragmatic and does not give up their ground easily. They are very congenial and charismatic magnet that always aspires to leadership among tribes.

An old Badibounka sage from lower Badibou District once advised me thus: "Son, he said, better keep you mouth short and everyone think you are a fool than open it for everyone to be certain of it." He added that when one speaks it should make others want to listen and it should be worth talking about.

I visited a Badibounka studying in the USA and while we compared tribes he showed me an entry in his diary, which runs thus "I do not know where and when my end will come but I am certain my grave will be in Badibou." What could be more quintessential Badibounka than this fellow? For me the heart dwells in Njawara Badibou and my soul shall rest in peace in Badibou with its maker any time he chooses to receive me.

The Badinbounka is a visionary businessman in nature. Nearly all the successful business stalls at the grand Albert market in Banjul belongs to sharp minded Badibounkas businesses. Most of their children studying in universities abroad are either enrolled in economic or business administration courses.

A few now opt to read for a law degree, political science and agriculture. This stubborn and yet charismatic group can be comical. Ask any true red-blooded Badinbounka where he or she came from and one is certain to get a rhetorical answer full of pride.

The answer is normally, "Home!" What is it you want to know and why do you ask? The answer "home", exudes pride in themselves and detestation of intrusion into their affairs. On the other hand they are very congenial and comical.

They refer to Wolofs as their surwaringo and Fulas as their Fulandingos. They almost always assume superiority over other tribes. Hence their domineering nature is reckoned by most Gambians. They are hard working people who detest laziness.

Their women are the most beautiful and hardest working of all women in the Gambia. The quintessential Badibonka enjoys his favorite dish of Manankasi Nyelengo, (similar to coos coos) or Kobayi Nyelengo (from lily pods) with some Furindingo to go with. They love an early breakfast of Nete Kadango.

This is obtained from the local plants and is full of glucose saturated with vitamins A and C. It is nature's gift to the region. The ancient Badibounkas were among those to firstly resisted colonialism in the heydays of empire and blind rule by might. Yes, the Badibounka is Warrior by right and merit. They shed blood and lost illustrious sons in wars against colonial domination. Even though a late entrants to Western education, the Badibounka rank highest number among those schooled in the North Bank Region.

Without boasting about Badibounkas it is true they hold qualifications in many professions like law, medicine, teaching, nursing, business, writers and music. Yes, they are industrious indeed and are custodians of their culture and tradition beyond any other group in the Gambia. Marriage ceremonies, christening ceremonies, circumcision, ancient rituals dances, and dresses are still maintained in form as far back as the beginning of the Mandinka, Fula and Wolof tribes.

No wonder, the first head of state and president of the Gambia was none other than a Mandinka, the illustrious Dr. Dawda Kairaba Jawara, who is not a Badibounka, but a mandinka from Barajali Kunda further down the river Gambia. He was a gentleman and a democrat but fell victim of deception by tsars of political tug of war and jokers that was going on in the Gambia amid rampant corruption he could not curb without going against his principles of human right and belief that one not being guilty of a crime until duly proven so by his or her peers in a fair and open court of law.

This man upheld the Gambian constitution and stood for freedom of the individual, press and judiciary. He is the only African former president who left the post as poor as the poor man on the day he took power and in running the affairs of the Gambia to the time of his removal from the seat of government.

No wonder the new regime had him back from exile to have his retirement days in the Gambia instead of withering away in a foreign country that cares little about him since he was no use to them in executing dirty deals with the continent. Like it or not the people still love and welcomed him back to Gambia with joy and no malice against him personally.

Corruption was an inherent way of business life in those days and needed drastic draconian laws to curb it out. It is still as rampant in the continent as ever despite having been now independent for well over sixty years. The first vice president of the Gambia was none other than the late Mandinka quintessential indefatigable and seasoned politician sheriff Mustapha Dibba of Badibou Salekenye in the North Bank Region. He tried to rescue the country from the hands of swindlers wolves in sheep clothing and corrupt forces but could not wrest power from combined forces bent on retaining power in the Gambia.

He lost the country because it was rumored he had declared himself the sole if not the only rightful hire to the Gambian presidency and perhaps the only able to break the back bone of rampant corruption in Banjul and the country. This did him great disservice at polling stations and he never got to the dreamt throne or becoming the second president of the Republic of the Gambia, in shorts the realm.

He however served briefly as Speaker of the House of Representatives before his peaceful return to his maker in 2008. Two more stalwarts of the Badibou were Dr. Lamin Saho and Kalilu Singatheh. Both held various ministerial posts during the Jawara administration. Dr. Saho served, after the overthrow of President Kairaba Jawara, as Director of Air Atlantic and he also is founder of the Njaba Kunda Clinic, which delivers great Medical service to the Central Badibou and it surrounding hamlets.

Dr. Saho peacefully joined his maker in 2006. Foday Makalo also ceased the lime light for Badibou when he became the Junta's Administrative Secretary from 1995 until his abrupt disappearance in the later part of 1996 or there about. Some believed him massacred by his bosses others still hang onto the slim information that he is alive and well in Mali.

We all pray the later is the case. In summary, this is one Gambian community that is not afraid of AK47 and hates the dole; being under rated and is never moved by coaxing or the use of the carrot and the stick. They accept only equal footing and treatment and also respect while preferring to earn their own living.

Among the stalwart chiefs of the Badibous are Sefo Njanko Kinte, Sefo Nfamara Singateh, Sefo Sillah Dibba, Sefo Kitabou Singateh, Sefo Sheriff Kinte, Sefo Mama Tamba, Sefo Mustapha Dibba, Sefo Kende Dibba and sefo Fafanding Kinte. The later being the current bearer of the reigns in the Lower Badibou District. I hope this bit had given insight into the Badibounka and especially the Warrior Mandinka tribe of the Badibous.

Chapter 30

Difficulty I encountered

Bringing medical aid to my people

Allow me digress and bring this immigration tale in throwing light to my personal experience and difficulties encountered while fight to get resources to build Manding Medical Centre at Njawara, the Gambia. In nutshell I live less than a 5th grade human being homeless, jobless and wallowing in extreme poverty and destitution.

All my efforts crashed upon my head like a thunderbolt from hell and friends one way or the other deserted me. Only God and a few true friends buoyed my spirit in conjunction to my steely will that kept me going. Here is the straw that almost broke my back in my effort to bring medical aid to doorsteps of villagers. I braced myself and just when I was busy reviewing for the exam a bombshell note came from the UK Border agency at Cryodon. Here is the entirety of what it requested of me.

Home Office

UK Border Agency

P. O. Box 1875 NAC

Lumar House

40 Wellesley Road

Croydon, CR9 2BY

Our Ref C1024534

15 March 2011

Alhasan Sisawo Ceesay

82 Finchingfield Way

Colchester, Co2 OAU

Dear Alhasan Sisawo Ceesay

Your case is in the backlog of older applications that the UK Border Agency is in the process of concluding. The case Resolution Directorates (CRD) is responsible for your case. CRD aims to resolve cases by either removing individuals from the United Kingdom or grant them leave to remain in accordance with the existing law and policy. It is important that we hold the most recent information about your case.

We need you to send us some photographs and, if you have already done so, any original identity documents you have for yourself and any of your dependents along with any other documents listed below where applicable to you and/ or your dependents. Please send any additional documents that may be relevant to your application.

You should send four photographs for yourself and four photographs each for any dependents. The photographs must be passport sized photographs and should not be stapled or marked in any way. They should have a plain colored background. Write on the back of each photograph the name of each person in the picture and your Home Office reference.

If you have not already done so, send any identity documents including your national passport (valid or expired) and National Identity Cards for yourself and any dependants. You should send any Immigration Status Documents that may have been issued to you and any dependents by the Home Office or UK Border Agency (formerly the Border and Immigration Agency or Immigration and Nationality Directorate) with an endorsement indicating that the person named in it can stay in the United Kingdom.

If you are married or are in cohabitation relationship please provide details of your partner along with evidence of the addresses and immigration status. If you have children who were born in the United Kingdom you should provide a full birth certificate (long version) for each child.

If you have children who arrived with you or arrived in the United Kingdom after you, and have not already done so, you should provide a full birth certificate and/or national passport. Please provide evidence to show how long each child resided in the United Kingdom. If your child does not reside with you please provide details. You should note that if you send us information other than that requested above, this will be treated as information only and will not be accepted as "Further Submissions.' Further submissions to any previous claim must be submitted in person at our Liverpool Office.

Please send your photograph and any other documents along with the completed form sent with this letter, to the address at the top of this letter. You should do this within 21 days from the above date. If you do not send the documents requested above, we will consider your case on the documents available to us. We ask that you do not make routine telephone or written enquiries about the progress of your case, as this diverts our resources from resolving cases.

We will not confirm receipt of your reply to this letter or receipt of your photographs. Should we require any further information about your case; a UKBA colleague will contact you. You should however ensure you write to us if you change your address.

VOLUNTARY RETURN

If at any stage in the process you decide that you want to return voluntarily to your country of origin, help and advice for people who wish to permanently return home voluntarily can be obtained from International organization for Migration (IOM). The IOM is an independent international organization that may be able to help you with paying for flight ticket, travel arrangements (which includes booking flights, help with documentation and arranging travel to and from airports) and airport assistance (both departure and arrivals). Also, depending on your case, reintegration assistance to support the sustainability of your return may be available.

Reintegration assistance can be used to help for a variety of things depending on your needs, such as additional luggage; short-term accommodation needs, setting up a small business, job training, work placements education and vocational training.

Return to the United Kingdom

People who have previously broken the United Kingdom immigration laws can have any future applications to come back to the United Kingdom refused for up to 10 years following their departure from the United Kingdom.

The exclusion period will be shorter if you leave the United Kingdom of your accord and it does not apply in all categories of entry clearance application.

If you intend to make a visa application abroad to return to the United Kingdom in the future, you may wish to take advice about this before making a decision to leave voluntarily. To obtain a visa you will need to meet the requirements of the Immigration Rules.

Yours Sincerely

NAC

Case Resolution Directorate

UK Border Agency

In response, I gathered all what was required to be submitted to NAC in the above letter. I wrote the following reply before contacting an Immigration lawyer to help me with the case. I then ran to one of my best friends, Asfque Ahmed in seeking the help of an immigration solicitor. We contacted the Khan Solicitors in London.

Chapter 31

IN RESPONSE TO NAC AT CRYODON

With a place to put my head I braced myself for full-blown review in preparation for the PLAB exam due in June 2011. A few days after just when I was busy reviewing for the exam a bombshell note came from the UK Border agency at Cryodon. In response, I gathered all what was required to be submitted to NAC in the above letter.

I wrote the following reply before contacting an Immigration lawyer to help me with the case. I then ran to Ashfaq Ahmed, one of my best friends, to seek help of an immigration solicitor.

We contacted the G.K. Associates Immigration Law firm located in London to advise and also stand in for me. Mr. Zubaid on receiving and after reviewing my documentation presented him suggested that I submit it directly to NAC as no lawyer was addressed in their letter to me. He felt that it will best and cheaper and would save time. I did as advised and sent all my documents along with my expired Gambian passport 001393 under recorded delivery on the 16/4/11 to the UK Border Agency, P. O. Box 1875 NAC, Lumar House, Wellesley Road, Croydon, CR9 2BY, London. The letter bellow accompanied the documentation and passport to NAC.

NAC DOCCUMENTATION

82 Finchingfield Way 3

Black Heath

Colchester, Essex, CO2 OAU

8/4/11

UK Border Agency

P. O. Box 1875 NAC

Lumar House

40 Wellesley Road

Croydon, CR9 2BY

RE: In response to your letter dated 15/3/11

Dear Sir/Madam

Thank you for your letter of the 15/3/11, which I received today; in response I submit the following. I did reply to Ms. Coker's letter of 18/3/04 as per enclosed on the 26/3/04 herein enclosed copy.

As my situation stands its paramount that I get the PLAB certification to enable me practice medicine. That conundrum suffered seriously because of my not being allowed to work to pay for my exam fees and support my family back home in Gambia. Neither the Gambia Government nor any other organization was able or willing to help in this matter.

Worst, the GMC had wrong information regarding entry on website of the American University of the Caribbean University School of medicine to cause it recant recognition of my PMG. However, thank God, both the American University and UK GMC have resolved the situation. My PMG is now recognized and I am allowed to take the PLAB and would be eligible for registration upon completing parts 1& 11 of the PLAB exams.

See enclosed. Dear sir/ Madam, life had been such an unexpected set back due to unforeseen circumstances such as coming to the UK with a visitor's visa only to find it could not be reverted to "student visa Status." My salary being suspended forced me to fend for my family and the education of my daughters. I am most grateful to the Brits for helping me pay some of the schooling of my daughters caught in between this nightmare of mine. No matter what happened I am grateful to England.

I wrote a few books amongst them is Country for President, Tribe and Party. This I now found according to the enclosures had added more troubles to my already turbulent life. I did write in believe that democracy should be bases of governance and not tribe and AK47 as is the norm in current Africa.

The books have not sold much and hence my economic state remain below that of a church mouse. I had to borrow money from kindhearted friends to pay for the attempts I made at the exam. When no further help came to me I resorted to endure life of the homeless because of the following threats most recent of all are the enclosed declarations made by the Attorney General of the Gambia on 10/01/11and lately by the head of state at a meeting with the Gambia media.

I enclose copy of what awaits civil servants that resign to further their skill or future in the West. It is my hope the above brief explanation of my encounters would help you give me a favorable consideration to stay until the storm in the Gambia settles. Hence, being one who wrote extensive on what I believe should be the democratic governance in our countries I now find myself a possible target for arrest as per attorney General's pronouncement of 10/01/11.

I am so fearful for the safety of my children that if this revealed truth is brought to attention of the officials my family may become victims. Hence, my wife Fatou Koma-Ceesay, and our three daughters (Famatanding Ceesay, who was born at Colchester in Essex on 17/09/91 while I was doing my clinical clerkship, Binta Ceesay 18 and Roheyata Ceesay 13 years old were born in the Gambia) walk the streets with fear in their hearts but dare not say so to any fear of what may follow.

I please appeal for your kind consideration to allow me stay until its safe for my family and me. Thank you very much for being kind and patient in this unusual case of mine before you. Bless your hearts.

Yours Sincerely

Dr. Alhasan Sisawo Ceesay, MD

Gambian

The above along with most of the required documentation were sent on 16/4/11 to the UK Border Agency under recorded delivery mail.

Chapter 32

In steps my God sent Samaritan solicitor

Life for me has been a balancing act at dizzying heights on the high wire of life. Life was at this stage akin to that of moving one step forward followed by three behind. A blurred line ran in-between the two hillocks. It was not until the arrival of Dr. Angela Stull and her husband Attiq Raman that some forward momentum became realized. It came about after my having appealed to Ashfaq Ahmed, a good friend of mine, seeking the help of a lawyer to fight my pending case that has been on going with the Home Office since 2004.

I had responded to the Home Office's March 15th 2007 as reproduced above. I was more than surprised to learn that UK Border agents were in Essex at my Colchester address wanting to speak with me face to face. This set alarm bells ringing in my head for it connote that the officers were there to arrest and proceed on deportation processing.

Ashfaq Ahmed who felt sorry that life had been so much of an uphill battle for me drew the above God sent Samaritan couple's attention upon my case. Dr. Angela is a lawyer specialized in Immigration matters and cases, especially visa related cases. I met the couple after husband Attiq set up a meeting for me to talk to his wife Dr. Angela Stull.

I liked her the moment I set eyes on her. She came through as some kind human being that would understand the pains, needs and aspirations of the downtrodden. She was very sympathetic and caring and above all willing to listen to my dark days' story on this planet. Dr. Angela was vividly moved on knowing that I had to spend nights at a park in Manchester.

After half an hour listening as well as interjecting the period with clarification questions Dr. Angela told her husband that she would take up my case to enlighten the Home Office and to plead for them to consider giving my case a prospective granting me leave to remain in the UK. They made it very clear that the service was not free and that it would cost at minimum, five hundred pounds sterling. That agreed they requested all former correspondence along with my latest dealings with the Home Office.

I agreed and gladly deposited sixty pounds sterling towards the bill being money I collected from friends to Dr. Angela Stull of Lloyds Solicitors. In addition Dr. Angela requested that I provide her with all recent news and political development occurring in the Gambia and what effect my having written has on my returning home then. Hence on the following Monday I submitted every bit of correspondence that transpired between the Home

Office and I. I dispatched the following e-mail thanking Dr. Angela Stull thus.

From: alhasanceesay@hotmail.com

To: angela@hotmail.com

Date; wed.22 June 20011

Dear Angela,

Thank you very much for being so kind to take on my case. It has been long and acidulous journey but I will fight on to bring good to my family and rural villagers. I will be most grateful if you help sort my visa problem with the Home office.

I left a copy of my book, 'the legend against all odds', at the front desk for you to have a bird's eye view of a tried life I led since birth. Sections relating experience I had with the Gambia since 1982 arc marked for your review. In regards to the five hundred pounds sterling payment I have started begging for help and it may come in drips but rest assured I will pay up.

Again, God bless and I will certainly bring any cash I happen to collect. Cheers and my regards to Attiq. This was followed by an almost endless stream of update emails political state of the day and copies of threats to prosecute all who wrote about human right violations in the Gambia.

My book, Country for the President, Tribe and Party, was hot on heels of African officials who turned pseudo monarchies or dictators with blessings of AK47. These rulers have mindlessly ruined lives of millions upon millions of peasants in addition to wanton destruction of property and life. They glamorize their wantonness at the expense of farmers while forcing intelligentsia to flee or leave in servitude.

AK47 is disgrace to Africa and has caused many intelligentsias suffer poverty, homelessness and even death from hands of autocratic dictators ruling the continent. During one of our regular secessions I pleaded for Dr. Angela to give me a letter that would give teeth to my appeal for donations. And she gladly gave the following note to help my cause.

Lloyds Solicitors

580 Stockport Road

Manchester, M13 0RQ

Telephone: 0161-248-8050

Date: 29 June 2011

To whom it may concern

Dear Sir/Madam:

RE: Mr. Alhasan Sisawo Ceesay, MD

This is to confirm that our firm is handling the immigration matters for Dr. Ceesay.

We are currently working with UKBA to resolve his case but as he's legal representation, it could take some time to sort out, though we hope not. Lloyds Solicitors is a private law firm and as such we do not subscribe to legal aid.

Those clients coming to us must pay privately. We try to keep our rates as low as possible and work with the client. Dr. Ceesay is looking for contributions to defray the costs of the legal work performed on his case. If you wish to contribute you can make checks payable to Lloyds Solicitors.

We are happy to provide you with a receipt. If there are any questions about this matter, please do not hesitate to contact me.

Yours faithfully

Dr. Angela J. Stull

Immigration Consultant

Lloyds Solicitors

With this letter in hand I left the office happy and braced to raise the five hundred pounds sterling expected of me. This coincided with the month of Ramadan along with a massive economic down turn and joblessness most people were experiencing. Fund raising became an uphill battle, which allowed few pennies and pounds to trickle towards my efforts instead of bulk amounts I looked forward.

I was able to make another forty pounds sterling down payment later on with lot of friends promising help after Ramadan. Mean while Dr. Angela Stull let her pen and expertise go to work on the case and eventually releasing the following superbly documented coveted letter in my behalf to the Home Office.

On the 14/9/11 Dr Angela sent me the following e-mail updating me on action taken in my behalf. It read:

From: Angela Stull

To: Alhasan Ceesay

Date: 14/9/11

Dear Dr. Ceesay,

Yesterday I made further representations to the Home Office regarding your case. I sent it by recorded delivery and it should get there today or tomorrow.

I am hopeful we will get a reply soon. I have a copy that I can give you on what I submitted. Let me know when you want to come by and I will have it at the front desk. I will only be in the office on Thursday for a few hours because of other duties. So let us hope for the best.

Kind Regards,

Angela

The letter further exhumes kindness and Angela's concern for others this benevolent lady has at heart. Dr. Angela's coming into the picture exudes compassion and needed protection for me as at the time my forward momentum was like standing still.

Fate somehow or somewhere brought Samaritan Angela to help me solve this nightmare and ongoing impasse between the Home Office/ UK Border Agency and I. Reading a copy of it lifted a ton of lead weight off my shoulders as it buoyed my spirit while throwing a glimpse of hope of my ever seeing my wife and children sooner than eons to come. The letter is reproduced for your perusal.

Lloyds Solicitors

580 Stockport Road

Manchester, M13 0RQ

Date: 13 September 2011

UK Border Agency

P. O. Box 1875 NAC

Lunar House

40 Wellesley Road

Croydon CR9 2BY

Dear Sir/Madam:

Re: Alhasan Sisawo Ceesay: Gambia

We represent Dr. Ceesay in the continuation of his case Dr. Ceesay received was dated 15/03/2011 stating that his case was in the CRD and there was no time frame for when his case would be resolved. Dr. Ceesay replied to that letter but has received no further information and as he is living on the streets, we ask that you please try to process his case as soon as possible.

As Dr. Ceesay has no fix abode and all correspondence should be sent to our firm. Dr. Ceesay has been in the United Kingdom since 2000 and through a series of circumstances and misfortune he has been unable to regularize his status.

Initially, he counts on the support of his benefactors Mr. and Mrs. Robinson, who had their own, registered charity, but Mrs. Robinson is deceased leaving a sick husband behind. This proud and vigorous man now wears tattered clothes, sleeps on the floor or on a park bench and survives on the kindness of strangers.

We would argue that there are quite compassionate and compelling circumstances regarding his case and ask that you allow him to remain in the United Kingdom. Dr. Ceesay's immigration history is as follows:

Dr. Ceesay entered the UK on 6 January 200 to clear the PLAB; his intentions after the PLAB were to pursue the MRCP. He applied for an extension of stay which granted on 9 June 2000. A further application for extension was granted on 13 September 2001. In the letter from UKBA it stated that Dr. Ceesay had permission to stay for a maximum of 4 years to enable him to undertake postgraduate studies.

During these periods, Dr. Ceesay took the PLAB and was unsuccessful in passing. He then had no money to pay for the test. Another extension was applied for on 10 February 2002. A decision was not made until 17 January 2003 for that case and it was refused.

Dr. Ceesay contacted the local MP, Bob Russell, for help in this situation, as he did not understand when he had been refused.

A further application was submitted in 2004 for further leave to remain. Since this time Dr. Ceesay has tried to regularize his status. As he has not been able to afford legal representation, he has tried to manage this on his own with no resolution.

Moreover, during Dr. Ceesay's time in the United Kingdom, he ran afoul of the Gambian government, as he was highly critical of their policies toward the poor villagers, the delivery of health care and a dictatorship. Actually he had always been an outspoken advocate but had not come to any physical harm when he left the country.

However with the current actions of the Gambian government led by president Jammeh Dr. Ceesay is fearful of his life and that of the family he left behind in Gambia. Dr. Ceesay established a medical center in Njawara, which was dedicated to serving rural areas. The funding came in part from the United States and United Kingdom and his own proceeds from his literary works; no money was received fro the Gambia government. They could see more than 500 patients in any given week.

The clinic also gave information on hygiene, preventive medicine, sexually transmitted diseases and family planning. They gave free treatment to elderly, children and pregnant women.

Female genital mutilation is widely practiced in Gambia and Dr. Ceesay was an advocate against this procedure so he came into a lot of conflict even with the population he served. As the clinic was entirely dependent upon funding from outside of the country, Dr. Ceesay was

always critical of the depravity and indifference the government showed towards the poor. Whenever anyone asks for money he or she must always have a proposal and provide the source of funding and expenditures, etc.

Naturally donors would want to know why the local government was not supporting such worthwhile cause. Dr. Ceesay did not hold back his criticism of the government so naturally he drew a lot of attention within Gambia and outside of the country.

It is certainly arguable that Dr. Ceesay would be categorized as a public figure. Dr. Ceesay's views have not changed and he would not be able to remain quiet about the situation if forced toreturn. Dr. Ceesay is a publish writer which classifies him as a public figure as well.

His books have been published in the United States and are widely available. He has written one book of fiction to raise money for the clinic and the others dealt with his education journey.

(The legend against all odds) and the establishment of the Manding Medical Centre in Njawara and his writings of democracy in a book called: 'Country for President, Tribe and Party.' In that particular book he stated that democracy should be the basis of governance and not the tribes and their use of an AK47.

He writes about the systemic human rights abuses and poor governance on the African continent. The book certainly incensed the authorities and now leads him to believe that he should be in fear for himself and his family.

There have been statements made in the media from the Attorney General and President Jammeh of Gambia where it is stated that he vows to prosecute and expel public servants who left the country for the sake of pursuing better opportunity overseas.

Amnesty International has stated that human right situation in Gambia is "Dire". They also go on to state that the "Gambian security forces routinely kill suspects and opponents of the government with impunity."
The United Nations High Commissioner for Human Rights report that the Jammeh government does not answer to anyone. Recently Dr. Amadou Janneh was arrested for sedition and treason for the distribution of t-shirts bearing the Coalition for Change Gambia logo and the statement, "End Dictatorship, NOW!!."

Dr. Ceesay, like Dr. Janneh is also a public figure known for his criticism of the government and would surely face the same fate were he forced to return. Dr. Ceesay would state that under the ECHR if returned to Gambia, his 2, 3 and 8th amendment rights would be violated. These issues should be given consideration in his case.

Whilst we understand that the Secretary of State has the right to protect her borders and control who comes into the country and remains, we would ask that all relevant factors be given consideration in Dr. Ceesay's case. We would ask you to remember that it was never Dr. Ceesay's intent to become an overstayed. He did not come to the UK as an economic migrant either.

He made legal entry into this country and continued to extend his stay for 3 years without incident. While it was not his goal to be employed, he did need to work to be able to pay for his exam and children's schooling but not once did he violated the law in taking up unauthorized employment.

He was determined to increase his medical knowledge and develop his skills through postgraduate training so that he may return to Gambia to continue his humanitarian work for the underprivileged and deliver better health care and train staff to the latest techniques.

As a doctor he would enjoy a relatively high position and a good life so there would be no reason for him to overstay. During his stay Dr. Ceesay has done his best to raise money so he can sit for the PLAB. He is now penniless. He has not engaged in any employment nor acted in any illegal manner. He has developed close ties to the UK in terms of his private life. He has no family to which he can turn to in this country.

He had depended upon the encouragement, support, spirit and strength from the community. These people who were once strangers are now as source of help and inspiration. Months passed without him receiving a decision to his queries.

Months passed without a decision to remove being made, and the months became year, and years succeeds year, so it is to be expected that this sense of impermanence will fade and the expectation will grow that if UKBA had intended to remove the applicant it would have taken steps to do so.

These factors do affect the proportionality of removal at this point and consideration should be given to him. During his time in the United Kingdom, the political situation has also worsened, human right are being violated on a massive scale, especially to those highly critical of the current regime.

Dr. Ceesay has been highly critical in his assessment of the political policies of the country and the need to find democratic solutions in order to move the country forward and enable everyone the chance to live a peaceful and prosperous life. Dr. Ceesay simply is not able to return to his country for fear of being persecuted, jailed and killed. We ask that you allow him to remain in the United Kingdom.

Dr. Ceesay will not be a person who will live off of benefits. He will write about the love and sincerity of the British people and its government and will no doubt serve the public and fill a need in the medical community of this country. We thank you for consideration of his case and await your reply.

Kind Regards

Angela J. Stull, J. D

Immigration Consultant

Lloyds Solicitors

Bless her heart. A million thank Angela! The above letter was accompanied with many substantiating evidence from the Media, Amnesty International, and West Afriooca.

United Nation High Commissioner for Human Rights. I reproduce a few of these to provide something to chew on or contemplate upon.

Media Foundation for West Africa (Accra)

Gambia: Justice Minister Threatens to Prosecute Exile Nationals

10 January 2011

Press release

Gambia's Justice Minister, Edward Gomez on January 7, 2011 issued threats to exiled journalists and rights defenders saying that they would be prosecuted if they returned for allegedly "painting a grim picture " of the country. Gomez, who was reacting to a publication in a privately-owned Daily News about an international campaign against the systematic human rights violations in the country, said: "we will wait here for them to come (home).

"The Justice Minister said the advocates were "evil members" of society" who have taken refuge abroad and were "putting every nonsensical story in newspapers and on radio to tarnish the good image of the government." Media Foundation for West Africa (MFWA) sources attributed the minister's threats to a campaign mounted by an exiled journalist Alieu B Ceesay and Scottish Society of Human Rights.

The sources said in December 2010 the campaign received a boost with 24 British parliamentarians appending their signatures to a motion calling on the international community to ensure that the deteriorating human rights in Gambia are improved.

On the repression of Gambians including abductions and gruesome killings, which was the basis of the motion, Gomez said those were mere speculations and unfounded allegations. I gladly made another down payment of sixty pounds sterling to Angela towards the bill and horrid away with letter to the Home Office in hand. On reaching my flat I prayed for relief before going through the letter line by line with broad smiles for a job well done.

Friends, family and I all hope and pray that this be the end of my nightmare caused by visa problems in one of the world's richest countries. The visa conundrum let my solicitor and to contact Hon. Gerald Kaufman, MP for Manchester to help us find way out of the nightmare. The president threatened to arrest and prosecutes all who left in search of greener pasture in the Diaspora.

It was very clear that those of us who about the poor governance and untenable state of affair were subject to retribution.The above speech by Gambian president has virtually exiled and rendered us nation-less as returning at this juncture would be suicidal.

My books, even though spoke the truth about human rights and governance in Gambia, were not welcomed by the regime as pronounced by the attorney general of the Gambia.I stayed at 284 Great Western for well more than six months before the Home Office through intervention of Dr. Angela Stull, my solicitor gave the following response to a long standing request I made since 2004.

Dr. Ceesay & wife Fatou Koma-Ceesay

The above speech by Gambian president has virtually exiled and rendered us nation-less as returning at this juncture would be suicidal. My books even though spoke the truth about human rights and governance in Gambia was not welcomed by the regime as pronounced by the attorney general of the Gambia. It would be six months since my solicitor represented me in the case at the UKAB.

Friends normally teased that I needed the constitution of an Ox and hide of a Rhinoceros to fight the Home Office foot dragging with my application for change of visa status. Hence, darkness veiled my eyes with impunity upon reading my solicitor's 16 March 20012 email. Please acquaint yourself with that sad information as reproduced below.

Angela Stull

To Alhasan Ceesay

Dr. Ceesay,
I did want to speak to you about your case. I am not getting any kind of reply from UKBA and unless we file a judicial review nothing is going to happen.

UKBA keeps saying that they have no record of an application and if they don't then we could not win the Judicial Review. So I am thinking that an asylum case is about the only way for you to go.

There are strong arguments for you and at least we would get a decision and you could get in front of a judge. Think about it and then come see me so we can move forward.

Regards
Angela

The search for a needle in a hay stalk continues in the letter below to hon. Gerald Kaufman, MP for Manchester. Dr. Angela's letter states thus:

Lloyds Solicitors

580 Stockport Road

Manchester, M13 0RQ

Date: 13 September 2011

From: Angela Stull

Sent: 16th March 2012 16:23

To: 'Kaufmang@parliament.uk'

Subject: Immigration mater for constituent Dr. Alhasan Sisawo Ceesay

Attachments: Ltr to HO 09 2011 doc. Signed FOA doc

Dear Mr. Kaufman

Our firm represents Dr. Ceesay with regard to his immigration mater. Dr. Ceesay has been in the UK since 2000. He applied for extensions that were granted up and until 2003. In 2004 he applied for a further extension and no decision was made on that application. He received a letter from UKBA in March of 2011 that his case was in the legacy backlog. He submitted pictures and provided further information that was requested.

Dr. Ceesay is an educated man who acted as a humanitarian in his home country of Gambia. He provided free health care to the poor and was highly critical of their health care policies. He had well respected benefactors in the United Kingdom who sponsored his visit and then fought for him to stay. Unfortunately Dr. Ceesay's sponsor passed away, which left him alone leaving on the street for the last several years.

Since his stay in the UK, he has run afoul of that government for his outspoken criticism of the current regime. He is also published author so he is very visible figure in that country and not able to return.

He came to me last year and I took on his case pro bono. Members of the community as well as myself have given him food and shelter when possible.

I attach the letter we sent to UKBA on 13 September 2011 which gives the background on his case. I have never received any acknowledgement from the UKBA. He and I would be very grateful if you could look into this matter. Kindest regards,

Angela J. Stull

Immigration Consultant

On receiving copy of the above I help my hands high towards the sky and begged God to anoint my case and give this honorable man's intervention some positive rewards for my family and country.

I cannot tell how much heart ache there was in me at this time. My daughters had grown and needed to attend university but my dire financial state was blocking if not delaying their entry to college.

Already my elder daughter, Famatanding Ceesay's admission to do her pre-med courses at Alpena Community College remained in limbo.

I had no money to either pay for her first semester or air ticket fare due to my being unemployed. I sent Hon. Gerald Kaufman, MP for Manchester the following email note right away.

To: Gerald Kaufman, MP

From: Dr. Alhasan S. Ceesay, MD

Date: 12/4/12

Dear Sir,

I am Dr. Alhasan Ceesay, a Gambian. My Solicitor Dr. Angela Stull at the Llyod's Solicitors in Manchester recently contacted you on my behalf regarding application I had before the Home Office since 2004. I now leave in the streets of Manchester because of visa problems.

My state became more precarious by death of my sponsor and now declaration made by my home country's Attorney General (see attached) regarding those of us who wrote exposing poor governance and lack of respect for the rule of law in the country. Amnesty International and others have documented some of the stifling of freedom and democracy in the country.

Those of us who imbibe democratic ideals from America or Europe and are using it to help our people realize fruits of democracy normally fall at loggerheads with the AK47 regimes in our regions. They are scared stiff scared of change that would bring meaningful democracy and rule of law.

Hence folks like me trying to do the little we can to help elevate state of our people before fading away are seen as traitors. A T-shirt with label, 'Coalition for change' now landed Dr. Amadou Janne and co to life imprisonment. That would never happen in Britain as there is freedom in UK. I have since 1967 been involved in trying to bring healthcare service to villagers.

Do not use http://, www. Or Google) will show how far that went. I put myself through university and medical school and returned to the Gambia to help bring much needed medical service to villagers on graduating as a Doctor in 1993.

I set up a village self-help health organization (NGO) Manding Medical Centre and by it have treated more than 9000 villagers free of charge before coming to the UK to do 2 things, which are (1). Improve my medical skills to the MRCP level and (2). Internationalize my NGO to boost our objectives. The later caught on well as we are a charity (FRIENDS OF MANDING Reg: 1088136) both in Colchester UK and Alpena USA.

On top this I authored several books with hope of raising money to fund our operations. Dismal sales hampered that state. One of my books, 'Country for president, tribe and party' ruffled feathers back home. I am now one of those easily labeled 'treasonable acts' for telling it as it's in our regions.

It is in the light of this sad state of affairs that I seek your personal help in letting me have a place to stay until reasonable people come to the helm in Gambia. I do need to be allowed to stay so as to achieve the medical training and above my goals for the rural man. Rest assured that I will continue to do all I can to bring the medical Centre at Njawara, Gambia to fruition.

I hope that this snippet about me and my effort would deserve your helping me get on with my objective for family and villager. Thanks a million for taking time to consider this appeal. Regards
Yours Sincerely
Dr. Alhasan S. Ceesay, MD

Life for me has been a balancing act at dizzying heights on the high wire of life.

Chapter 33

Creation of Manding Medical Centre, Njawara, NBR, the Gambia

When God wants to destroy someone, He first made him an unusual dreamer. So Gandhi had his dream of people solving social deference none violently and Martin Luther king, jr. held onto his admirable dream of children of Jews and Gentile, black and whites holding hands and living in harmony spearheading peaceful cause for mankind.

There are the Albert Schweitzer's and mother Theresa's of the world dreamers who spent their lives believing in their dreams for mankind. My dream, since 1956, was the simple goal of providing medical aid to those far and in remote villages.

The villager, who is forced to walk miles on end to seek medical aid for his already dying child, wife or friend, deserves a better health system. Something I saw in 1956 left an indelible mark in my mind and I have since then asked and prayed that God help me bring part if not full solution to the kind of tragedy that was passing right before me. I was hopelessly unable to give relief except to comfort those involved.

In 1956, while on my way to Saba village, I met an anxious father carrying his son and his almost dead pregnant wife on the back of donkey heading for the health center at Kerewan village, another three or more miles from where I met him.

The child was vomiting yellow stuff, he was sweaty, his eyes were reverted backwards and the pregnant lady groaning every time the mule moves. There was some greenish fluid dripping off her lapper. She could barely hold the ropes controlling the donkey.

I went to Kerewan later that evening and asked about the status of that family, only to be told that the boy passed away half a mile to the dispensary and the lady was referred to the central hospital in Banjul but the family had no money to pay for her transportation nor was the River ambulance available as it was undergoing maintenance at the Dockyard.

To cut a long story short, both child and mother died because of lack of medical facilities or modern medical aid to the villager. One or all of those lives could have been saved and remain beneficial to the country than the fate that befell them. I prayed and grieved with the family for months and redoubled my efforts at school in other to solve such development in future.

I committed myself to medicine from that day on and never regretted making such a challenging decision in my life. Hence, when on the day I was taking the Hippocratic Oath, I not only swore to uphold all therein but to make sure that God help me not to ever deviate from my commitment and promise to be part of the solution in the health services of the Gambia, to foster health education for the villager, and to complement the existing medical facilities in the Gambia as well as ease the shortage of medical service personnel.

To many, except the dreamer, such Erewhons leads to failure as they turn to be white elephants. Some friends tease me by flatly promising to rise from their graves on the opening day of such an Alice in wonderland project. Let me make it crystal clear that I had no illusions about what was needed, or to be done and that the building of the hospital would indeed be a lifetime challenge I am fully ready to grapple with.

There would be a lot of well-wishers but very few will ever want to join until the opening day ceremonies. So first things first, I met an attorney friend Mr. Ousainou Darboe, a villager like me, on September 24, 1992, and pleaded for his assistance with the legal aspects of setting up a charitable foundation, Manding Medical center at Njawara village in the provinces governors elected while he prepared the memorandum and articles of association of Manding Medical Centre at Njawara village. Also, I met with the Lower Badibou district chief, Kitabou Singateh, who by the way was my primary school class mate at Kinte Kunda from 1953 to 1957, the District Authority, Commissioner and the kerewan Area Council. All of whom were more than delighted and did all they could under the law to help me set up a grassroots local advisory committee, which was headed by the commissioner, to assist the board and also let the villagers feel being part of the ongoing project.

At my home village, Njawara, a group organized itself and formed a pioneering committee to formally ask the Alkalo (village head/mayor) and the people of Toro Bahen village to donate the earmarked land between it and Njawara for the sole purpose of establishing the Manding Medical Centre on it.

The land issue was partially cleared by the first week of the appeal. In October 1992 Alkalo Omar Koi Bah of Toro Bahen along with Musa (Njabi) Bah and Sirimang Bah called my brother, Doudu Ceesay, the elders of Toro Bahen and I to officially inform us that the earmarked land of two plots have been donated to me for the sole purpose of erecting a medical center and hospital facility for the villagers of the region and Gambia. We thanked him for his foresight and kindness towards future generations.

I went back to my lawyer, Ousainu Darbor who by then had finished all work needed for the registration of Manding Medical Centre. We are forever indebted to Alkalos Omar Koi, Arfang Bah, Musa (Nyambi) Bah and resident Sirimang Bah, and the people of Toro village. Lastly but not the least our venerable able lawyer Mr. Ousainou Darboe, without whose kindness and legal mind the registration of Manding Medical Centre would have taken longer that it did assisted me.

I also express profound gratitude to Paramount Chief of Lower Badibou District, Kitabou Singateh, the commissioner, and the local district authority for their understanding and willingness to contribute positively towards our goal and growth. I submitted the registration application material to the Attorney General's Chambers at the Justice Department, Banjul, on October 22, 1992 and Manding Medical Centre was officially registered as an incorporated charitable organization under the companies Act, 1959 by the 27th of October 1992.

Manding Medical Centre' certificate of incorporation is number: 224/1992. With the completion of the paper work and registration of the center, I embarked on a blitz of letter writing informing philanthropists and organizations world wide about Manding Medical Centre and the need for assistance or donations of medications, equipments, medical videos with which to teach our cadre and villagers to become health worker or evangelist, or nurses and to help us build the center. To complete the establishment process, after the land was officially ours, I wrote to the following letter to the Ministry of Health informing them of the formation of Manding Medical Centre, a self –help health organization at Njawara, Lower Badibou, North Bank Division, The Gambia. Our temporal address was at 5B Ingram Street in Banjul, capital of the Gambia.

Manding Medical Centre

5B Ingram Street

Banjul, The Gambia

March 2, 1993

Permanent Secretary

Ministry of Health

The Quadrangle

Banjul, The Gambia

West Africa

Dear Permanent Secretary

Re: Application for the establishment of a Medical Centre at Njawara in the North Bank.

We are pleased to bring to attention the setting up of a self-help Health organization in the North Bank Division at Njawara village. The directorates and members of the organization would be more than grateful if the Ministry of Health would allow us establish Manding Medical Centre at Njawara village, Lower Badibou District of the Gambia.

Manding Medical Centre, when fully operational, will provide medical, surgical, gynecological and obstetrics, Pediatrics and other facilities to the villagers. It will also help ease the shortage of medical facilities in that region. Manding Medical Centre will have health education secessions in the villages as an effort to enlighten our youths.

Again, thank you for taking time to consider our application and we certainly look forward to a positive recognition of the need for such a center in the rural sector of the Gambia. Anxiously waiting to hear from your office at your convenience; regards

Yours sincerely

Dr. Alhasan S. Ceesay, MD

Director/Coordinator

Meanwhile the villagers grew more enthused and throngs of them attended our monthly health field trips or clinics. The attendance grew so large that we ended up listing the villages to attend in turn of nine villages per trip. This usually totals to a bit above 1,000 patients at a given visit.

I normally go on weekends with three doctors and at times four volunteer doctors along with nurses' aid Mrs. Mbee Sonko and Ida Njie to assist us do the job. The field trips/clinics start with an announcement by Radio Gambia giving the names of villages expected to attend and at which village health center. The clinic day starts with an early morning breakfast by the team and then a ride to the village health center where we would find the villagers and their sick ones assembled.

Every occasion starts with the offering of prayers and then the various village heads, in attendance help us in organizing the flow of people wanting to be seen by one of our team doctors. In most cases the day goes trouble free but at certain localities the political tension does make it very difficult to have such large groups of people without little arguments. Thanks to the Commissioner (s) for deploying the police or making them available to quell trouble and help us maintain order during these clinics. Commissioner Lamin Koma can tell you how rough things can be at some of these clinic centers.

He was trapped in one of these bad moments of people rushing to be in the front line of the queue to see one our doctors. The Ministry of Health finally sent us the following affirmative reply as thus: -

Ministry of Health & Social services

The Quadrangle

Banjul, The Gambia

Ref.P510/289/01(95)

Dr. Alhasan Ceesay

Manding Medical Centre

5B Ingram Street

Banjul, The Gambia

Dear Dr. Ceesay

RE: Application to establish a Medical Centre at Njawara

I acknowledge receipt of your letter of the 2nd March 1993 on the above-mentioned subject. I wish to inform you that this Ministry has no objection to your application to establish Manding Medical Centre at Njawara.

This initiative is in line with our national health policies and we would render our support in our joint efforts to improve the health of the people.

Signed: N. Ceesay

For Permanent Secretary

After several more field trips it was suggested we apply for a None Governmental Organization (NGO) status. It was believed that if we become and NGO, help would come our way quicker. I went to work on this suggestion and arranged for Tango Secretariat Centre to send one of the United Nations voluntary program officers to come and evaluate our performance relative to the objectives of Manding Medical Centre.

This was accepted and a field trip was set up for September 12 to 22, 1995. Radio Gambia made the announcement well ahead of the time for our arrival and the following was the outcome of that august gathering of September 21 &22, 1995.

Chapter 34

Tango Secretariat trip report

On Manding Medical Centre,

September 21 – 22, 1995

A field trip to Kerewan at the North Bank Division was organized by the Manding Medical Centre Executive Director Dr. Alhasan S. Ceesay in conjunction with Tango Secretariat Centre to see the organization's activities and meet the members before recommending the organization as a member of Tango.

On September 21, 1995, two meetings were organized in two big centers where members gather to air their views and experience from the organization. Alkalos, chiefs, imams, women, men and youths attended these meetings.

The key leadership from five villages in their speeches showed interest and support for the project and organization. Alkalo of Toro Bahen Omar Koi and chiefs donated the land for the constructing of Manding Medical Centre, the hospital and its ancillaries. The two meeting was highly attended and successful.

The Tango (UNV) program officer Mr. Muloshi on behalf of Tango gave a keynote speech on Tango's operations and activities as an umbrella organization and urged members to work hand in hand with the organization in their efforts to develop their villages and North Bank area.

The three meetings with the commissioner during the field trip on our courtesy call were successful and encouraged the executive Director of Manding Medical Centre, Dr. Alhasan Ceesay, to cooperate with the strict, especially the commissioner who is one of the advisors in the local committee.

The commissioner thanked Tango for making the purpose of the mission clear to him and promised that he will try by all means to cooperate with Tango in the area of Technical advice and institution capacity building. Clinic day was organized on September 22, 1995 at Njawara and 150 people attended and got treatments.

RECOMMENDATION

Looking at the caliber of leadership and developmental activities in comparison to some NGOs; tango members Manding Medical Centre organization need consideration since they have already activities with a promising future. Looking at the composition of the Board, they have people with a great vision.

They have strong membership and backup at the grassroots levels. The organization has chosen to do what is right at the right time and their concentration in one area is vital and a good starting point. Any success achieved by any organization depended on good leadership and discipline. Manding Medical Centre has quality leadership and deserves NGO status.

Signed: M. Muloshi

UNV Program Officer

We were delighted by the recommendation made by the United Nations voluntary Program Officer in the Gambia. We redoubled our efforts to contact organizations seeking help worldwide. In between letters and monthly field trips to different select health centers we were blessed with visits from interested friends and groups or representatives of similar organizations in the globe.

I had several telephone calls to Dr. Edward Brown, an official of the World Bank in Washington, D. C. responsible of the bank's health affairs at the time. He was very receptive and had several added discussions with Dentist Melvin George, then Director of Medical and Health Service for the Gambia, on how the bank could help in the financing of the building of Manding Medical Centre.

These talks went on well and Dr. Edward brown gave me his promise and personal commitment to helping the project and that we have to start in a small scale and the building will have to be done in several well planned phases. Dr. Sidi C. Jammeh, an Armitage School colleague promised to help keep the momentum at the bank alive; by consulting and constantly reminding Dr. Brown of the need to help us with the project.

Among our guest were a couple from Colchester, Essex, UK, Lorna V. Robinson and husband Keith Robinson were very impressed by our project and enthusiasm of the ordinary villagers about Manding Medical Centre. They fell in love with the idea and objectives of the self-help health organization and promised to help as much as they could.

We had by this time submitted application for NGO status and ACCNO Secretary replied thus:

ACCNO Secretariat

Dept. of Community Development

13 Mariner Parade

Babjul, the Gambia

September 12, 1994

Ref.CD/ACCNO/Vol3/(183)

Dr. Alhasan S. Ceesay

Director/Coordinator

Manding Medical Centre

P. O. Box 640

Banjul, the Gambia

Dear Sir,

RE: application for an NGO status within the ACCNO framework

Please find enclosed a self-explanatory letter from the Ministry for local government and lands concerning the approval of your application for NGO status.

ACCCNO Secretariat congratulates your organization for successfully completing the registration process and wishes you a fruitful relationship in the field of development. Thank you for your cooperation

Yours Faithfully

Musu Ngujo

For: ACCNO desk Officer

Cc: file & R/File

Replies from our worldwide appeal letters did not pour in money nor did it materialized beyond promises to help in due course. Hence, I decided to open up a pharmacy at my expense at my residence in the Bundung area of Serekunda using the proceeds from its sales to finance the health field trips and activities of the organization.

This meant spending an extra three to four at the pharmacy daily after eight hours at the RVH before rejoining my family. All drugs used for the treatment of patients at our field trip clinics were purchased from sales I made at the Bundung Pharmacy.

A local agency, known as IBAS, lent me D8000, interest free, which was used in buying drugs and paying for transportation for the project's activities. The loan was completely repaid well ahead of the allowed sixteen months period given by IBAS. We are obliged and grateful to Aja Ndey Oley Jobe and management of IBAS for their kindness to assist us at the time.

Just when things were about to be financially complete for us to start the first phase of building the various sections of the hospital, came the unexpected coup d'etat of July 22, 1994. The reaction from would be our donors and supporters or sponsors were swift and equally unexpected.

All those who were considering giving the project a chance sited likelihood of sudden national unrest and instability as reasons for their withdrawal of promised aid and participation while some suggested my waiting until after the transition phase of the coup d'etat before they would reconsider reopening our files with them.

Again it resorted to legend or case of the chicken the egg, which came first as no one, knew when the transition would end and we kept our fingers crossed hoping that daylight will be ours in not far distance. It was a severe blow to our hope and for getting the type of interest and support that was engendered for Manding Medical Centre would be difficult to match after such crisis that occurred in the Gambia.

Many were acting in conjunction with their governments, which were not sure of what the future under military rule would be for the Gambia. All prospective and possible international sources earmarked for Manding Medical Centre were either frozen or evaporated into thin air with the coup leaving me floating in the middle of the ocean of despair without a life jacket except God's merciful hands. I knew the villagers would grow restless if nothing happens in the direction of building the center.

I called an emergency general meeting with members from most of the villages and told them of the new challenge and development and this information not only fell on deaf ears but left their spirits dampened. Interest waxed and waned at some quarters but I kept on trying my best not to be despondent like the others have shown.

I kept the organization alive under very limited funds raised from the pharmacy at Bundung until my trip to the UK in January 2000. Before leaving the Gambia, the Commissioner for north Bank Division and chairman of the local advisory committee for Manding Medical Centre, Mr. Lamin Koma, gave me the following letter to assist me in my fund raising drive while in England and possible other European countries. It read thus:

The Commissioner

Kerewan Village

North Bank Division

The Gambia, West Africa

June 15, 1998

TO WHOM IT MAY CONCERN

I hereby write to testify and confirm that Manding Medical Centre is a self-help health project situated at Njawara village, North Bank Division. As the Commissioner of this division I was elected as the Chairman of the local advisory Committee of the Manding Medical Centre.

As I am concerned, I am aware of this self-help project since it took off the ground, by the able hands of Dr. Alhasan S. Ceesay, a born citizen of Njawara village. The purpose of the establishing of such a medical centre is to provide medical attention/care to all Gambians irrespective of religion, tribe, nationality or gender and age within the country and sub-region.

It is in these regards that this office writes to seek for your assistance in providing support in cash/kind to make this medical centre a reality. I look forward to your continued support and cooperation.

Signed: V. Baldeh

For Commissioner

North Bank Division

The new millennium started with good omen for Manding Medical Centre.

I have been invited to go to Europe and America on a fund raising trip for the center but could not because of my commitment with the Royal Victoria Hospital (RVH). I needed a longer vacation period to be able to travel and keep my job at the same time. Above all my family needed the monetary support, which would fade away if I lost the post at the RVH.

Hence, to my delight and greatest timely occurrence I heard from my long-standing friend in Colchester, Mrs. Lorna V. Robinson, inviting my wife and I to come to the UK to attend the wedding of their younger daughter on January 9th, 2000. Coincidentally, I had just started my annual leave, which was to finish on the 26th of January 2000.

The excitement mounted when we received a fax from the visa officer at the British High Commission in the Gambia requesting that we report to the visa processing office with our passports on Tuesday 8.30 am January 4th, 2000 for processing of our visas for our pending travels to the UK. This took me by surprise because of the casual way we had discussed the possibility of such a trip.

So when we got the telephone call followed by the said fax from the visa section I was caught off guard and had to rush through all the preparations for my wife and I to travel to UK without a second thought on whether adequate arrangements were being made for my eventual pursuit of a postgraduate degree (MRCP) in internal medicine. Hind side has it that I needed to discuss this aspect with the visa concilor and request for eventual student visa status or leave to remain until my completion of the post graduate degree I wanted to pursue.

God's ways and timing are best for every occasion. I was yearning to get a way out of the financial limbo the center ran into since the change of government in the Gambia. Now that opportunity was suddenly thrown on my laps by Lorna Robinson's open-ended invitation for my wife and to attend their daughter's wedding ceremony in the UK.

Interested donors started being weary about Military rule and possible restlessness that may ensue. Hence, Manding Medical Centre literally lost all its prospective overseas support as well as sponsors most of who had cold feet after the July coup d'etat of 2004. I ended up running the center from my meager salary of D1500 or seventy-five pounds sterling per month and of literally hard labour with long hours at a time. The other source was from what little I could make from sales at the Bundung pharmacy. To cut a long story short we were granted visas to travel to the UK.

We left the Gambia on the 6th of January 2000 on a new footing and challenge to bring back some life into Manding Medical center while in England. I got on the ball as soon as the wedding ceremony was over. I obtained a three-year study leave from the Management Board of the Royal Victoria Hospital in Banjul.

This gave me all the time I needed to try to rekindle interest in the center and thereby inject into Manding Medical center cash flow it needed to help us meet or our targeted goal and objective for the farming community in the North Bank Division of the Gambia. It was more like a miracle entering this new concrete and direct ways.

Help from my host Lorna Robinson of Colchester, Essex, UK further anointed my hands. Lorna and I wrote several letters to various places, including celebrities and organizations, most of who replied in the negative because of perception they had about the political climate in Gambia since the coup d'etat of July 22nd 1994. Nonetheless some hinted being interested at a later date, meaning when the solders return to camp.

A few donated small amounts plus hospital items. By now it became clear that we have to counter the perception most, on this side of the isles feel or had about the Gambia at the time.

This dreadful start did not alarm me much for I am fully aware of the wrong information about the average African in the village, who like most, is just a decent human being trying to earn an honest living for himself, family and community.

Villagers are least interested in all the political gimmickry shrouding and clothing their lives. I do not at all blame the rest of world for getting sick and tired of helping and not seeing any tangible good come out of it and worse some African politicians and regimes show no interest in helping move the African people onto better and modern rewarding modalities of life. They offer more lip service than opening avenues for progress.

How many knew that the Ethiopian starvation was politically orchestrated by the then Mangestu regime? Genocide regime and the heartlessness of some African politicians made me feel sick. To remove any possible skeptics regarding Manding Medical Centre and its objectives we decided to have it registered as a charitable organization in the UK under the name of Colchester Friends of Manding charitable trust. The Robinson knew a solicitor who would be so kind to help us with the legal aspect of the registration process with UK charity Commission.

They spoke to Mr. Bruce Ballard of the Birkett long Solicitors to come to our aid. This kind gentleman, like my lawyer friend, Mr. Ousainou Darboe, gladly agreed to help and sent us a draft of the Trust deed. After a series of changes were made on the draft he forwarded our request to be registered in the UK as a charitable organization helping its twin partner or parent group, Manding Medical Centre at Njawara village in the Gambia, West Africa.

Meanwhile, we concentrated our activities through media campaign effort to call attention to existence of Friends of Manding and their desire in building a hospital for Manding Medical Centre at Njawara, the Gambia. Again we ran into a very gentle heart in the person of Miss Helen Anderson of Colchester who was the Community website editor for Essex County.

She went head over heels regarding the idea of helping others so far away when approached by Lorna Robinson. Helen thought the idea wonderful and at the same time helped us have our own website and also had an article published by the Evening Gazette which had a large reader circulation.

In the same vein I got the interest of Dr. Linda Mahon-Daly, Dr. Peter Wilson, Dr. Laurel Spooner, Dr. Richard Spooner, Dr. Philip Murray, Dr. Barbara Murray, Dr. Fredric Payne, who by the way was our Medical superintendent under who I worked at the RVH during the later part of colonial Gambia, along with many surgeries in the Colchester area. These were my Good Samaritans of the day who worked acidulously to make Manding Medical Centre become a reality for the villagers in the Gambia.

Dr. Linda Mahon-Daly helped distribute letters about Manding Medical Centre to nearly all her colleagues in the Colchester Borough and so did Dr. Laurel Spooner. Bless their hearts for kindness and job well done. The news article published by the Evening Gazette brought us another very helpful and kind person, Mr. Malkait singh who is an ophthalmologist and had made several trips to the Gambia before knowing about the Friends of Manding.

He was delighted to join Neville Thompson, Connie Thompson, Lorna Robinson, Keith Robinson, Loenard Thompson, Mark Naylor, Barbara Philips and others as pioneering members of Friends of Manding. Mr. Malkait Singh and I grew to be very good friends and he had since given me lots of personal monetary help to cater for my exams and family back in the Gambia. I am very grateful for interest and kindness, and concern he showed about my family.

A few months after the formation of Friends of Manding, Dr. Laurel Spooner spent a week in the Gambia vacationing and doing some fact finding about the center. During which time she visited Manding Medical Centre at Njawara in the North Bank Division.

The villagers were happy to meet her and thanked her about good work being done in Colchester regarding Manding Medical Centre. Everyone was happy about the news that people in the UK were poised to assist Manding Medical Centre goes forward in its drive to provide medical aid to villagers.

A meeting of member of the Friends of Manding was scheduled for the first week of February 2001. Mean while our solicitor continued pressing for registration of Friends of Manding, which is the arm and Manding Medical Centre's Colchester branch support group, as charity in the UK.

Dr. Laurel Spooner suggested we start with small-scale form of the center and then gradually expand as funds become available. This consideration would be studied in full and deliberated upon by the committee during the forth-coming February meeting.

Chapter 35

What is Manding Medical Centre?

Manding Medical Centre is a self-help village health organization founded by Dr. Alhasan S. Ceesay, located at Njawara village in the North Bank Region of the Gambia, West Africa. Its objective is to provide medical service to the villagers by providing efficient and affordable medical aid to all people in and around the Gambia, especially the rural sector. We are dedicated to relieving suffering and ensure effective treatment for villagers and all attending Manding Medical Centre at Njawara, NBR.

ESTABLISHED

The Manding Medical Centre is founded by Dr. Alhasan Sisawo Ceesay, a native of Njawara village in 1992, because of sheer shortage of medical service to the region and the preponderance of premature deaths by children from Malaria, malnutrition, diarrhea, and worm infestations. These childhood maladies account for almost 25% of Gambian children's death before the ripeful age of five years.

The Gambia Ministry of Health officially recognized the Centre in 1995 and prior to which it became a None Governmental Organization (NGO) on September 12th, 1994.

In addition, the Manding Medical Centre now has Friends of Manding Charitable Trust, Colchester, Essex, UK as its arm and liaison in the UK and the European Union countries. The Friends of Manding is a registered charity in England and Wales.

Its registration number is 1088136 since August 21, 2001. In similar development and purpose, Dr. Avery Aten heads the Friends of Manding Alpena Charitable Trust, Alpena, Michigan, UAS since May 2005.

MISSION STATEMENT

Suffering in another human being is a call to the rest of us to stand in fellowship. It requires us to be there and it is a mystery, which demands the spirit of caring, sharing and our presence. Our duty as healthcare professionals is providing medical care, which is a fundamental right of all human beings.

This village health organization is dedicated to providing medical aid to the rural sector and farming community in the Gambia. It will compliment the health service in the Gambia in addition it will promote preventive medicine in the hinterland of the Gambia.

MEMBERSHIP

Well over twenty thousand villagers, comprising of farmers, village heads, and chiefs, the Kerewan Area Council, Commissioners and local District Authority are now fully active enthusiastic members of Manding Medical Centre. All are welcomed to join the endeavors of the center. People from the rest of the globe are more than welcomed to participate or share with us our dream in bringing much needed medical service to people in desperate state because of lack of medical facilities.

Activities

Manding Medical Centre tries to alleviate some of the above mentioned health problems and situations by having bimonthly health field trips/clinics to villages teaching them about health, preventive medicine and hygiene that would help reduce the number infected and the vectors responsible for these diseases.

We encourage antenatal and postnatal attendance of clinics by mothers and we treat the sick amongst them with minimum charge to not so elderly and pregnant young ladies. The service is free to children, the very elderly, and the indigent needing emergency treatment. The rest pay amounts well below tat in private practice. Money accrued is subsequently used to buy drugs with which to treat the patients and for other projects of the center. When in cession the center treats well more than 1000 patients per field trip to the villages.

We provide free information and advisory service on aids and sexually transmitted diseases (STDs) to the young, all patients, their relatives and friends. We also plan to have a Nursing School in due course to augment not only staff but also the government health centers when the need arises.

Immediate goal and appeal

The villagers are very enthused about the center and Toro Bahen village, next to Njawara village, has donated two plots of land for the building of the center and its ancillary units, which is now leased to manding medical center for ninety-nine years. More than 2000 children die tragically from malaria and other childhood ailments stated above for shortage of health services.

We are eager to start building the children' and maternity wings of the proposed Gambia General Hospital at Manding Medical Centre and do need raise the required 900,000 pounds sterling to accomplish our goal. Ten bags of cement cost thirty pounds sterling or $60 (sixty us dollars). Also we would be most grateful if we could be assisted with medicines and equipment to facilitate our work.

Hence we implore you to kindly support our yearning to build the children' and maternity wings of Manding Medical Centre. We are dedicated to providing medical aid to the villager, especially children.

We are investors in people and you are invited to join the endeavors of Manding Medical Centre at Njawara village, the Gambia, West Africa. Help us make a difference and beacon of hope for the villagers. Please give generously. Today's hope can be tomorrow's reality.

We want to contribute positively towards the health services of the Gambia, and with this center in place it will create greater health awareness and privation by the villagers. Cash contributions of any amount should be sent in the name of Manding Medical Centre, to the Friends of Manding charitable Trust, 82 Finchingfield Way, Blackheath, Colchester, Essex, CO2 OAU, and England.

It is vital to be certain that Dr. Alhasan S. Ceesay is informed of your contribution via email thus: alhasanceesay@hotmail.co.uk Your kindness and humane consideration to help save lives will always be deeply appreciated and grateful for by the villagers, the Gambia and I.

Overseas links

The Friends of Manding in Colchester, Essex County, UK, is a local group of residents, doctors, and nurses who regularly visited the Gambia and is in support of Manding Medical Centre.

Manding medical center through the auspices of the Friends of Manding recently received recognition and registration by the UK Charity Commission. They serve as support and our liaison in the Europe Union. The Friends of Manding in behalf of Manding Medical Centre at Njawara has been entered in the central Register of charities with effect from August 21, 2001; the registration number is 1088136 for England and Wales. Also, a similar charitable trust, the Alpena Friends of Manding Charitable Trust of Michigan, USA, has been established in Alpena, Michigan in June 2006. It's headed by Dr. Avery Aten a resident physician chairman of the Women and newborn of the Alpena Region Community Health along with the medical community of Alpena.

Chapter 36

Manding Medical Centre Milestones

Manding Medical Centre has been in my mind's drawing board since the early 1950s but it took off in earnest when I returned to the Gambia, after graduating from medical school in 1992. The Centre is registered as a charity with the Attorney general's Office, Department of Justice, Banjul, The Gambia, since 1993. The Gambia Ministry of Health also recognized it in the same year. Toro Bahen village, Lower Badibou, NBD, Gambia, donated two huge plots of land for the location of the center in 1993.

Our none governmental (NGO) status was approved in 1994. On September 21, 1995 Tango Secretariat sent a United Nations voluntary program Officer, Mr. Muloshi on field trip to evaluate the organizational and extent of support for Manding Medical Centre at Njawara village. Mr. Muloshi's recommendation after two days field trip to the region stated thus; "Looking at the caliber of leadership and development activities to some NGO Tango members in comparison to Manding Medical Centre, the organization need consideration since they have already activities with a promising future.

Looking at composition of the Board, they have people with a vision. They have strong membership and backup at grass root levels. The organization has chosen to what is right at the right time and their concentration in one area is vital and good starting point.

Any success achieved by any group or organization depends on good leadership and discipline. Manding Medical Centre has high quality leadership and deserves NGO status". It was not until my travels to the UK in 2000 that the Friends of Manding Charitable Trust was formed and registered as charity in England and Wales by the UK Charity Commission.

Friends of Manding is the extended arm of Manding Medical Centre at Njawara, The Gambia. They serve as our liaison in the UK and the European Union. Please browse thus: friendsofmandinggambime.btck.co.uk, to learn more or for further information about our work and organization.

We are still on fund raising activities to earn enough to enable us build the children' and maternity units of the hospital at Manding Medical Centre at Njawara. In May 2005, 11 American students and their instructor Mr. Thomas Ray visited Manding Medical Centre at Njawara. Additionally, input from has now resulted in Alpena City, Michigan, USA, twining by proclamation with Njawara and Kinte kunda villages in Gambia respectively on the 5th

of December 2005. In June 2006, Dr. Avery Aten, Chairman of the Women and Newborn of Alpena Region Health Community along with the medical community of Alpena commenced processing application for a charitable Trust to be named Alpena friends of Manding Charitable Trust, Michigan, USA.

This will soon be finalized and up and running to help Dr. Alhasan Ceesay in the provision of medicine and educational assistance to schools in the Lower Badibou district, the Gambia, West Africa. In August 2008, Dr. Alhasan Ceesay and the Badibou Cultural Dance Troupe will visit Alpena and other cities in Michigan for fund raising drive to enable the building of the Manding Medical Centre children and maternity units at Njawara village.

Dr. Richard Bates, an Obynge, and a number of medical professionals involved in obstetrics and Gynecology at Alpena, Michigan joined Manding Medical Centre's crusade on 17/08/07. Manding Medical Centre became a template for districts elsewhere and villagers to nurture, develop further and handover to the next generation. This None Governmental Health Organization epitomizes a developmental watchtower for the region. Manding medical center at Njawara village is now a pulsating source of hope, jobs, training and superb medical service to the region.

Everyone knows that government alone does not move things fast enough. Society must be radical and pragmatic to pitch into its development. We know all too well that the developed world got where it's because private efforts were self prophetic and projects like Manding Medical Centre goes long ways to initiate and stimulate community to work together for a positive agenda for its people.

Manding Medical Centre is a positive good that help our regions to cross the road. We thank everyone for making it possible that our center became a platform and guide in rejuvenating our regions. We now provide medical service to all Gambians and none Gambians domiciled in the Gambia.

We will create more jobs as need arises. This was the reason why I gave my life's comfort for reward that will benefit most needy villagers. It came through determination and kindness of many people worldwide. There are some things only governments can do but together communities through collective initiatives can achieve at least fifty percent of their developmental needs in addition to government effort.

Chapter 37

An appeal to the International community

Dear Readers,

The above information about Manding Medical Centre is included in this work only hoping that it will help spread the word more extensively and draw awareness to a greater community of people and readers of my work. It's believed that lots of good people out there may want to participate or give to the cause and goal of the center should they be aware of its existents for the villagers.

Hence, I am appealing for help and participatory support from all able to extend their hearts to make this much needed medical endeavor to come to fruition for the rural sector of the Gambia. Who knows you might even end up coming to bask in our beautiful sea sides and relish Gambian generosity.

Music for me is reaching out to help others and my patients are yearning for your kind participation and donation in cash/kind. Thanks a million for considering our appeal. God blesses your heart(s). I write with believe that by it money can be generated to provide a much needed medical service to the rural sector.

Writing about the Manding Medical Centre may course some Good Samaritan and any wanting to leave foot prints on the sand of time for a good cause to come to our assistance to help us meet the goals of the center at Njawara village, the Gambia, West Africa. My head, heart and soul are devoted to my family, the Gambia and Manding Medical Centre. It is not a God given calling but a mere conviction that our rural folks deserve better health service than currently available and hence human calling to want to contribute positively to bring resolution of some of our rural health service inadequacies.

I never had an angel come down to me nor have I ever heard the voices of God saying, "Ceesay, you must do so and so" as many mocked Manding Medical Centre emanated from sheer conviction that it is a dutiful way of doing the right thing for curbing premature deaths of children before reaching 5 years of life from malaria, water born diseases, and warm infestations; and in the same vein providing both pre and postnatal care to the pregnant. Hence, portions of proceeds of sales in all my work go to help meet the center's operational costs and in providing scholarship to indigent indigenous rural candidates due course return to serve rural Gambia wishing to read for a medical degree or agriculture and Medicine. Signed: Dr. Alhasan S. Ceesay, MD

Email: alhasanceesay@hotmail.com

Chapter 38

A tribute to Lorna V. Robinson

As friends and family bit farewell to a unique, caring, sharing and rare angel of mercy, allow me share a snippet or bird's eye view about Lorna Valerie Robinson with whom I started the push for Colchester Friends of Maning Charitable Trust to serve as liaison in the European Community for Manding Medical Centre at Njawara Village, Gambia, West Africa.

Mrs. Lorna Robinson and I met through her job as a general nurse at the then Essex County General Hospital in Colchester in 1990, when I was a trainee doctor at the Essex County hospital. She and husband Keith Robinson became my friends and they visit my family in Gambia annually.

In my village Lorna becomes the modern Pipe Piper of Hamlin town as children with bright eyes swamp her from all sides. One could hear chorus of children singing, "Auntie Lorna is here. Welcome to Gambia, Auntie Lorna". The Robinson's became my England and together we set to catch a dream of providing medical aid and service to Gambian villagers in the North Bank Region. Lorna and I have since 2000 worked acidulously to make the coveted dream of providing medical service come to fruition for the villagers.

It was Lorna Robinson's joint efforts with, nurses, doctors Laura Spooner, Richard Spooner, Barbara Murray, Philip Murray, Linda Malhon-Daly, and Malkait Singh along with Colchester residents Connie Thompson, Neville Thompson, and Keith Robinson which led to the formation of the Colchester Friends of Manding Charitable Trust, which, with help of a solicitor was registered in England and Wales as a charity by the UK Charity Commission in August 2001 and our charity number is 1088136.

The Colchester Friends of Manding Charitable Trust serves as extension of Manding Medical Centre at Njawara and doubles as our liaison in the European Community. Lorna spent countless weekends either selling material such as toys, cloths, coats or anything she could lay her hands on as long as she believes it will generate money for the building of the children and maternity units of the Manding Medical Centre at Njawara in Gambia.

She continued to promote the course of the above by holding weekend bazaars at different places in Colchester and with ladies at Bingos. Influence of this Good Samaritan group in Colchester reverberated and led to the formation of a similar charity group in America, with Dr. Avery Aten heading that effort.

Through his leadership emanated the Alpena friends of Manding Charitable Trust in Michigan, USA, and it was approved in 2005. All of which came by because Lorna, the lady of mercy, would not rest while the indigent goes without the most basic things in life. Lorna was one willing and delighted to help others.

She used to say, "In life we most extend our hearts to others and with compassion reach the needy." For my villagers she was hope and knowledge that someone so far away, whom they have never met, cared about them. Lorna was concerned that millions suffer needlessly for not having means of proper healthcare, clean and safe water, food, and good shelter etc.

She more than any wanted to help the villagers from descending into a downward spiral of deepening healthcare deprivation. When am in low spirit she would quote Albert Schweitzer, "Any who proposes to do good must not expect people to move stone away from his path but most accept his lot if even a few more are placed on his way". It was this unique caring angel the villagers and I lost on the third of March 2010.

Loosing Lorna V. Robinson left me feeling having lost one of the best persons, outside of my family, I ever known. She was a kind soul of unswerving determination to share the little she had with others less fortunate needing help.

Lorna stood by my cause in thick and thin moments of my stay in the UK, when most had given up on my mission for the villagers and me. The provision of medical care to the rural sector in Gambia is more than a responsibility; it is a sacred duty and trust to me.

It is a call I have dedicated my life and would work on archiving it for as long as it may take to accomplish. I will never let my villagers or the memory of Lorna V. Robinson down because of trepidations and like her I believe in looking to the well being of the less fortunate, especially villagers. One cares on trying, upon reflecting on all the children and villagers who sincerely need this healthcare.

Hence, I repeat, Lorna Robinson, no trepidation will stop or hold me back. Finally, my family, villagers, in fact the entire Gambia and I miss and deeply mourn her premature and untimely departure from mother earth. May she rest in eternal peace with her maker and may we the living without fail or fear able to follow her high and shining examples of the indefatigable, Good Samaritan she was in life. I hope you will join me to keep goals of Manding Medical Centre of providing medical aid to villagers and Lorna's memory and legacy alive for others to copy. Lorna thanks for sharing your life with us and for loving us. A million thanks and goodbye for now!

Signed: Dr. Alhasan S. Ceesay, MD,

Founder/co-ordinator

Manding Medical Centre,

Njawara, Lower Badibou,

The Gambia, West Africa.

Email: alhasanceesay@hotmail.com

Chapter 39

An ode to my Family

Family is no oddment but one's dearest flesh and blood. This ode goes to my kith and kin of the Njawara Ceesay kunda dynasty. First, praises be to the Almighty God for letting us descend to this Garden of Eden through Sisawo Ceesay and his brother Abdulie (Baba Salah) Ceesay and their respective wives.

Both were devoted, loving parents who taught us to seek knowledge, faith and be responsible participants in our communities wherever we may find ourselves. Equal thanks go to our mothers who stood by these men and helped them steer us in the right direction for a better tomorrow.

Binta Ceesay is now the oldest matriarch of the family and our gratitude and appreciation goes to her for enduring all of us through the decades. She has always been a buffer and like our parents a very straightforward person who does not take sides when it comes to dealing with us her younger siblings. Bravo to Binta Ceesay for being an envied bright example to the family.

Dodou Ceesay is the oldest patriarch male child in the family. He, although a mandinka, having spent three quarters of his life within the Fula tribe tends to perceive life in that light. He is my brother of the same father and mother. He is a very quite and shrewd fellow and well versed in the Quran. He is in fact the Oustas at Njawara School. He too is moral support to all of us despite our philosophical divergences.

One of his daughters, Dr. Fataou Ceesay, is now a welcome addition to the family's pride of doctors. While her sister Yaramu Ceesay is a qualified nurse currently manning one of the private clinics in the Kombo area. The elder of his children Alagie Mama Ceesay is now a drug enforcement officer in the Kombo districts.

I am next oldest in the family in this Njawara Ceesay Kunda clan and there is enough about me in my books that can fill the back of a stamp. I just believed in reaching out to touch others and bring help, hope and relief to their lives.

Hence one of the reasons why I became a medical doctor and proprietor of a village self-help health NGO, Manding Medical Centre at Njawara village, north Bank Region, the Gambia, West Africa. My elder daughter, Famatanding Ceesay has just been accepted to commence her premed studies at my former Alma Mata, Alpena Community College, Alpena in Michigan USA.

She would be leaving shortly for the United States. Omar Ceesay, the gentleman of the family, is next oldest and a headmaster at one of the Primary Schools in the Kombo enclave. The guy is so nice and gentle that I used to tease him as Baba Sallah incarnated. His attitude is carbon copy of his father Abdulie Baba Sallah Ceesay. The mannerism, laughing, and humaneness are akin to none other than Babab Sallah Ceesay.

He is not the arbitrator but the easygoing fellow of the Njawara Ceesay Kunda dynasty. Ismaila Sisay, the genes of his mother persist in him. He is a nice fellow but of a no nonsense type among the clan. Thank God he is not violent but does not let anyone push him around. He is forth in line when it comes to affairs of the clan. He is also a headmaster in the Kombo enclave. He like his father Baba Sallah Ceesay is skilful entrepreneur and at times too competitive. He now runs his own private school in the Kombo.

Our fifth in line male child of the Njawara Ceesay Kunda clan is none other than Ebou Ceesay. He is a technocrat and very gifted electronics. He once manned the Gambia's earth satellite for years before becoming Director of Operation at Gamtel House in Banjul, capital of the Gambia, West Africa. If there be any financial endowment or call luck in the family, it went to this fellow.

We all praise him for help he quietly gives to the members of the clan at various times for various reasons. Ousman Ceesay, nick named "OS" is the youngest living male child of the clan. He too is faring well but another carbon copy of the old man Baba Sallah Ceesay. He is easy going but not a laidback fellow.

He is a hard worker and a not cutthroat competitor. No, no I am not forgetting our sisters. Jainaba Ceesay is next older lady to matriarch Binta Ceesay. Jainaba is one girl that epidermises and archetype of her mother. We have had our moments but still remain good friends and team members of the clan.

Isaou Isata Ceesay is our last sister on Sisawo Ceesay's linage. She is warm at heart and very easy to relate to, even though the Fula syndrome shrouds her. She participates fully in all activities of the Njawara Ceesay Kunda clan.

Mariam Ceesay is Huley Ndongo's elder daughter for Baba Sallah Ceesay. Mariam is an easygoing girl. She has amiable attitude and personifies the old man Baba Sallah. She too is contributor to the clan. Last but not the least is Hawa Ceesay, the youngest girl of Huley Ndogo. She is very intelligent and smooth operator. She has an exemplary character but fierce defender of her tuff. She too contributes to day-to-day function of the Njawara Ceesay Kunda Clan.

All said and done there is no way I will exchange any of the above for another kin. They are very kind, team like most of the time, and share lot of good qualities and examples to help propel the next generation of the Ceesay family at Njawara.

We are not financially rich but have abundant love, care, and participatory zeal than most in the **village.** Bravo to Njawara Ceesay Kunda. May God grant us unity, longevity and above all prosperity with peace in this life.

Chapter 40

The Epilogue

Dear reader, in the final analysis one can see from the above sample of activities that a village Bantaba is a forum almost larger than itself where the locals make epic decision, if not history, in pursuit of cohesive and peaceful living. The above hotchpotch, farrago or call it mélange of topics are thoroughly discussed and sticky points ironed out by debating openly until all or most agree with a final solution to a problem which may be of marital in nature, tribal, or out right dispute about landownership.

 It's a place where people talk openly as they express their views on topics or tradition. Here disputes are jointly and fairly brought to reconciliatory term catering to all involved. Hence freedom of speech is highly adhered to in local villages, as has just been portrayed. The creeping in of Western style settling of disputes is now encroaching on a very sophisticated effective African way that the villagers used to handle very complicated case as would be perceived in today's jurisprudence concept. It is my hope this work opens doors that were left partially ajar by the colonial era.

The world needs to know the real truth about Africa from fiction that most outsiders and writers tend to lean on in an effort to entertain instead of presenting true facts to their readers and audiences. The above intoxicating cocktails of Bantaba activities and stories call them classic village parliament in action, all reminds us of a highly sophisticated and advance democratic governance societies Africa had always enjoyed.

The ignorant still insist in stereotyping as well as scapegoat the African as primitive in primordial times. These stories are the ancient and powerful way Africans keep records as these interprets our world. It is my hope that releasing the village Ginny from the bottle as above would inform at the same time entertains readers.

It shows how village life reflexes balance and harmony amongst people and nature. In short, love and communal action energies villagers. The fascination in living in a village is that one soon finds oneself surrounded by endearing people that root one with nature.

The villagers have control about themselves caped with an unfailing backup system from the communities. The positivism of the villager emanate from self-love and duty-bound obligation of being part of the community and the neighbors. Culturally they are tired to the same umbilical code of behavior and norms. You are always a welcomed guest to Njawara village.

I hope you will, in due course, treat yourself to the gratifying visit and satisfactory discovery that the American students' trip revealed. My Alpena by and large mirrors the Alpena Community student Leadership class's Njawara experience. God blesses the sister-city relationship between Alpena, Michigan, Njawara and Kinte Kunda villages in Gambia, respectively. Logo on www.friendsofmandinggambimed.btck.co.uk to learn more about our projects for the region. Again, I reiterate profound gratitude to all who purchase this work as portions of proceeds from it will go to help us build the children and Maternity units of the Manding Medical Centre's The Gambia General hospital and to, in future, provide scholarship to indigent rural candidates wishing to read for a medical or agricultural degree and return to serve the rural sector of the Gambia, West Africa.Cheers and thanks a million for believing and participating in our dream of providing medical aid to villagers.

Chapter 41

I rest my case

Paul in a letter to Timothy 2 said, "I have fought a good fight, I have finished my course, and I have kept the faith." I hand this work for publication for you to be judge of the ravages of the years and how my life was that of extreme ups and downs. In reality, I am very grateful to God even though my life met with various misfortunes, the most unbearable being the delay in my becoming a physician.

My life as witnessed in these pages was an assembly of trials and tribulation emanating from roadblocks placed on my path by inhuman laws and unfortunate dark circumstances. Life has taught me to submit to divine decrees, whatever they may be from God.

I feel on the whole overly rewarded and delivered even though I had no family here in England nor was I as lucky as others who can feel and experience the warmth of their wives and children on daily basis. I succumbed to it as the way things were going to be for me and lived with this state of affairs while in Manchester, England. I experienced various turns of fate, enough for ten elephant loads, while on the little moat of the silver sea called England.

With my travels I was able to see Europe, the Americas and have learnt a great deal from it as well as experienced numerous unforeseen adventures thrown on my path. My life in England was pain; fear of deportation, hunger, extreme poverty due to joblessness, solitude and missing my wife and children I loved dearly. I had a huge sense of duty in relation to the villagers and was not ready to fail them because of personal comfort or pleasures.

Consequently Manding Medical Centre and benefits to be accrued from it became my most if not the only occupation and direction in life. Here is Manding Medical Centre if managed well it will do justice to rural health service for the next generation of Gambians to build upon. The medical center is now a recognized charity in both the United Kingdom and America.

I am committed to serve the villagers so that life of the children and young people would be better than mine when I was young. I hope Manding Medical Centre becomes a model testimony of the boy from Njawara village who doggedly struggled to become a doctor and despite various twists of life is able to provide medical aid and service to villagers in rural Gambia. May be this will strengthen some other fellow to strive to do better than I did to bring health and happiness to the region.

I hope my adventure persuades youngsters that man is capable of a lot more than he thinks he is capable of. Our footprints must be inspirational to give heart to new coming Gambian generations. Twenty years ago none would dream of thinking me becoming an author or to challenge powers as I did in this little frame and life of mine. I met a beautiful Maraka girl while I was in Monrovia, Liberia, West Africa.

Fatou Koma is daughter of Elhaj Ansuman Koma and Jalian Ture of Kindia, Guinea Conakry. Her positive attitudes towards me lead our meeting on weekends at Cousin Sainabou Jobe's home. We started going out together and very soon I had the courage to ask her hand in marriage.

There was no bone of contention with regards for my love for her. She was the darling of my heart at first sight and I was not going to let a fly land on her from that day onwards. We had a simple wedding because her father did not quite approve of me because of fear for his uneducated but very pretty daughter being dump at one stage of the marriage for another educated city girl.

I, in the long run, allied his fears and he ended up being one of my best friends and confidants I had up to the day he went to his maker. Fatou Koma-Ceesay and I are blessed with three beautiful daughters, princesses Famatanding Ceesay, Binta Ceesay and Roheyata Ceesay.

All of who, unlike me, had their schooling start at the age of five. The elder girl is aspiring to become a doctor and had been admitted to start her premed courses at Alpena Community College in Alpena, Michigan, USA. Together Fatou Koma-Ceesay, the children and I went through all the tragedy of hunger, poverty and other sad experiences my sojourn in the quest of the Golden flees for the villager brought to us.

 Fatou Koma-Ceesay initially hated Manding Medical Centre for she felt it consumed me and took me away from her and the children. The call got me entangled in a web of unfortunate circumstances and laws. The marriage had at one point almost spiralled to its end as wife' move became questionable. Nonetheless she remained a good mother and wife who took care of the girls in my absence. My mother in-law was battered by confusion and as to why Fatou stuck it out with me under such immense hardship.

Love is stronger glue! We loved each other and so we were able to stand by the other in good or bad times and my trip to England was the worst ever in our connubial life. It caused great turbulences in the marriage but I stuck with it for love's shake and the children who I love dearly. Today, we are back together as family under the same roof while planning and supporting future of our darling girls.

God bless Fatou Koma-Ceesay's heart and be reassured of endless love I have for her. For now Dalliance said it best for me when he said, "Say of me what you will and the morrow will judge you, and your words shall be a witness before its judgment and a testimony before it justice. I came to say a word and I shall utter it. Should death take me ere I give voice; the morrow shall utter it. That which alone I do today shall be proclaimed before the people in days to come."

I wrote with the hope the life enshrined herein will serve not only as an inspiration to the despondent but a lesson never to allow this sort of experience it passed through this planet. I wrote in the hope that life enshrined in my books will serve not only as an inspiration to the despondent and downtrodden but a lesson never to allow this sort of experience it passed through this planet.

I wrote because I felt that my life has something worth revealing to the world to engender tolerance and understanding between people and their governments. I risked revealing today for all of us to learn from it and move to a better and rewarding future. Among the forces of life is one that stands a certain lofty peak a few is endowed with or able to explore its heights.

Ambition urges us to leave the lower surface of earth where the ordinary people live and ascend to heights that pierce the heavens. This mission has led to numerous Erie paths but for me this Pell-mell towards a better medical service for the neglected villager was a worthwhile adventure.

I am profoundly grateful and indebted to my wife Fatou Koma-Ceesay and our daughters, princesses Famatanding Ceesay, Binta Ceesay and Roheyata Ceesay for enduring all the pains that we went through in thick and thin times during my sojourn to America and England. Also my deepest gratitude goes to Cousin Yata Sey-Corr for helping keep my family hopeful.

God bless her heart eternally. I forgive my own brothers and sisters who refused to cater for my family in my absence. Hello, hats off to Roheyata Corr-Sey and Kombo Sey kunda!

THE WAY OF A DREAMER

Back in the Gambia a friend decried my efforts as nothing but a dream that I persistently chased. I let such observers know that it only takes time before my dream become fruitful. Here are a few examples: I left the Gambia in 1967 as a nurse and returned; after insurmountable roadblocks as a medical doctor. While practicing in the Gambia I further created two worthy entities, namely (1) The Gambia Health Credit Union, which today provides needed financial assistance to all health workers i.e. Nurses and Health Inspectors country wide. (2) In addition I created NGO Manding Medical Centre at Njawara village, Lower Badibou to help provide a much needed medical aid and service free of charge to villagers who could not afford to pay private clinics. With the help of visiting doctors the centre has treated more than 9000 villagers free of charge since its inception in 1993.

On returning to the UK, I again with help of resident nurses and doctors in Colchester Essex setup the Friends of Manding Charitable trust in Colchester UK. This was recognized and registered as a charity in England and Wales by the UK- charity Commission in 2002.

In the midst of which I published my first book 'The Legend Against all Odds' and now has published more than thirty eight novels. To further cement my goal for the villager I was able to convince the Alpena City Council to form a sister city link with Njawara and Kinte Kunda villages in the Lower Badibous of the Gambia in 2005.

This was made easier after my being awarded on May 5th, 2005 'Distinguished Graduate Award' by Alpena Community College. My web site: friends of Manding gambimed continues to lure people to Njawara to see what help they could give the villager.

Today, I am not only an author of several books; Google search: Dr. Alhasan Ceesay/books to view of purchase as contribution to rural healthcare; portions or sales from these books go to support goals of Manding medical Centre at Njawara. I am indeed a dreamer and will continue to dream fir my people.

If the above is dream then here is another step to help see through me. I am humble to let you know I am now a Publisher and my company in the UK is 'PUBLISH KUNSA LTD' and one can have their work published by logging on to our web site; www.publishkunsa.com. Again two pounds sterling from any book published by my company goes towards scholarships and rural healthcare as stipulated in terms of contract we would work on manuscripts. Dreams must be activated and not wasted.

I cannot fly without wing but can make artificial wings to let reach higher hits that loafers never can dream of. Allow the dream to force you into action. Yes, I too have a dream, which is simply that every hamlet in the Gambia be bequeathed good healthcare, safe drinking water, enough food and chance to a solid education for every child.

Yes. Education is power and a mover. I sacrificed my life to endure depravity, humiliation and solitude in other to bring medical aid to villagers. With all these I am busy trying to get more medical skills and experience before heading to Gambia, home , sweet home.

With this tit-bit I can freely and willingly encourage you to dream but not to let it remain at that. A life with trials or challenge is like an orchestra without conductor and it very defeating if not boring indeed. One must act for the good of self and any community we find our selves.

An old village sage once advice that 'A good person and at best a leader never yield to failure but only learns from it to move forward. Grand Pa Bajoja Ceesay told me that; "One willing to do good should not expect people to remove obstacles or stones from their path; but such leaders must accept it calmly in the event these place more boulders on our way."

This is what a dream turns out. At first it becomes a lonely avenue full of heartaches, which eases gradually as the good things unfold from one's relentless efforts to make the dream becomes fruitful and rewarding.. Simple its life 99.9% very hard work full of stumbling.

Do not we all dream of going to heaven? Well the path to such respites need challenging theological and spiritual discipline. Hence we earthly dreamers dabble with ideas of landing on Mars and eventually colonizing it. So allow me ask, what is your dream for mankind, especially Africa?

Can Africa ever be free of ignorance, self subtenant, corruption and misuse of the tribe? These just few multipronged toxic dragon heads African must dream to remove from our midst. With better education and discipline Africa can overcome and progress. Dreamers are doing utmost to slay the pestilent dragon hindering life in the villages of rural Africa.

We must remove the monster of retro ration for the shake of the future generation. Again grandpa Bajoja Ceesay advices that we stay the good cause and never be taken by detractions. I am no millionaire but have a million dreams worthy of pursuing for my people. Would you dream along with me? Glad to let you know hard work yields rewarding fruits.

Dream and be in control of not only your own life but be a source of hope and inspiration while contributing positively to your community. Do not be carried along by current get rich quick and live selfishly. Life is to be shared even with dreamers. Time is not mine and life will continue for the villager. Success comes slowly and brings with it contagious hope that serves as blue print for other.

The fate of mankind is up to each of us. Do not succumb to idleness. Use youthful opportunity to develop out of ignorance, and corruption by having courage to bring change to the people. Be the change you want in others. Expect resistance on your path to bring change. A useful proxy in fulfilling a dream is not letting it wane away. Always think it possible and work hard at its realization.

Be warned to think what could be done and not that which cannot be archived. Matrix of success lies in hard work with guided ski full knowledge. I will work on my dream and morrow will be my judge along with benefits accrued from it. I hope my last footprints of my journey on earth will inspire people towards doing well and sharing their worth with others. From one villager to another may this wish be true for rural Gambia.

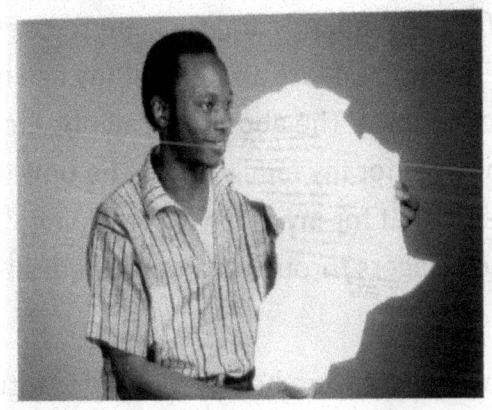

Dr. Ceesay holding Africa

Chapter 42

My endearing life and about the author

For a while in my native innocence all I had was erudition and wit, which always misfired. Everything I touched came to nothing but failure, whatever I tried to achieve came crashing down on my head. At any given moment some mishap befalls me and nothing surprised me anymore.

I took my current plight with stride and smiled as fate taunts me. I remain poor but my in extinguishable strong will enabled me face life squarely and took me through these dark days. The twist of fate abated but my age had advanced beyond retrieval. The above apocalyptic life is indeed trying moments for my family and I. The only passion I have, aside that for my family, is providing medical service to villagers through Mandlng Medical Centre.

My dream spawns better future health service for future generations. I never write expecting a best seller but to inform and share ideas. I am certain readers will enjoy my work, as it may enlighten as well entertain than most books found in bookstores. It is hoped that in writing another would be spared of very sad experience I had before being able to provide much needed medical aid/service to Gambian villagers.

Browse: www.beehive.totalessex.co.uk/gambimed or contact alhasanceesay@hotmail.com

To view/purchase books: amazon.com Dr. Alhasan Ceesay books.

You are invited to join a live saving cause for a much-needed medical service in behalf of Gambian villagers.

Mrs. Fatou Koma-Ceesay

Dr. Ceesay and his father, Mr. Sisawo Ceesay

Mrs. Famatanding Tarawale, Mother

Mrs. Binta Ceesay, sister

Dr. Ceesay and wife Fatou Koma-Ceesay

Miss Famatanding Ceesay, Daughter

CHAPTER 43

TEMPLATE FOR REGIONAL DEVELOPMENT

Manding Medical Centre became a template for districts elsewhere and villagers to nurture, develop further and handover to the next generation. This None Governmental Health Organization epitomizes a developmental watchtower for the region.

Manding medical center at Njawara village is now Badibous' pulsating source of hope, jobs, training and superb medical service to the region. Every one knows that government alone does not move things fast enough. Society must be radical and pragmatic to pitch into its development. We know all too well that the developed world got where its because private efforts were self prophetic and projects like Manding Medical Centre goes long ways to initiate and stimulate community to work together for a positive agenda for its people.

Manding Medical Centre is a positive good that help our regions to cross the road. We thank every one for making it possible that our center became a platform and guide in rejuvenating our regions. We now provide medical service to all Gambians and none Gambians domiciled in the Gambia. We will create more jobs as need arises. This was the reason why I gave my life's comfort for reward that will benefit most needy villagers. It came through determination and kindness of many people worldwide.

There are some things only governments can do but together communities through collective initiatives can achieve at least fifty percent of their developmental needs in addition to government effort.

Miss Binta Ceesay, Daughter

Miss Roheyata Ceesay, Daughter

CHAPTER 44

LORNA V. ROBINSON: AN ANGEL OF MERCY

There are certain moulds God broke them moments after He finished making them. Mrs. Lorna V. Robinson was one of these unique, caring, sharing and rare angels of mercy. Mrs. Lorna Robinson and I met through her job as general nurse at the then Essex County General hospital in Colchester, Essex County in 1990, when I was a trainee doctor at the hospital. She and husband Keith Robinson became my friends as far back as in the 1990s and one of their annual pilgrimages is visiting my family in the Gambia, West Africa. This benevolent couple has since been my Colchester if not my England.

Together we set to catch a dream of providing medical aid and service to Gambian villagers. I left at the end of my training to serve my country in 1992. In December 1999 Mrs. Lorna Robinson sent an invitation for my wife and I to attend wedding of Miss Fiona Robinson, her younger daughter, to gentleman Reeves.

Keith, Dr. Ceesay, Lorna Robinson

We have since 2000 worked acidulously to make the above goal come to fruition, especially for those in the rural sector of the North Bank Region of the Gambia. It was Lorna's joint effort with, nurses, Doctors Laurel Spooner, Barbara Murray, Richard Spooner, Phil Murray, Linda Mahon-Daly, Peter R. Wilson, Malkait Singh and residents of Colchester, which lead to the formation of the Colchester Friends of Manding Charitable Trust.

It was registered as a charity in England and Wales in 2001. The charity number is 1088136. This charity acts as liaison in the European Union countries for Manding Medical Centre at Njawara village in the Badibous of the North Bank Region, the Gambia.

Since its conception, the Friends of Manding Charitable Trust had busied itself on weekly or bimonthly Gambi-barzaars in an effort to help raise money for building of both the children and maternity units of the center. Mrs. Lorna Robinson spent countless week-ends either selling material such as toys, coats and anything she could lay her hands on as long as she believes it will generate money for the building of the children and maternity units of the center.

She spent most of her retirement time organizing activity for the center to help promote our cause. She sent books, spectacles, pens and pencils along with medication for the centre's use. The influence of this Good Samaritan group in Colchester reverberated and lead to the formation of a similar charity group in America, which is lead by Dr. Avery

Aten, Alpena Friends of Manding Charitable Trust, Michigan, USA, was formed in May 2005. All this came about because Mrs. Lorna V. Robinson, the lady of mercy behind the wheel, would not rest while the indigent goes without the most basic things in life.

Here is how Lorna views her part during one of many conversations we had about the need to share worth and ourselves with other less fortunate than us. She simply said, "Ceesay, I feel delighted and warm at heart in helping others, like the villagers. I strongly believe good use could be made from my work and experience I had at the NHS over years. I will try to recruit as many retired nurses to our cadre as long as they listen to my please.

The other secrete is that such activity keeps me young, participating and contributing to the needy. I feel alive and forever growing. In life we most extend our hearts to others and with compassion reach the needy." This tit bit tells about the unselfish nature of Mrs. Lorna V. Robinson who through the years since her retirement gave her all to help others, especially the villagers' breath a sigh of relief and to have hope and knowledge that someone far away they never met cared about them.

Lorna continued saying, "It brings joy to my heart when I share the little I have with the needy. It helps to uplift the despondent. Millions suffer needlessly for not having means of proper health care, clean and safe water, good shelter and chance to attend schools.

I want to help you get the villagers from a downward spiral of deepening health deprivation. I certainly take hope in people like you and your stand to help your folks back home in the Gambia." It was this unique caring angel that I lost on the third of March 2010 for she returned peacefully to her maker on this day.

The above was my Lorna and now I cry, when shall we be blessed will another like her? Losing Lorna Robinson left me feeling that I lost the best person, outside of my family, I ever known. She was a kind soul of unswerving determination to share the little She had with the little guy needing her help. She stood by my cause in thick and thin moments of my stay in the United Kingdom.

The provision of medical care to villagers is more than a responsibility; it is a sacred trust for me. I will not the villagers or memory Mrs. Lorna V. Robinson down because I believe in looking to the well being of the less fortunate. One carries on trying on reflecting on all the children and villagers who need this health care.

Hence no trepidation will hold me back. My family, the villagers and I miss and deeply mourn her premature departure from mother earth. May she rest in peace with her maker and may we the living without fail or fear able to follow the high shining examples of indefatigable Good Samaritan she was in life.

I hope you will join me to keep her memory and legacy alive for other to copy while we continue taking medical aid to villagers in rural Gambia.

Lorna V. Robinson thanks a million and goodbye for now.

Signed: Dr. Alhasan S. Ceesay, MD

Manding Medical Centre, Njawara

The Gambia, West Africa. E-mail: alhasanceesay@hotmail.com

Dr. Alhasan S. Ceesay graduating from the American University of the Caribbean School of Medicine, 1992

Dr. Ceesay holding Africa

L – R: Dr. Alhasan Ceesay, Prof. Sul Nyang, Mr. Cloyd Ramsey and Prof. Francis Conti, 1984

L R: Mrs. Fatou Koma-Ceesay, Famatanding Ceesay Alagie Ceesay, Binta Ceesay and Roheyata Ceesay

Chapter 45

Photo Gallery of my Somali Samaritans

Angels like Mahmud Adam, Faisal Alin, Abdinnisir Hassan, Abdal Rhaseed, Noora Suqulle, Asusu Mohamed, Othman Shati, Ahmed Abdhi, Ahmed Aboud, Abdurhaman and Yusuf Mohamed Ali, deserved to be classed as paragons of kindness.

These Somalis are among many who refused to let me bit the dust because of foot dragging visa problem. They encouraged me by sharing food they had with me and made certain that I persevere for a brighter day for family and country. These are people who help lift my feet when my wings could not remember how to fly away from hardship. Faisal would on week ends prepare hot and well spiced Spaghetti and meat, or buy food for me from the next door restaurant.

Abdinnisir in almost tearful manner would push me into going with him to get food. On top of this generosity these folks let me stay in their flat at 284 Great Western Street, Manchester while my lawyer fight not only to untangle my nightmare but to get the Home office act on change of status request I made to that office as far back as in 2004. Yusu Ali, alias: 'open Ali' normally knocks my door while asking, "Ceesay, are you ok? "Open door!"

He would then hand me food, fruits, sugar or tea and at times small cash with it.. Like wise Faisal and Othman Shati encouraged me in like manner as they were constantly at my door during Ramadan making certain I had food to break fast with. Mrs. Noora Sugulle refuses to be left behind in this benevolent trail of wingless Angels. She contacted friends and seek their help to get some cash for me to send to my beleaguered family back in the Gambia.

God blesses their hearts and my family, villagers and I look forward to the day we can serenaded and thank them for being so generous and kind towards. Their humanness enables me over the pains of solitude, destitution and life of a homeless in one of the world's richest countries.

Faisal, a soft spoken kind gentleman is one of my best friends and an Angel without wings.

Dr. Alhasan Ceesay having a warm friendly hand shakes with Mr. Abdinnisir Hassan. He is a gentleman and my Somali Samaritan

L- R: Mahmud Adam and Abdinnisir Hassan, Liverpool, 2009. Mahmud is another unique kind and generous soul that stood by me throughout my Manchester days.

Yusu Mohamed Ali

Alias: 'Open Ali" the kind hearted.

CHAPTER 46
ABOUT THE AUTHOR

I was born at Njawara Village, Lower Badibou District in the North Bank of the Gambia. I am a scion of a Mandinka and Fulani tribe and am one of five siblings.

I had my education at Kinte Kunda, then Armitage High School, ending up as a registered nurse at the Royal Victoria Hospital, Banjul, before embarking to the USA on my medical degree quest.

I graduated from the American University School of Medicine in Montserrat, West Indies, in 1992 and returned to the Gambia to start setting up a self-help village health NGO Manding Medical Centre.

The Gambia Government and the Badibou local authority register NGO Manding Medical Centre. The centre has treated more than 9000 patients free. In addition I created

The Gambia Medical Health Credit Union in 1993 which continues to serve and provide loand to medical staff.

I am married to Fatou Koma-Ceesay and we are blessed with three beautiful girls, Famatanding Ceesay, Binta Ceesay and Roheyata Ceesay. Unlike me, all of them started school early without the roadblocks I had to cross in my early years. I am currently a medical officer at the Royal at the Royal Victoria Hospital on study leave. It is my hope that this work will inspire others and bring much needy help to providing medical service to rural Gambia.

You are urged to log onto: http://friendsofmandinggambimed.btck.co.uk to learn more about my work with villagers. One can log onto www.publishkunsa.com to view or purchase my books sales from which go to support goals and operation of Manding Medical Centre at Njawara village, the Gambia.

Dear reader I hope you enjoyed navigating through the piece of work I am contribute for all of us makes case for change in attitudes of government and the governed.

For now, Dalliance said it best for me when he said, "Say of me what you will and the morrow will judge you, and your words shall be a witness before its judgement and a testimony before its justice.

I came to say a word and I shall utter it. Should death take me ere I give voice, the morrow shall utter it. That which alone I do today shall be proclaimed before the people in days to come." I wrote with the hope the life and position enshrined herein will serve as not only an inspiration to farmers, the despondent but also a lesson never to allow these shameful international jigsaw games continue as experience to pass through this planet.

I felt that it is worth writing about the above because it is something worth revealing to honourable men and women to engender change, tolerance and understanding between people and governments. I risked speaking out for all of us to learn from it and move forward to a better and rewarding future.

Have your manuscript become a book by submitting it for possible publication to acquisitions publishes Kunsa. Com

Please contact us to expose your work globally.

www.ingramcontent.com/pod-product-compliance
Lightning Source LLC
Chambersburg PA
CBHW050247170426
43202CB00011B/1588